AFTER PLATO

AFTER PLATO

Rhetoric, Ethics, and the Teaching of Writing

EDITED BY
JOHN DUFFY
LOIS AGNEW

UTAH STATE UNIVERSITY PRESS
Logan

© 2020 by University Press of Colorado

Published by Utah State University Press
An imprint of University Press of Colorado
245 Century Circle, Suite 202
Louisville, Colorado 80027

 The University Press of Colorado is a proud member of
the Association of University Presses.

The University Press of Colorado is a cooperative publishing enterprise supported,
in part, by Adams State University, Colorado State University, Fort Lewis College,
Metropolitan State University of Denver, Regis University, University of Colorado,
University of Northern Colorado, University of Wyoming, Utah State University, and
Western Colorado University.

∞ This paper meets the requirements of the ANSI/NISO Z39.48-1992 (Permanence of
Paper)

ISBN: 978-1-60732-996-1 (paperback)
ISBN: 978-1-60732-997-8 (ebook)
https://doi.org/10.7330/9781607329978

Library of Congress Cataloging-in-Publication Data

Names: Duffy, John, 1955– editor. | Agnew, Lois Peters, editor.
Title: After Plato : rhetoric, ethics, and the teaching of writing / John Duffy, Lois Agnew.
Description: Louisville, Colorado : University Press of Colorado, [2020] | Includes biblio-
   graphical references and index.
Identifiers: LCCN 2020001749 (print) | LCCN 2020001750 (ebook) | ISBN
   9781607329961 (paperback) | ISBN 9781607329978 (ebook)
Subjects: LCSH: English language—Rhetoric—Study and teaching (Higher) |
   Rhetoric—Moral and ethical aspects.
Classification: LCC PE1404 .A395 2020 (print) | LCC PE1404 (ebook) | DDC
   808/.0420711—dc23
LC record available at https://lccn.loc.gov/2020001749
LC ebook record available at https://lccn.loc.gov/2020001750

Cover illustration © Enola99d/Shutterstock.com

The editors of this book, Lois and John, wish to thank their families for their love and support.

CONTENTS

AFTER PLATO

INTRODUCTION

John Duffy and Lois Agnew

In the popular narrative, familiar to all who have read Plato's *Gorgias*, the character of Socrates is sent forth to engage a trio of Sophists—Gorgias, Polus, and Callicles—in a public debate concerning the nature and morality of rhetoric. It isn't much of a contest. Socrates easily dispatches the first of his two interlocutors, showing Gorgias to be an amiable charlatan, unclear on the nature of that which he professes to teach, and Polus a naive hothead whose arguments about oratory are confused and contradictory. Callicles proves a more formidable adversary, amoral and contemptuous of Socrates's philosophy, which he regards as a pursuit unworthy of mature adults. By the end of the dialogue, however, Callicles, too, is vanquished, growing sullen and silent as Socrates expounds on his ideas of justice, virtue, and the good life. As for rhetoric, Socrates dismisses it as "pandering," "cookery," and a "counterfeit" art, "useless in establishing the truth" (Plato 1960, 44). So does Plato introduce the famous division—locating philosophy, knowledge, and truth on the high side of the river, with rhetoric, ignorance, and duplicity occupying the lower, muddier bank.

This searing indictment of rhetoric, which has achieved a historical staying power that might have surprised even Plato, has preoccupied rhetoricians for centuries, raising questions about the place of ethics in rhetorical theory, practice, and pedagogy. After Plato, rhetoric became something of a dirty word, signifying dishonesty and insincerity, as in the expression "give me truth, not rhetoric." After Plato, rhetoric was understood as cheap ornamentation, as in the command "spare me the rhetoric; just say it plainly." After Plato, rhetoric was construed as the opposite of productive activity, as in the headline "governor calls for action, not rhetoric." These and similar denunciations are part and parcel of the accepted narrative, in which Plato effectively separated rhetoric from ethics.

And if Plato's views of rhetoric were more complex than the popular narrative admits, which they were, and if rhetoricians long ago rejected binary thinking about the relationship of rhetoric and ethics, which

DOI: 10.7330/9781607329978.c000

they have, there yet remains the challenge for those of us who teach and study writing to think past popular conceptions to delineate for ourselves the relationship of rhetoric and ethics as this has been enacted in own historical time and place, in our own cultural moment.[1]

How do we understand the relationship of rhetoric and ethics at a moment when objective truth is under assault, reason is derided, racism is intensifying, conspiracies are rampant, and authoritarianism is on the rise in the United States and Europe? What does it mean to be an ethical speaker and writer in conditions of strident polarization, economic inequality, mass incarceration, and environmental destruction? What sorts of arguments would the ethical speaker or writer make in addressing these conditions? What stories would she tell? What principles would guide her choice of metaphors, analogies, allegories, or ironies?

For teachers of writing, other questions present themselves. Should we be teaching practices of ethical rhetoric in our classrooms? Is that part of our charge, another of our many responsibilities? If we would answer "yes" to such questions, what deliberations would follow? What decisions? What choices would we make, for example, in our first-year writing classrooms, our Writing Across the Curriculum (WAC) programs, our writing centers, our teacher training courses, and elsewhere?

Such questions compel us to address more basic questions: What do we mean by the words *ethics* and *ethical?* These are familiar, even commonplace terms. We encounter them, perhaps use them, in contexts of civic life, policy debates, commercial transactions, religious discourses, and personal communications. But what do we mean, exactly, by these words? What do we mean by "ethical rhetoric?" What theories, principles, concepts, or experiences organize our understandings and our practices? How have our conceptions of the terms *ethics, ethical,* and *ethical rhetoric* been influenced by recent scholarship in such areas as feminism, transnationalism, postmodernism, non-Western ethics, and other schools of thought?

We are not, of course, the first to ask such questions. In his review of scholarship on the relationship of ethics and rhetoric, William Duffy (this collection) references writings in philosophy, public sphere theory, and new rhetoric, citing such figures as John Dewey and Jurgen Habermas, Richard Weaver and Kenneth Burke, Wayne Booth and Sharon Crowley. In the field of what is now called writing studies,[2] publications such as Sheryl I. Fontaine and Susan M. Hunter's *Foregrounding Ethical Awareness in Composition and English Studies* (1998), James E. Porter's, *Rhetorical Ethics and Internetworked Writing* (1998), and Frederic G. Gale, Phillip Sipiora, and James L. Kinneavy's, *Ethical Issues in College*

Writing (1999) have explored intersections of ethics and rhetoric from a variety of theoretical, philosophical, historical, and ideological perspectives. More recently, ethics has been the subject of scholarly inquiry in Krista Ratcliffe's *Rhetorical Listening: Identification, Gender, Whiteness* (2005), Ira Allen's *The Ethical Fantasy of Rhetorical Theory* (2018), and John Duffy's *Provocations of Virtue: Rhetoric, Ethics, and the Teaching of Writing* (2019), to name but a few of many.

This essay collection is intended to extend and enrich such conversations. Featuring chapters by some of the most accomplished scholars in the field, *After Plato* explores the diversity of ethical perspectives animating contemporary writing studies, including feminist, postmodern, transnational, non-Western, virtue, translingual, and other perspectives, and examines as well the place of ethics in our classrooms, writing centers, prison education classes, and other settings for the teaching of writing. Collectively, the chapters demonstrate the integral place of ethics in writing studies and provide a roadmap for moving forward in conversations about ethical rhetoric that will play an essential role in the future vitality of our field.

PLAN OF THE BOOK

Section One: Historical and Theoretical Perspectives

After Plato is arranged in two complementary sections. The first section, Historical and Theoretical Perspectives, offers seven chapters that explore different frameworks for developing an ethical rhetoric in writing studies. In the first of these chapters, James Porter argues that the revitalization of rhetorical ethics can be furthered through reframing Western rhetorical history. Porter contends that the ethical force of rhetoric has been diminished not by accident but by the deliberate suppression of strains of the Western rhetorical tradition that asserted rhetoric's integral role in ethical decision-making. Porter seeks to reclaim a historical lineage that creatively imagines the intrinsic relationships among language, ethics, and the public good. Although this important strain of thought has been elided as a result of the persistent impulse on the part of thinkers such as Peter Ramus to diminish rhetoric's power, Porter argues that recovering ancient notions of rhetoric as both *techne* and praxis can recapture the emphasis on rhetoric's transformative potential that has been obscured by dominant versions of rhetorical history.

Porter's essay is followed by William Duffy's "Practically Wise and Good: Understanding *Phronesis* as a Rhetorical Virtue," in which Duffy connects rhetorical action to the subfield of moral philosophy known as "virtue ethics." The chapter begins with an acknowledgment of the challenges of defining rhetorical ethics and agreeing on whose judgment matters in that ongoing determination. Duffy's response to that challenge begins with the search for an internal ethical standard that resides in the field, a quest that takes him to Aristotle's virtue of *phronesis*, which arises from the notion that "to choose the right or most expedient course of action in most situations requires the ability for good deliberation." Duffy maintains that the value of *phronesis* lies in Aristotle's understanding that the particularities of circumstance always matter, an issue that "falls squarely in the realm of the rhetorical." While Duffy notes that *phronesis*, like other rhetorical virtues, is not completely relative, it provides a framework for cultivating an ethical disposition that facilitates appropriate responses across varying rhetorical contexts.

In concert with the other writers in this section, Lois Agnew begins with the disciplinary assumption that rhetoric and ethics are intrinsically connected but considers the question of "precisely where our field's connection to ethics lies." Although many prominent Western rhetoricians have conceived of style as a central resource for grounding and furthering rhetoric's ethical potential, competing strains in rhetorical history have viewed excessive attention to language use with suspicion. Agnew's exploration of Western rhetorical history supports her argument that style should be imagined "as a focal point for revitalizing the ethical potential of language," a goal that has assumed increasing urgency in the present day.

Bo Wang suggests that Confucius's perspectives on "the self, human relationships, speech, and ritual practices" can usefully inform conversations about ethical practices in rhetoric and writing studies today. Wang argues that "the *Analects* can be read as a virtue-oriented rhetoric" and offers a methodical discussion of the central ethical principles found in Confucius's text. In Wang's view, the complex concept of *ren* can be seen as the key to ethical rhetorical engagement, since "the concern for the good of others makes the exemplary person irreducibly communal and relational." Although she acknowledges interpretations that have emphasized Confucius's ambivalence toward eloquence, Wang advances the compelling argument that the significance of language in Confucius's system can be more fully understood through tracing the intricate connections among the cultivation of *ren*, ritual practices, and speech.

Rasha Diab seeks to "provoke further discussion of the *(trans)national* in a world that prides itself on the compression of time and space, border crossing, transnational identification, and a global community."

Diab's investigation of the border offers a framework for interrogating the material reality that is often elided by the terms used to discuss transnationalism. She interrogates how we can read differently the (in)visible presence of national doxa that informs our perception of and discourse about the movement of bodies, bodies of knowledge, technologies, and capital across national borders. Drawing on Seyla Benhabib and Denise Ferreira da Silva, Diab centers relationality to explicate how we "include an other in our spheres of attention, intention, and ethical consideration." Diab calls for a relational ethics, which is "a manifestation of a moral philosophy, a relational worldview, and an interdependent, relational self."

Xiaoye You, in turn, explores questions about the ethics of translingual practice. You begins his chapter with a discussion of ancient thinkers such as Confucius, Plato, Aristotle, and Diogenes, who not only engage directly with issues of cultural difference but also use multilingualism "as resources in their composing process." The recognition that "writing often matters tremendously to the writer and his or her community" creates an opportunity for greater awareness of the high stakes that are at play whenever monolingualism is asserted as the norm without acknowledging the potential value of embracing the range of resources that multilingualism makes available to writers and audiences. In light of the ethical complexities surrounding translingualism and its potential compatibility with the expedient goals of neo-liberal capitalism, You proposes that the field encourage students to develop a cosmopolitan perspective that not only encourages an appreciation for multilingual/ translingual language practices but also cultivates a relational awareness across sociopolitical boundaries.

The section concludes with an ambitious vision of the role of rhetorical ethics in addressing a world plagued by division and environmental destruction. Jacqueline Jones Royster and Gesa E. Kirsch offer strategies for ethical action defined by rhetorical listening and response, the pursuit of productive interactions and collaborations across multiple levels of difference, and the exploration of possibilities for a more just and peaceful society. Although Royster and Kirsch draw from their work in feminist rhetorical studies in exploring the questions at hand, they insist that this ambitious project requires an intersectional approach; their inspiring call for awareness of "hierarchies of difference in human value systems and practices" establishes a foundation for the "deliberate decentering of the primacy of human beings and the primacy of Western ontologies, theories, and practices" that they consider central to their ethical project. Their extensive discussion of how rhetorical studies can pursue this goal offers practical steps for re-inscribing ethics as a central concern of our field and offers a call for action that brings a note of hope in troubled times.

Section Two: Disciplinary and Pedagogical Perspectives

The second section of the book, Disciplinary and Pedagogical Perspectives, builds on the theoretical foundations established in the first, examining how ethics is conceived and enacted in the institutional spaces in which we teach and assess students.

The section begins with Robert J. Mislevy and Norbert Elliot's "Ethics, Psychometrics, and Writing Assessment: A Conceptual Model," which outlines the challenges of addressing the topic of ethics and writing assessment. The authors respond to this challenge by establishing a framework for assessment defined by "a sense of reason tempered by consequence, convictions revisited by reflection, and fairness enacted in communities" and then use their framework to design ethical writing assessments. Although the authors issue a "warning label" concerning the fact that the technical nature of their expertise gives rise to a chapter that is "complex at times in its use of terminology," their explicit attention to the ethical principles underlying their work supports their view that a multidisciplinary approach to writing assessment has tremendous value in illuminating the complex, relational, and ethical nature of all communication.

Michael A. Pemberton shifts the conversation to the writing center, addressing the unique challenges in determining ethical courses of action in the context of the tutorial sessions central to writing center pedagogy. His chapter offers a critical discussion of the complexity that surrounds the notion of "the good" in writing centers, particularly as any absolute ideal is persistently challenged by the highly contextual nature of every writing center interaction. Pemberton's introduction of William Lillie's list of ethical standards serves as a provocative framework for a consideration of how key principles might be applied to establish an ethical system that is fully situated in and attentive to the ever-changing demands of the writing center tutorial session.

Vicki Tolar Burton considers what it means to bring ethical considerations into Writing Across the Curriculum/Writing in the Disciplines (WAC/WID) pedagogy. Drawing from Michael Hyde's notion of ethos as a means for establishing "dwelling places," Burton argues that WAC/WID programs provide opportunities to explore "the concept of disciplinary discourse as a dwelling place of disciplinary ethics." This insight entails an awareness of the ways writing within disciplines supports the discovery and instantiation of values that guide particular fields and also of how teaching students to write according to the standards of particular disciplines should be seen not simply as an endeavor to acquaint them with a set of rules and generic expectations but instead should be more broadly conceived as "the places where their professional character (ethos) and knowledge develop and where they learn to write as ethical citizens of their field." Burton makes a thorough and compelling case for the ways students and faculty engaged in WAC/WID initiatives can benefit from greater awareness of how their encounters with disciplinary discourse provide a means to engage with rhetorical ethics.

Don J. Kraemer takes up the complex and relational nature of rhetorical ethics. Kraemer applies "the revisionary zeal in Plato" to the context of teacher training, as he considers what it means to apply the goals of Plato's "democratic city" to a TA training program in which the "citizens," teacher and students, hold widely different values and professional objectives. Kraemer's case study of a single student demonstrates how an ethically responsive approach to teacher training obligates both teacher and student to commit to an honest exchange of ideas that will open the door to new insights and perspectives. While Kraemer's proposed method of "pedagogical hospitality" in teacher training does not offer a remedy to the ethical challenges that can arise in a TA training program, which Kraemer frankly acknowledges, the method does provide a productive way forward for imagining the type of "city" an ethical teacher education program can create for prospective teachers.

Paula Mathieu proposes mindfulness as an alternative framework for developing ethical responses to the life circumstances we encounter. Mathieu argues for the importance of rhetorical and pedagogical strategies that support self-awareness, by which she means the cultivation of a personal presence that facilitates "conscious and purposeful" action. Although Mathieu acknowledges that "mindfulness is a tool that in itself is neutral," she argues that aligning mindful practices with ethics can lead to a type of consciousness that purposefully enables us to "reduce suffering in ourselves and others." In addition to explicating a theory of mindful ethics, Mathieu's chapter offers insight about the role of writing in promoting mindful practices, and she suggests a variety of contemplative teaching practices that teachers might adopt in mindful writing classrooms.

Our field's scope is not limited to the academy but requires a consideration of the ethical issues that can arise as students and faculty engage with community partners. Patrick W. Berry addresses the pressures that emerge as the outcomes of prison literacy programs at times deviate from the expectations of those who participate in them. Berry calls for a thorough consideration of the imagined function of higher education in prison, insisting that such an investigation requires that we "listen rhetorically to how discussions about higher education in prison are framed, interrogate the cultural logics that inform them, and create spaces for alternative understandings." Berry argues that rhetorical listening, which fosters an understanding of the range of perspectives of participants in prison literacy programs, is an eminently ethical stance, as it fosters resistance to a limited and limiting model of prison education.

Section Two concludes with John Duffy's "Toward a Common Tongue: Rhetorical Virtues in the Writing Classroom." Duffy argues that while writing studies is characterized by a rich diversity of approaches to the teaching of writing, what is common across our various pedagogies is the teaching of what he calls "rhetorical virtues," or the discursive enactment of such qualities as truthfulness, accountability, intellectual generosity, intellectual courage, and other such traits and disposition. By way of illustration, Duffy compares two seemingly distinct approaches to the teaching of writing—community-engaged pedagogy and new media pedagogy—to show how each is grounded in the teaching of rhetorical virtues. Duffy concludes by arguing that teachers of ethical rhetoric have an indispensable role to play in repairing the toxic condition of contemporary public argument.

EPILOGUE

In his wise and engaging epilogue to this book, Frederick Antczak acknowledges that the place of ethics in writing studies is something of a moving target, responsive to transformations of theory, politics, economics, and other urgent forces. And yet it is possible to view present challenges, Antczak writes, as versions of earlier contentions or to understand that everything that was old has been made new again. However, if questions concerning the relationship of rhetoric and ethics are enduring and unresolved, Antczak argues that the appropriate response should not be to deny

> that understandings can grow and deepen; nor is it to be skeptical about whether debates can progress. Indeed, sometimes they progress so much that they begin to connect to, even anticipate, other contemporary discussions. Scholarly inquiries into the ethics of rhetoric in writing studies and in communication ramify so often and powerfully that they practically career toward interdisciplinarity. These sorts of connections

seem like signs of making real headway, as well as a rough map of future directions—although, of course, it was ever thus.

We offer *After Plato* in that spirit, proposing that the very old, indeed, the ancient quandary of the place of ethics in rhetorical theory and pedagogy has been made new again by contemporary situations that pose new questions, challenge new audiences, and call for new expressions of ethical rhetoric. We hope you will find value in the understandings and insights offered in this collection as you work out your own responses to the urgent ethical challenges facing our students, our colleagues, and our society in the twenty-first century.

NOTES

1. We use the pronouns "we," "our," and "us" to refer in the broadest possible sense to anyone who teaches or studies writing, as well as to those who administer writing programs.
2. We use the term *writing studies* inclusively, intending that it stand for each of the various disciplinary labels that have been applied to the teaching and study of writing, such as composition studies, rhetoric and composition, and others.

REFERENCES

Allen, Ira. 2018. *The Ethical Fantasy of Rhetorical Theory*. Pittsburgh, PA: University of Pittsburgh Press.
Duffy, John. 2019. *Provocations of Virtue: Rhetoric, Ethics, and the Teaching of Writing*. Logan: Utah State University Press.
Fontaine, Sheryl I., and Susan M. Hunter, eds. 1998. *Foregrounding Ethical Awareness in Composition and English Studies*. Portsmouth, NH: Heinemann.
Gale, Frederic G., Phillip Sipiora, and James L. Kinneavy, eds. 1999. *Ethical Issues in College Writing*. New York: Peter Lang.
Plato. 1960. *Gorgias*. Trans. Walter Hamilton. London: Penguin Books.
Porter, James E. 1998. *Rhetorical Ethics and Internetworked Writing*. Greenwich, CT: Ablex.
Ratcliffe, Krista. 2005. *Rhetorical Listening: Identification, Gender, Whiteness*. Carbondale: Southern Illinois University Press.

SECTION ONE

Historical and Theoretical Perspectives

1

RECOVERING A GOOD RHETORIC
Rhetoric as Techne *and Praxis*

James E. Porter

Does it bother you as much as it bothers me that the US news media and public still define *rhetoric* as lying, manipulation, and deception, as the opposite of truth, honesty, facts, and wise judgment—in others words, as innately *unethical* versus *ethical*?

It has been over fifty years since publication of the English translation of Chaim Perelman and Lucie Olbrechts-Tyteca's *The New Rhetoric* (1969)—a bold, innovative effort to recover a broader, more positive view of rhetoric and its civic role. Since that time the field of rhetoric has worked hard to reestablish itself as a worthy, distinctive, and valid area of study with significance for public discourse—as it once was. We have made *some* progress at the university, but in the public realm, not so much. We are still stuck with the negative view: rhetoric is lying, the opposite of ethics. Something has gang aft agley.

In this chapter I conduct a historical frame analysis that attempts through historical inquiry and critique to understand how our current situation came to be: How did rhetoric come to be viewed as lying, deceit, manipulation? How did ethics become so disconnected from rhetoric? In a short chapter it is not possible to answer these questions completely or satisfactorily. What I will do, rather, is consider a few key historical moments that speak to the question:

1. The Greek and Roman classical conception of rhetoric as both *techne* and praxis, involving rhetoric and ethics as complementary, integrated arts serving the public good,

2. The influence of Ramism, in the sixteenth century, and its disastrous effects on the meaning and placement of the study of rhetoric in the Western higher education curriculum,

3. The formation of the modern US research university, in the late nineteenth and early twentieth centuries, which established the current disciplines and departments for higher education (rhetoric, of course, not among them).

DOI: 10.7330/9781607329978.c001

I'm aware of the danger of cherry picking historical moments: you run the risk of oversimplifying a complicated story, making a smooth, clean narrative where one is not to be found. I hope to make my narrative clear without doing injustice to the richness, complexity, and nuance of the issue. What I hope to show is some key moments that contribute to rhetoric being viewed as unethical—with the aim, of course, of suggesting how we might change the view. The way down is also the way up.

making

My argument overall is this: rhetoric is a *techne*, but it is also a praxis. That is to say, rhetoric should aim at practical, transformative connection with the world. The purpose of rhetoric is not just to make a symbolic artifact: a speech or a piece of writing, a Web page or a weaving. That constructed symbolic entity is expected to *do* something. Its purpose is to do good work in the world, to provide value or benefit for somebody, to change the world from its current state to some better state. To inform us. To make us warm. To stop an injustice. To praise the worthy. To keep the peace. And because rhetoric aims ultimately at some improvement, some change in the state of things, it invariably involves a judgment about what that good should be, and that decision requires ethical reasoning. The good state is the *telos* of rhetoric, its final cause.

Several Greek and Roman classical rhetoricians said this quite clearly and emphatically in a number of places—most notably Isocrates, Cicero, and particularly Quintilian, who defined rhetoric as "the art of speaking well" (2006, 2.13.38) or "a good man speaking well" (2006, 12.1.1). That definition insists that the rhetor must first be a virtuous person—*vir bonus*—or else he will not have the credibility (ethos) to compel an audience. But "speaking well" has a second important meaning, considered by Quintilian in *Institutio* (2006, 11.1.8–10) and by Cicero as well in *De Oratore* (1948). The good speaker must be guided by her public position and by her duties and obligation to the polis. The rhetor should be a leader speaking for the good of the polis (Walzer 2003, 2006).

Over a long period of time, the ideas that rhetoric involved ethics, that rhetoric was concerned with the public good, that there was an ethic *inside* rhetoric were lost. (Well, not so much *lost* as *intellectually sabotaged*.) Rhetoric as *techne* (art) became confused with *tribe* (mechanical process) and lost its connection with praxis. Rhetoric became associated exclusively with text-as-expression rather than text-as-action. We have to fix that. But it won't be easy because, as I will discuss, the Western intellectual tradition has treated rhetoric badly and because rhetoric remains housed in an institutional structure (i.e., the modern university system) that is fundamentally hostile to it.

METHODOLOGY: HISTORICAL FRAME ANALYSIS

To examine this question, I use a critical approach that exposes and then questions the foundational category systems we have inherited—the frames or terministic screens that have established themselves over time as the way things are, as unexamined reality. These frames are built into our everyday uses of language and are perhaps even, as George Lakoff (2008) argues, hardwired into our brains. It is just such a frame that over-determines our understanding about rhetoric and its relationship with ethics and that puts those terms into a particular configured relationship, one that has proven very difficult to change:

ethics : rhetoric :: truth : lying

Ethics is to rhetoric as truth is to lying. There are, of course, many variants of this analogy frame that help support the classification system:

philosophy : dialectic :: rhetoric : persuasion

philosophy : interlocutor (engaged co-equal participant) :: rhetoric : audience (passive, subordinate)

language : thought :: packaging : content

Frame analysis has been explicitly articulated as a methodology by Erving Goffman (1974) and by George Lakoff (2008). But the version I am using is a looser kind of frame analysis that is probably closest to Michel Foucault's archaeological analysis (1972), particularly because it examines the classification systems in which key terms (like *rhetoric* and *ethics*) appear, how and why those systems are modified (in particular what power dynamics are in play at the moment of modification), and finally, how the system becomes reified into institutional structures (like the university).

The purpose of the methodology is to expose the often hidden (forgotten, suppressed, or denigrated) "other" that the dominant classification system obscures. It aims to expose and challenge the moments when the essentialized categories (such as those related to race, gender, and sexuality or to disciplinary formations) and classification system emerged and became established politically and institutionally. I will use this method first to examine the historical configuration of rhetoric and ethics within the Western rhetorical tradition and second to propose an alternate view of that configuration—a historical counter-story.

The alternate view actually lies *within* the Western intellectual tradition and even within the work of some of the key figures of that tradition, particularly Isocrates and Quintilian. To put it another way, *there is already an alternate view of the relationship between rhetoric and ethics in the*

Western rhetorical tradition that needs to be recovered—what we might call *a good rhetoric*, a view that sees rhetoric and ethics as necessarily intersecting and overlapping arts. Over time many historians and scholars of rhetoric, several of whom I cite here, have made this point. Mostly, I am echoing arguments that have already been made in the field.

RHETORIC AS *TECHNE* AND PRAXIS

Here is the key frame shift: rhetoric is not only a *techne*, it is a praxis.

In classical Greek thought, *techne* refers to the skill or craft of making something, including making a speech. But be wary of simple definitions of complex concepts: the simplicity can hide histories, complexities, power moves, cultural nuances, and the tensions and ideological battles involved. You have to understand the battles—and also the conceptual system, the ideological grid, what Foucault call the discursive formation in which the term sits. *Techne* as opposed to what? In relation to what? Within what system of knowledge or human activity? In what system is *techne* configured?

The earliest uses of the term *techne* connect it with Greek gods and goddesses who have the gift of art and technology (Atwill 1998): for instance, Prometheus's knowledge of fire, which he shared with humans—and then was punished for it. The person with *techne* knows how to do something technically and materially, and that art has a value and the person shares it. The shared thing is useful and beautiful, and it intervenes in human affairs in a way that changes the world. Socrates explicitly identifies as *technai* such activities as playing the harp, generalship, piloting a ship, cooking, medicine, managing an estate, smithing, and carpentry. Poetry is a *techne*, medicine is a *techne*, carpentry is a *techne*, professional writing is a *techne*. Notice that this art is not just for art-ists (in our sense of the word); it refers to artisans, skilled craftspeople.

Because *techne* makes things that work in the world, it must address both materiality and the possibility of changing conditions. The carpenter who makes a rudder must think about the conditions of the sea, the size of the ship, the depth of the port. He needs to make a rudder that can perform its function, deal with change, and be sustainable, last. That is the art/*techne* of rudder making (Plato n.d., 390d; Wild 1941). Because *techne* deals with fluctuating conditions, like the sea, it is not perfectly predictable or certain; it does not generate a guaranteed outcome. You can build the best rudder in the world, but if it hits a rock your ship will go belly-up anyway. *C'est la mer. Techne* deals with fluid and fluctuating and unexpected circumstances, matters on the ground, educated guesswork—and with *probability*, not with idealized, static, or abstract certainty (Atwill 1998).

Techne includes the technical/material facet as well as a critical/ intellectual facet: it includes *theoria* (broad philosophical knowledge), but it also involves knowledge of material and tools, as well as principles of construction and design. For rudder making, that means knowledge about the properties of wood, knowledge about carving tools, knowledge about design and shaping—as well as knowledge about the physics of the rudder. It means knowing how to position the hand holding the knife to leverage just the right amount of scraping and shaping of the wood. There is a physical embodied craft involved.

What is *techne not?* *Techne* should not be confused with *tribe*, which is the mechanical/algorithmic repetition of a task (Wild 1941), or with *kakotechne*, or false art, chicanery, eristic, manipulation, deception, lying (Quintilian 2006, 2.15).

And, of course, rhetoric is frequently equated with both of these things. Quintilian addresses this point quite clearly in *Institutio* (2006, 2.15), when he notes that we do not define the field of medicine based on the malpractice of quacks, and we do not define poetry based on the drivel of bad poets, so why do we use the term *rhetoric* to mean *bad rhetoric?* Yes, of course there are instances of bad rhetoric all over the place (sad). But that is not what *rhetoric* is.

Nor is *techne* merely a "knack," a practical technique that one simply copies from one situation to another. Here is the vital distinction between a technician and a craftsperson or artisan. A technician copies, follows rules and rote procedures, but does not know why or when to use them or, most important, how to adapt them for different situations and uses. *Techne* requires a deep understanding of audience and context of use; it requires an integrated, transdisciplinary view of the arts: rhetoric intersects integrally with politics, ethics, philosophy, design. These arts are not isolated, they are not disciplines; they are *arts*, and as such they are interrelated.

If you read Aristotle's *Rhetoric* (2006) by itself, rhetoric seems like its own distinct sphere with an emphasis on the productive side of speech making. But if you read it alongside *Politics* and *Nicomachean Ethics*, all sorts of interconnections emerge: the three texts are really one big text (Johnstone 1980; Porter 1998). The common aim that ties them all together, the *causa ultima*, was the good of the polis.

What is the ultimate purpose of rhetoric—or its *telos?* For a discussion of *telos* in the classical realm, we need to look at some of Aristotle's other works: *Physics, Metaphysics, Posterior Analytics.* (Some of Aristotle's most interesting and important statements about rhetoric are *not* in *Rhetoric.*) What Aristotle (2006, 194b33) calls the *final* cause is "the end (*telos*), that for which a thing is done." Health is the final cause of walking: a person walks in order to be healthy. Walking is the means; health is the *telos*.

So what is the *telos* of rhetoric? For classical rhetoricians it often meant the good of the polis, the civic good. In *Panathenaicus* (n.d., 12), Isocrates says that the purpose of rhetoric is "the good of the state" and "the needs of the commonwealth." Cicero's and Isocrates's critique of philosophers is that while they may have advanced thinking skills (*theoria*), they are "not able to contribute to the common good" because they make philosophizing the ends rather than the means. Doctors must have episteme—scientific knowledge of the body and of medical research—but they should never forget that the ultimate object and aim of their art is healthy bodies. Their art requires epistemic knowledge, but their *telos* is very much situational, located in the healthy body of the patient and the overall public health of the polis. The purpose of the good oratory, according to Cicero in *De Oratore* (1948, Book I, 34), is to "lead people out of their brutish existence in the wilderness up to a condition of civilization as citizens . . . to give shape to laws, tribunals, and civic rights . . . to uphold the safety of countless individuals and of the entire State."

The classical rhetoricians—particularly Isocrates, Cicero, and Quintilian but also, in a way, Aristotle—emphasized this view. And philosophers of praxis have emphasized this approach as well, including Hannah Arendt, Pierre Bourdieu, Paulo Freire, and, earlier, Karl Marx. Rhetoric involves reflection, symbolic construction/production, and action directed at something or someones to be transformed.

Thus, to summarize: in the comprehensive classical view, rhetoric is

- a craft (*techne*)
- involving multiple kinds of knowledge
- that produces an object (e.g., a speech)
- that acts in the world, bringing about a positive change (praxis),
- and that serves a greater good (*telos*).

Of course, the key implication of this notion of rhetoric, for our purposes, is that the rhetorical enterprise is deeply entwined with ethics, understood as the process of dialectical reasoning and wise judgment (*phronesis*) about what is good, better, best.

RHETORIC AND RAMISM

So what happened to this broad educational *paideia* (Jaeger 1939) and to the comprehensive, integrated view of rhetoric and ethics? Cicero (1948, 3.16.60–61) blamed Socrates/Plato for dividing "wise thinking" from "elegant speaking"—or to put this in terms of the arrangement of canons, for disconnecting *inventio* from the other four canons:

> Socrates [Plato] separated the science of wise thinking from that of elegant speaking, though in reality they are closely linked together [. . .] This is the source from which has sprung the undoubtedly absurd and unprofitable and reprehensible severance between the tongue and the brain, leading to our having one set of professors to teach us to think and another to teach us to speak.

We can see signs of this "reprehensible severance" throughout the history of rhetoric—for example, in Augustine's *De Doctrina Christiana* (1997). Augustine's comprehensive rhetoric does include a discussion of invention, but he draws a hard boundary between *ars inuendi* and *ars proferendi*, that is, between the art of invention (for Augustine this meant exegesis, scriptural interpretation) and the art of presentation. In Augustine's framework, the prelate must first interpret scripture and determine the lesson to be learned and the proper behavior to follow—that is the art of invention, which Augustine treats in Books I–III of *De Doctrina* (written in 397 CE). Then, in a second stage, the prelate determines how best to preach the gospel to sinners and to the congregation—that is the art of rhetoric, which is an art of presentation and style, packaging the scriptural truth for presentation to different audiences (a discussion that was written later, in 427 CE, as Book IV of *De Doctrina*). Here we see the division between ethical reasoning (based on scriptural exegesis) and rhetoric, which comes after and is designed to persuade the congregation to heed scriptural truth.

Thus in this linear two-step model, the process of determining what is right, true, and just (ethics) is disconnected from preaching it or presenting it (rhetoric). Truth/ knowledge is discovered through some inventional method prior to rhetoric—whether that method is divine revelation, scriptural exegesis, literary interpretation, philosophical dialectic, scientific analysis, or big-data aggregation. You bring rhetoric in later, as the instrumental means for presenting truth/knowledge to the ignorant pagan or the sinful Christian or the uninformed audience. There is the split between truth and presentation, between content and packaging.

So the seeds of the division were already planted—introduced by Plato, exacerbated by Augustine—to separate invention and dialectic, and therefore ethical reasoning, as something distinct from rhetoric. However, it was largely because of the attacks on rhetoric by Peter Ramus in the mid-sixteenth century that the split became firmly established and the academic curriculum was reorganized to instantiate the split.

Peter Ramus, or Pierre de la Ramée (1515–72), was a sixteenth-century French scholar of rhetoric and logic who made his mark by attacking Aristotle, Quintilian, and Cicero for their approach to rhetoric but also, more broadly, for challenging how they configured rhetoric alongside other arts (in particular, logic, ethics, and politics) and for their model of education.

The apocryphal story about Peter Ramus is that his scholarly career began in 1536, with him defending his thesis by stating that "everything Aristotle ever said was false." Whether Ramus actually said that is uncertain, but what is certain is that in series of widely read works (by sixteenth-century standards), Ramus viciously attacked Aristotle, Quintilian, and Cicero for their "muddled" rhetoric: *Aristotelicae Animadversiones* (1543), *Attack on Cicero* (1543), and *Arguments in Rhetoric against Quintilian* (1549). Ramus earned an appointment as Regius Professor of Eloquence and Philosophy at Collège de France. By all accounts he was an impressive speaker whose "public lectures were attended by huge crowds" (Ong 1958, 34). Ramus's conversion from Catholicism to Protestantism in 1561 disqualified him from his teaching post at a Catholic university in Paris. He died in Paris in August 1572, murdered during the St. Bartholomew Day's massacre, when a number of prominent Protestant figures were attacked and killed by Catholic mobs (Ong 1958, 1973).[1]

Ramus is sometimes classified as a humanist, but that seems odd given his attacks on the integrated humanistic literacy curriculum, the Greek *paideia*, and the Renaissance *studia humanitatis*. Walter Ong (1958) describes Ramus as a kind of teenager rebelling against the authorities of his time and place, particularly scholasticism, Aristotle, rhetoric, and Catholicism. Ramus was arguing against scholasticism, but he was not exactly for humanism either: he was an advocate for a curriculum based on strict division of the arts. Logic, he argued, should not be taught alongside rhetoric. In fact, *ars inveniendi* does not belong in the art of rhetoric at all, and the *topoi* as described by Aristotle are useless, period, and should not be taught at all.

Peter Ramus instituted "a diagrammatic structure for representing knowledge"—or what was called *methodus*—that became the basis, ultimately, for the formation of disciplines (and departments) in the modern research university (Triche and McKnight 2004, 39). Numerous scholars have tracked exactly how Ramus's *methodus* worked to divide knowledge—but from the point of view of rhetoric, or any *techne* actually, the result was disastrous: Rhetoric was curricularly divided from the art of reasoning (dialectic), and both were divided from ethics (character; the art of determining "the right thing to do"). What was left to rhetoric was a fairly narrow set of concerns related to the canons of *dispositio* and *elocutio*: arrangement/organization and style/expression (which included grammatical correctness).

One place where we can see Ramistic division strongly articulated is in his *Arguments in Rhetoric against Quintilian* (1549). Ramus was incensed about what he viewed as Quintilian's "confusion" between ethics and rhetoric (and also between logic and rhetoric). The art of thinking, he argued, should not be confused with the art of speaking or presenting: "We should distinguish the art of rhetoric from the other arts, and make it a single one of the liberal arts, not a confused mixture of all arts [. . .] rhetoric is not an art which explains all the virtual qualities of character. Moral philosophers speculate appropriately and judiciously on the numerous problems involving the moral virtues [. . .] Quintilian's definition of the orator is as a result defective" (Ramus 1549, 80, 84–85).

The Ramistic approach treats every subject topically and discretely—in essence, does not admit overlap, intersection, or complexity among the parts. The principle used to justify discrete disciplines—*methodus*—became a god term in later Enlightenment treatises (e.g., René Descartes's *Discourse on Method* [1998]), though the term "had been banned as barbarous by early humanists" (Eisenstein 2005, 78). Ramus structurally separated the study of rhetoric from the study of logic: establishing two distinct arts, one concerned with eloquence and elocution and the other with the art of finding and discovering valid arguments. As Chaim Perelman (1982, 7, 3) points out, this nice neat division, arising from "contempt for rhetoric," was "an error that was fatal for rhetoric"—but we might also see it as a fallacy harmful to logic as well, removing it from the realm of civic discourse and practical, situated argument.

Separating *ars inveniendi* from rhetoric had the effect, de facto, of eliminating questions related to purpose, audience, civic responsibility, and the question of the good: Toward what ultimate good is our rhetorical effort directed? Not the business of rhetoric to answer that question. Ethical decision-making belongs elsewhere—and for Ramus that elsewhere was Christian theology. Thus ethics, too, was a casualty of this curricular impetus to divide, though the separation of ethics from rhetoric had other causes as well. Ethics—then it was called moral philosophy—was "scanted" in the new curriculum because, well, there was no ethics outside of Christian theology. In other words, in the

Christian university, ethics was moral philosophy, and moral philosophy was a topic for theology. So the classification system of the Christian university coupled with Ramistic *methodus* conspired in the disconnection between rhetoric and ethics.[2]

The Enlightenment philosophers of the seventeenth and eighteenth centuries accepted the Ramistic binary between logic/thinking and rhetoric, with rhetoric being . . . *despised* is not too harsh a word. The Royal Society of London, founded in 1660, provides plentiful examples of hostility to rhetoric, seeing it as having to do with unnecessary ornamentation, elaborate expression, and metaphoric bombast. Thomas Sprat (1958, 111), one of the founders of the society, referred to rhetoric as "this vicious abundance of Phrase, this trick of Metaphors, this volubility of Tongue, which makes so great a noise in the world." John Locke (1959, 146), another prominent member of the society, called rhetoric "that powerful instrument of error and deceit [intended] for nothing else but to insinuate wrong ideas, move the passions, and thereby mislead the judgment."

From the Royal Society, we inherit the windowpane metaphor for language: language use should be clear, precise, accurate, and denotative—that is, as clear as a windowpane. *Perspicuity* this was called: the style that would transfer meaning as clearly, directly, and briefly as possible, with no embellishment or bombast, no emotional appeal—in essence, no rhetoric. The Royal Society did not invent hostility to rhetoric, but it certainly contributed to enshrining the degraded notion of rhetoric as false, as trickery, as ornamentation, and as a means of hiding the truth rather than revealing it (Halloran and Whitburn 1982).

Of course, during this period there were many humanist advocates for a broad, integrated rhetoric that included invention, ethics, logic, moral reflection, and civic engagement. There were many defenders of the classical *humanitatis* model, including, among others, Desiderius Erasmus, Thomas Wilson, and Giambattista Vico. However, Ong's compelling argument (see also Perelman 1982; Sharratt 1991; Triche and McKnight 2004) is that ultimately the Ramistic view defeated them all, at least in regard to the immense influence of Ramism on the university's understanding of knowledge, its disciplinary classification system, and its dismissive view of the role of rhetoric.

VICO AND PUBLIC RHETORIC

Giambattista Vico is an especially important counter voice during the Enlightenment, directly responding to the hostility directed at rhetoric.

Vico's two key works—*On the Study Methods of Our Time* (1990), written in 1708–9, and *New Science* (2000), published in 1725—are arguments for an integrated, transdisciplinary curriculum that promotes rhetoric, ethics, and public engagement. Vico was an advocate for the *studia humanitatis*, for an integrated approach to rhetoric and ethics, and for what he called "synthetic thinking" or "synthetic imagination," a form of intellectual inquiry that applies a transdisciplinary approach to the understanding of the role of knowledge in human affairs (Bevilacqua 1972).

Vico's *On the Study Methods of Our Time* is a direct response to René Descartes's *Discourse on Method* (1998), which rejected the logical system of Aristotle, questioned the value of topical or inventional thinking, and questioned the enterprise of rhetoric. Descartes's *methodus* goes a step further than Ramus's in rejecting all "inherited ideas"—he had no use for philosophy, poetry, theology, ethics, or rhetoric. Rather, one starts analysis with the observing/thinking self, who observes nature and builds knowledge analytically without recourse to traditional bias or cultural prejudice.

Contra, Vico argued that culture and tradition are critical components of knowledge. Vico was by no means hostile to the new science, but he saw scientific method as only one form of epistemic knowledge making. Vico was opposed to Cartesian mechanical philosophy—that is, the extreme form of the methodology that rejected all non-scientific forms of knowledge—and argued for the value of the diverse forms of knowledge included in poetry, imaginative thinking, theology, and rhetoric.

Like most true humanists, Vico does not fit conveniently into a single disciplinary category because, by definition, he works across categories: philosophy, law, rhetoric, history, theology, social science methodology, poetry (Burke 1985, 3). The study of law drove him toward practical application, and he was a historian and a historical methodologist, working to understand how the past intersects with and enlightens the present. Vico was dismayed by what he saw as the new university curriculum that was neglecting important areas of study, including rhetoric, culture, literature, history, theology, and ethics—and a curriculum that was also disconnecting itself from public affairs and from understanding of audience/culture: "Our chief fault is that we disregard that part of ethics which treats of human character, of its dispositions, its passions, and of the manner of adjusting these factors to public life and eloquence" (Vico 1990, 33).

Like rhetoric, ethics was getting pushed to the side in the new science curriculum as having no basis in scientific method and as not constituting a form of knowledge. As Albert R. Jonsen and Stephen

Toulmin (1988) point out, during this period, the casuistic method of addressing difficult questions of ethics was rejected by the new scientists as pseudo-knowledge and pseudo-methodology, as not meeting the standards for Cartesian methodological rigor, as not properly a discipline in the university. Jonsen and Toulmin argue that the new science failed to understand the vital importance *technai* like rhetoric and ethics have in the public realm of probable knowledge, where scientific methodology cannot provide answers to questions about "what we should do."

PURE KNOWLEDGE VERSUS PRACTICAL KNOWLEDGE

The argument between Vico and Descartes reveals a tension that has always been present in Western education: between an idealistic view of education (or a philosophical view, aimed at *veritas, theoria,* or *Wissenschaft,* in the nineteenth-century German university model) versus a more practical view aimed at *bonum* or *civitatem,* civic involvement, embodied engagement with the world and all its messiness, diversity, and imperfections. This was the battle between Plato's and Isocrates's two different academies in classical Athens. It was the battle between scholasticism and humanism in the Renaissance. And in the late nineteenth century it was the battle between the German disciplinary research university model and the land-grant university mission that emphasized the practical, applied arts of agriculture, technology, and mining. In a sense this tension between pure knowledge and practical knowledge is built into the very institutional history of the university—and into the history of rhetoric. It is not necessarily a bad thing, unless practical knowledge is neglected altogether.

We see this tension between Plato's and Isocrates's competing schools in classical Athens. Isocrates's school focused on rhetoric. Plato's school focused on a variety of subjects, with rhetoric a fairly minor concern. Where the two schools differ, profoundly, is in their view of truth and in the relationship between truth and rhetoric. For Plato, truth comes first and is absolute. Rhetoric is dangerous in its tendency to obscure the truth in its effort to flatter the audience (as he saw it). In Isocrates's model, rhetoric is the necessary tool for arriving at truth, through interaction with audience.

In the Isocratean model, rhetoric and ethics are very closely intertwined—and their common *telos* is "the best course of action" for the polis. Isocrates focuses on the character of the rhetor, on building and maintaining productive relations (the phatic purpose), and on promoting justice. According to Isocrates (n.d., 12), the purpose of rhetoric is "the good of the state" and "the needs of the commonwealth." The ultimate goal of the rhetorical enterprise is social harmony, concord (*homonoia*), or what Aristotle termed "the good of the state": "Isocrates linked rhetoric to the articulation of wise governance and civic conscience" (Poulakos 2004, 75; see also Benoit 1991; de Romilly 1958).

Put bluntly, your ultimate purpose as a rhetor—or as a public relations executive—is *not* to persuade the audience of your message or to sell your product. Your purpose is a *phatic* or irenic one (Porter 2017): to keep the peace, promote the common welfare, make society better for everybody.[3]

The Platonic model favors the ideal, the abstract, and the theoretical—and is less focused on the material, the technical, the economic. In the Platonic model *techne* (making things) is not as important as *theoria* (which, in Greek, means to wonder, behold, observe, speculate). In the Platonic model the focus is on "studying about" rather than "engaging" or "intervening in." The Platonic model can lead to a posture of impatience with the world, disdain for and disengagement with the world because the world can never quite measure up to the ideal.

RHETORIC IN THE MODERN DISCIPLINARY RESEARCH UNIVERSITY

Despite Ramism and *methodus*, up until the mid-nineteenth century rhetoric was a dominant feature of the US college curriculum, as Sharon Crowley (1998, 33) points out: "American colleges required all students to take four years of instruction in rhetorical theory and to engage in regular supervised practice and oratory and written composition." What happened to rhetoric in the curriculum?

From the mid-nineteenth century on, American universities embraced a new model of education. The idea of "knowledge for its own sake" became a primary focus for the emergent late nineteenth-century American university focused on the German disciplinary model, sometimes called the Humboldt Model (after Professor Wilhelm von Humboldt, a philologist/linguist at the University of Berlin in the early nineteenth century). This model emphasized disciplinary *Wissenschaft*—systematic research and scholarship. Knowledge and truth became the standards, not practical usefulness. The professoriate focused less on social and political matters and more on becoming subject matter experts and specialized researchers (Hawkins 1979; Neem 2017; O'Boyle 1983; Oleson and Voss 1979; Ringer 1979; Veysey 1965, 1979). Practical engagement with the world was *not* what higher education was about.

Organizationally, it was deemed important to organize faculty into distinct disciplinary specializations—and here is where we see Ramism come to full curricular and organizational fruition. By the 1890s the departmental system and its emphasis on academic majors became the norm in a number of key research institutions (Veysey 1965).

The English major was born at this time, as a belletristic literature major, at Harvard University under the leadership of Francis James Child. Donald Stewart identifies the mid-nineteenth century as a pivotal time, especially the years 1851 to 1876, when Child served as Boylston Professor at Harvard University. As Stewart (1982, 120) tells the story, "As the years passed, he [Child] increasingly questioned the legitimacy of oratory and composition as university subjects, because they were too elementary." Child's preference was the philological study of folklore, particular English and Scottish ballads; "he was intent on raising the study of English literature to the status of a solid academic discipline" (Stewart 1982, 120).

English fought a hard battle with the classicists at Harvard but eventually won out, establishing itself by 1920 as the premier humanities department in the new disciplinary university. The focus of this education was not, as formerly, the study of *belles lettres* for purposes of public rhetoric but instead the study of literary works from an aesthetic viewpoint: the focus was on studying literature as art—or what Crowley (1982, 33–34) describes as "the rise of aesthetics and the fall of rhetoric . . . the bourgeois appropriation of rhetorical education." Along with the departure of rhetoric came the departure of ethics instruction, or "the development of character" (Crowley 1982, 35).[4] Concomitant with the fall of rhetoric was the rise in linguistics, perceived as a more scientific approach to the study of language.

What we see in the structure of the modern university, as it came into being in the early twentieth century, is the ascendancy of the Platonic view of truth coupled with a nineteenth-century German university model based on disciplinary knowledge and scientific *methodus*, focused on research, taught through the lecture, and codified into a departmental institutional structure. Instruction in rhetoric, ethics, and dialectic (or informal argument) has no clear place in this curricular model because these were old *techne* arts from the classical era that had no disciplinary status in the modern era. Ethics and logic, if they were taught formally at all, were handled in the Department of Philosophy, but there ethics instruction largely become instruction about the history and theory of the philosophy of ethics rather than the formation of character and the practice of ethics for social purposes. So while rhetoric was, up until the mid-nineteenth century, the core of the higher education curriculum, it has no clearly defined place in the modern disciplinary university.

Johann Neem (2017) characterizes this organizational shift as a matter of *humanities disciplines* replacing *humanism*, as "organized bodies of inquiry and knowledge triumph[ing] over the liberal arts." Our modern notions of the humanities disciplines are not at all the more traditional notion of *humanitatis* developed by the classical rhetoricians and articulated and defended by Vico and others. So when we use the word *humanities*, we have to be careful to distinguish which version we are talking about: the old integrated/transdisciplinary version or the newer modern disciplinary version? The modern university is based on a disciplinary approach to the organization of knowledge that divides the study of history, philosophy, literature, and languages into distinct departments—with rhetoric left out of the mix, dismissed as the embarrassing vestige of an older, now disreputable paradigm.

James L. Kinneavy was very much aware of the practical consequences of university structure and its impact on instruction in rhetoric and ethics. For Kinneavy (1988, 109), rhetoric was "the practical bridge linking the humanities to the ordinary citizen of the *polis*. Without the practical link of rhetoric, the liberal arts can be viewed as somewhat removed and esoteric . . . The exile of rhetoric from the humanities may be the reason why the humanities now find themselves in disfavor in our society." Kinneavy worried that without a practical linkage to the polis—the linkage that rhetoric provides—the pursuit of knowledge tends to proceed without sufficient attention to practical realities, embodied experience, and real moral questions: that is, ethics.

CONCLUSION

So that is one theory about what happened to ethics vis-à-vis rhetoric in the university curriculum and also in public consciousness. But what do we *do* about this?

Our Teaching

First and most obvious, when we teach rhetoric, we need to be teaching ethics, too. But ethics in the curriculum has to be more than simply a special topic, an isolated two-week instructional module, or an occasional special course offering. Ethics must be taught as integral to all discussions of rhetoric throughout the rhetoric, writing, and communication curriculums.

In my teaching experience, students are generally not familiar with the idea that, as an art, rhetoric and writing contains within it principles for a rhetorical ethics or a communication ethics. (Such as: Speak the truth. Let others speak, and listen carefully to what they say. Treat your audience with civility and respect. Accurately and fairly represent the sources, data, and research you use in your writing.) In other words, they are not aware of the idea that the *techne* of rhetoric includes ethical obligations—as does the *techne* for medicine, poetry, shipbuilding, engineering, computer science, and other disciplines. It seems they have not been exposed to the idea that in practicing a *techne*, what they produce in their writing must serve some larger purpose outside of themselves. In other words, they are unfamiliar with this radical idea: you are not writing for *you*, you are writing for *others*. What good will your writing/ speaking achieve for the polis?

There are ethical systems and standards that are not sectarian, not tied to a particular religious tradition, not deriving only or mainly from religious sources, not only a matter of personal preference. Rather, as the Greeks showed us, ethics is connected with *techne* of various types. There is a moral obligation within the *techne* of medicine, the *techne* of engineering, the *techne* of business, the *techne* of computer science, the *techne* of rhetoric. There is a right way to practice each art, and each art has implicit in it its own ethical requirements vis-à-vis the purpose and *telos* of the art.

In the classical Greek tradition of the *paideia*, the goal of rhetoric was very clearly a social goal, a social ethics, geared for the good of the polis. Now, of course, we can disagree about what path leads to the good of the polis. My path? Your path? Some other path? Of course we have different opinions about that. But that is where rhetoric comes in handy: it is the means by which we interact, negotiate, and resolve our differences—or at least chart a path that we will take together.

And why would students be familiar with ethics or the notion of a rhetorical ethics? First, as far as I can tell, ethics is not systematically offered in the university curriculum, at least not at public research institutions. The university itself may be a little sketchy about what ethics is, whether it is an academic subject and, if so, who should be teaching it. The dominant assumption seems to be that ethics comes from somewhere else, outside of disciplines: typically, from your religion or some set of religious codes, your particular culture, your family heritage or personal upbringing. And so ethics and rhetoric have been shuttled to the sidelines and divided from a number of fields where they are fundamentally essential: business, law, engineering, and science.

We can teach ethics as integral to instruction in rhetoric, writing, and communication—but beyond that we have to rethink/reframe our view of rhetoric altogether, seeing it as praxis as well as *techne*. That reframing means we have to profoundly change how we talk about writing and how we evaluate it. Does the writing present its message clearly? Well, yes, *perspicuity* is an important principle of good writing—it is a stylistic principle that serves the worthy goal of helping the audience understand something—but it is not the only or the main principle. That question represents the Royal Society view, the current traditional view that assigns to rhetoric the charge of getting out of the way.

From an ethical/praxis point of view, the measure of a good piece of writing is this: What good work does it do in the world? What value or benefit does it provide for its audience and for all of us? *Cui bono?* The *telos* of the writing lies somewhere in the world, in people and communities, not on the paper. We need to move from the degraded, limited, instrumental notion of rhetoric as packaging (i.e., rhetoric as referring only to the words on the page or the images in the video) to a view of rhetoric as embodied performance in the world, as action and interaction in the world for the good of others, for the good of the polis.

Our Institutional Location

We are also disadvantaged by our typical institutional locations in the modern disciplinary university. Most of us probably do not encounter the kind of hostility to rhetoric that Peter Ramus, René Descartes, and Thomas Sprat delivered in their time. The university is nicer to us now because we do important things that are loathsome to most people (e.g., teaching writing). But we should not forget that most of us live in a disciplinary structure that is hostile to rhetoric, to all *techne* really.

If you are still located in an English department, you are in a structural location not friendly to the art of rhetoric. The disciplinary framework you are likely to encounter, as Crowley shows us, is historically one born out of confusion between *techne* and *tribe*; a lack of regard for practical, applied knowledge; and a fundamental hostility to rhetoric. It is not a structure that is ever likely to provide adequate support for the *techne* of rhetoric—it just isn't in the DNA—and, with increasing financial pressures on universities and particularly on humanities disciplines, that situation is only likely to get worse.

The English department has never been a happy home for rhetoric—and I believe this institutional location has contributed to our field being distracted from what should be its primary focus: not on texts as aesthetic artifacts but on production, on public engagement, and on relationships as built and maintained through symbolic actions. Which is to say, rhetoric as *techne* and praxis. We have been in an institutional location that regards practical work, client-based projects, community engagement, focus on tools of production, and similar factors as intellectually deficient. Rather, we should be in a location focusing on what language does (as action) and for whom and where and when rather than on what it is (as statement).

Fortunately, the twentieth-century disciplinary research university seems to have run its course, as the old categories and disciplinary alignments become more and more disconnected from public needs. We are seeing the disintegration of the old early twentieth-century disciplinary model of the humanities, a model that divided philosophy, history, literature, and languages into separate departments. That could be a good thing—I'm all for eliminating humanities departments as long as we preserve *humanitatis*: that is, the holistic integrated critical thinking that teaches and promotes rhetoric as ethically responsible direct engagement with the problems and issues of the world.

We have to preserve what is fundamental to the *techne* of rhetoric: What is best for students? While that is an excellent audience-centered question, an even better question from the standpoint of *techne* as praxis is this one: What is best for society? What kind of rhetors does society need, who know how to do what for whom? Yes, we have to think about our students' needs, but ultimately our job as rhetoric instructors is to think about the good of the polis: What kind of rhetors does the world need? Our own *telos* as instructors should be better, more ethical rhetors in the world.

In many ways, the students are ahead of us. I see the Miami University students breaking the stranglehold of the disciplinary mind-set, insisting on transdisciplinarity and practical education. They are choosing double majors and making their own hybrid degrees, cutting and pasting the pieces of the existing university structure to construct their own identities that make sense for their professional lives. What I see at Miami is students moving in the direction of an education based on *techne*, on making things, on internships and co-ops, on study abroad/afar (both international and domestic), and on practical engagement with the world. And, of course, rhetorical interaction is critical for this work. They are changing the model of education to suit their lives even if the university is slow to change itself. What role does a liberal art like rhetoric play in this? Rhetoric has always been about engaged, practical situatedness in the world. (Majors in technical communication and professional writing are one way rhetoric tries to bridge the liberal arts side of rhetoric with the practical needs of society.)

It should be a good time for rhetoric to reestablish itself as important, as vital to higher education, as contributing significantly to public needs and the public good. The key, I believe, is to put rhetoric and ethics, *techne* and praxis back together—Vico showed us one way; our majors in professional writing and technical writing are a promising step in the right direction, as are writing programs that emphasize civic engagement and community partnership. Online education can also be a way to break out of the constraints of the disciplinary, brick-and-mortar institution. The challenge for rhetoric in the twenty-first century will be to find or create an institutional location that values practical engagement with the world, that views such work as intellectually rigorous (as it is), and that respects the role of rhetoric in serving the good of the polis.

NOTES

1. Walter Ong (1958) thinks Ramus's martyrdom probably enhanced his reputation. Ramus was particularly revered by a small Protestant sect known as the Puritans, who imported his ideas to the American colonies. In fact, Triche and McKnight (2004, 40) trace the current structure of US public education back through Descrates to Ramus, whom they argue "flourished in colonial New England owing to the Puritans' appropriation of his ideas . . . , found a home at Harvard from its inception in 1636, and spread across New England townships and countryside, permeating New English institutions." Finally, they argue, "the Puritans' Ramist educational practices [became] the general model for US mass public schooling" (2004, 40).

2. Walter Ong (1958) views Ramism through the lens of theology, not through the lens of gender. But we can certainly see Ramism as a patriarchal/masculinist move to further separate masculine logic (rational discourse) from feminine rhetoric, assigning the more important role—discovery of truth and knowledge—to the masculine art. Rhetoric is necessary only as the vessel, an unreliable one at that, by which truth and knowledge are delivered. Rhetoric is a means of transmitting knowledge, not generating it. Rhetoric was also dismissed on the grounds of its association with persuasion (*pistis*). C. Jan Swearingen (1992) notes that rhetoric has always been associated with belief, feeling, expression, emotion, and persuasion—in Greek, *pathos, peitho,* and *pistis*—and thus has been historically denigrated as feminine and the opposite of rationalistic (masculine) discourse. Finally, related to the elevation of masculinist rationality and the denigration of rhetoric is the subordination or dismissal of the *phatic* aim (McKee and Porter 2017; Porter 2017), a view which posits that the primary purpose of rhetoric/communication is not to win arguments or compel resistant audiences but rather to build and maintain positive relations, achieve harmony and peace, and avoid war and conflict.

3. According to James L. Kinneavy (1982, 21), Isocrates's notion of the goal of rhetoric, its *telos*, was born in "the Athenian notion of a guest's right to protection and compassion," or what was known as *xenia*, the guest-friend relationship: your first obligation, the presumption, in your behavior toward an unknown person was that

you were to treat them well, with respect and graciousness, as a friend—because that unknown person might well be a god. The rhetoric of the open hand. The Greek term for guest/friend, *xenia*, means "guest friendship." And xenophobia is the opposite of that. To violate this principle was to invite the wrath the gods and was a common theme in Greek tragedy.

4.   There were dissenting voices who tried to maintain rhetoric and composition as an important and intellectually respectable enterprise in the modern university—Frederick Newton Scott at Michigan and Gertrude Buck at Vassar are notable examples. But they are exceptions to the general trend. In general, "rhetoric—the original heart of the liberal arts—was not included in the new arts and sciences faculties" (Kinneavy 1988, 108).

REFERENCES

Aristotle. 2006. *On Rhetoric: A Theory of Civic Discourse.* 2nd ed. Trans. George A. Kennedy. Oxford, UK: Oxford University Press.

Atwill, Janet M. 1998. *Rhetoric Reclaimed: Aristotle and the Liberal Arts Tradition.* Ithaca, NY: Cornell University Press.

Augustine. 1997. *On Christian Teaching (De Doctrina Christiana).* Trans. R.P.H. Green. Oxford, UK: Oxford University Press.

Benoit, William L. 1991. "Isocrates and Plato on Rhetoric and Rhetorical Education." *Rhetoric Society Quarterly* 21 (1): 60–71.

Bevilacqua, Vincent. 1972. "Vico, Rhetorical Humanism, and the Study Methods of Our Time." *Quarterly Journal of Speech* 58: 70–83.

Burke, Peter. 1985. *Vico.* Oxford, UK: Oxford University Press.

Cicero. 1948. *De Oratore.* Trans. E. W. Sutton and H. Rackham. Cambridge, MA: Harvard University Press.

Crowley, Sharon. 1998. *Composition in the University: Historical and Polemical Essays.* Pittsburgh, PA: University of Pittsburgh Press.

de Romilly, Jacqueline. 1958. "*Eunoia* in Isocrates or the Political Importance of Creating Good Will." *Journal of Hellenic Studies* 78: 92–101. DOI: 10.2307/628928.

Descartes, René. 1998. *Discourse on Method and Meditations on First Philosophy.* 4th ed. Trans. Donald A. Cress. Indianapolis, IN: Hackett.

Eisenstein, Elizabeth L. 2005. *The Printing Revolution in Early Modern Europe.* 2nd ed. Cambridge, UK: Cambridge University Press.

Foucault, Michel. 1972. *The Archaeology of Knowledge and the Discourse on Language.* Trans. Alan M. Sheridan-Smith. New York: Pantheon Books.

Goffman, Erving. 1974. *Frame Analysis: An Essay on the Organization of Experience.* Boston: Northeastern University Press.

Halloran, S. Michael, and Merrill D. Whitburn. 1982. "Ciceronian Rhetoric and the Rise of Science: The Plain Style Reconsidered." In *The Rhetorical Tradition and Modern Writing,* ed. James M. Murphy, 58–72. New York: Modern Language Association.

Hawkins, Hugh. 1979. "University Identity: The Teaching and Research Functions." In *The Organization of Knowledge in Modern America, 1860–1920,* ed. Alexandra Oleson and John Voss, 285–313. Baltimore: Johns Hopkins University Press.

Isocrates. n.d. *Panathenaicus.* Ed. George Norlin. Perseus Digital Library. http://www.perseus.tufts.edu/hopper/text?doc=Perseus%3Atext%3A1999.01.0144%3Aspeech%3D12.

Jaeger, Warner. 1939. *Paideia: The Ideals of Greek Culture.* 3 vols. Trans. Gilbert Highet. Oxford, UK: Oxford University Press.

Johnstone, Christopher Lyle. 1980. "An Aristotelian Trilogy: Ethics, Rhetoric, Politics, and the Search for Moral Truth." *Philosophy and Rhetoric* 13 (1): 1–24.

Jonsen, Albert R., and Stephen Toulmin. 1988. *The Abuse of Casuistry: A History of Moral Reasoning*. Berkeley: University of California Press.

Kinneavy, James L. 1982. "Restoring the Humanities: The Return of Rhetoric from Exile." In *The Rhetorical Tradition and Modern Writing*, ed. James J. Murphy, 19–28. New York: Modern Language Association.

Kinneavy, James L. 1988. "The Exile of Rhetoric from the Liberal Arts." *JAC* 8 (1–2): 105–12.

Lakoff, George. 2008. "Idea Framing, Metaphors, and Your Brain." YouTube, July 16. http://www.youtube.com/watch?v=S_CWBjyIERY.

Locke, John. 1959. *An Essay Concerning Human Understanding*. Ed. Alexander Campbell Fraser. London: Routledge.

McKee, Heidi A., and James E. Porter. 2017. *Professional Communication and Network Interaction: A Rhetorical and Ethical Approach*. New York: Routledge.

Neem, Johann N. 2017. "From the Humanities to Humanism in an Era of Higher Education Reform." *Process*, February. http://www.processhistory.org/neem-humanities-to-humanism/.

O'Boyle, Lenore. 1983. "Learning for Its Own Sake: The German University as Nineteenth-Century Model." *Comparative Studies in Society and History* 25 (1): 3–25.

Oleson, Alexandra, and John Voss, eds. 1979. *The Organization of Knowledge in Modern America, 1860–1920*. Baltimore: Johns Hopkins University Press.

Ong, Walter J., S.J. 1958. *Ramus, Method, and the Decay of Dialogue: From the Art of Discourse to the Art of Reason*. Chicago: University of Chicago Press.

Ong, Walter J., S.J. 1973. "Ramism." In *Dictionary of the History of Ideas*, ed. Philip Wiener. http://xtf.lib.virginia.edu/xtf/view?docId=DicHist/uvaGenText/tei/DicHist4.xml;chunk.id=dv4–06.

Pappillion, Terry. 1995. "Isocrates' *Techne* and Rhetorical Pedagogy." *Rhetoric Society Quarterly* 25: 149–63.

Perelman, Chaim. 1982. *The Realm of Rhetoric*. Trans. William Kluback. Notre Dame, IN: University of Notre Dame Press.

Perelman, Chaim, and Lucie Olbrechts-Tyteca. 1969. *The New Rhetoric: A Treatise on Argumentation*. Trans. John Wilkinson and Purcell Weaver. Notre Dame, IN: University of Notre Dame Press.

Plato. n.d. *Cratylus*. Trans. Benjamin Jowett. Internet Classic Archive. http://classics.mit.edu/Plato/cratylus.html.

Porter, James E. 1998. *Rhetorical Ethics and Internetworked Writing*. Greenwich, CT: Ablex.

Porter, James E. 2017. "Professional Communication as Phatic: From Classical *Eunoia* to Personal AI." *Business and Professional Communication Quarterly* 80 (2): 174–93. DOI: 10.1177/2329490616671708.

Poulakos, John. 2004. "Rhetoric and Civic Education: From the Sophists to Isocrates." In *Isocrates and Civic Education*, ed. Takis Poulakos and David Depew, 69–83. Austin: University of Texas Press.

Quintilian. 2006. *Institutes of Oratory* (*Institutio Oratoria*). Trans. John Selby Watson. http://rhetoric.eserver.org/quintilian.

Ramus, Peter. 1964 [1543]. *Aristotelicae Animadversiones—Dialecticae Institutiones*. Ed. Wilhelm Risse. Stuttgart-Bad Cannstatt: Frommann-Holzboog.

Ramus, Peter. 1986 [1549]. *Arguments in Rhetoric against Quintilian*. Trans. Carole Newlands. Carbondale: Southern Illinois University Press.

Ramus, Peter. 1992 [1543]. *Peter Ramus's Attack on Cicero: Text and Translation of Ramus's Brutinae Quaestiones*. Ed. James J. Murphy. Trans. Carole Newlands. Davis, CA: Hermagoras.

Ringer, Fritz. 1979. "The German Academic Community." In *The Organization of Knowledge in Modern America, 1860–1920*, ed. Alexandra Oleson and John Voss, 409–29. Baltimore: Johns Hopkins University Press.

Sharratt, Peter. 1991. "Introduction: Ramus, Perelman and Argumentation, a Way through the Wood." *Argumentation* 5 (4): 335–45.

Sprat, Thomas. 1958. *History of the Royal Society.* Ed. Jackson I. Cope and Harold Whitmore Jones. St. Louis, MO: Washington University Press.

Stewart, Donald. 1982. "Two Model Teachers and the Harvardization of English Departments." In *The Rhetorical Tradition and Modern Writing,* ed. James J. Murphy, 118–29. New York: Modern Language Association.

Swearingen, C. Jan. 1992. "*Pistis,* Expression, and Belief: Prolegomenon for a Feminist Rhetoric of Motives." In *A Rhetoric of Doing: Essays on Written Discourse in Honor of James L. Kinneavy,* ed. Stephen P. Witte, Neil Nakadate, and Roger D. Cherry, 123–43. Carbondale: Southern Illinois University Press.

Triche, Stephen, and Douglas McKnight. 2004. "The Quest for Method: The Legacy of Peter Ramus." *History of Education* 33 (1): 39–54. DOI: 10.1080/00467600410001648751.

Veysey, Laurence. 1965. *The Emergence of the American University.* Chicago: University of Chicago Press.

Veysey, Laurence. 1979. "The Plural Organized Worlds of the Humanities." In *The Organization of Knowledge in Modern America, 1860–1920,* ed. Alexandra Oleson and John Voss, 51–106. Baltimore: Johns Hopkins University Press.

Vico, Giambattista. 1990. *On the Study Methods of Our Time* (*De Nostri Temporis Studiorum Ratione*). Trans. Elio Gianturco. Ithaca, NY: Cornell University Press.

Vico, Giambattista. 2000. *New Science.* 3rd ed. Trans. Dave Marsh. London: Penguin Books.

Walzer, Arthur E. 2003. "Quintilian's '*Vir Bonus*' and the Stoic Wise Man." *Rhetoric Society Quarterly* 33 (4): 25–41.

Walzer, Arthur E. 2006. "Moral Philosophy and Rhetoric in the *Institutes*: Quintilian on Honor and Expediency." *Rhetoric Society Quarterly* 36 (3): 263–80.

Wild, John. 1941. "Plato's Theory of *Techne*: A Phenomenological Interpretation." *Philosophy and Phenomenological Research* 1 (3): 225–93.

2

PRACTICALLY WISE AND GOOD
Understanding Phronesis *as a Rhetorical Virtue*

William Duffy

Speech is the mirror of the soul; as a man speaks, so is he.
                                                    —Publilius Syrus

As rhetoricians and teachers of writing, how do we identify and, in turn, teach ethical rhetoric? Such a question begs any number of other questions, not the least of which is whether "ethical rhetoric" is something rhetorical educators would even agree can be defined as such. Two of the inevitable responses—Whose rhetoric? Whose ethics?—can easily be imagined as hasty retorts as much as sincere questions. After all, much of the Western rhetorical tradition is founded on the idea that rhetoric is the art of negotiating persuasion amid conditions of uncertainty, conditions that include competing sets of values. When arguments might ensue about such things as the merits of a proposed course of action, the legitimacy of an accusation, or the propriety of a controversial rallying call—situations that revolve around the deliberative, the forensic, and the epideictic—what counts as an ethical argument in classical rhetorical terms is often determined by the character of the speaker, which is to say that a rhetor's reputation is often the metric for assessing the ethical quality of his or her words—a point Plato's Socrates drives home when he scolds his young interlocutor in the *Phaedrus* for praising a speech delivered by Lysius, a mere sophist unworthy of acclaim.

In contemporary rhetorical scholarship, arguments about the ethics of rhetoric tend to rely heavily on the contingencies of situation and context. For example, the utilitarian ethic that underwrites the democratic rhetorical tradition highlights the importance of inclusiveness and accessibility for determining what makes rhetoric ethical, goals that require constant reassessment of a community's needs (Dewey 2012

DOI: 10.7330/9781607329978.c002

[1927]; Habermas 1991; Zarefsky 1979). Public sphere theorists tend to argue that ethical rhetoric is simply the consequence of normative semantic frameworks that have developed around particular moral traditions (Butler 2013; Warner 2002). Theorists of the "new rhetoric" have forwarded expanded conceptions of reason and rationality as defining characteristics of ethical rhetoric (Burke 1969; Gage 2011; McKeon 1987; Weaver 1985), although Chaim Perelman and Lucie Olbrechts-Tyteca (2011, 1378) are careful to emphasize that standards of language are always relative to "the habits, ways of thoughts, methods, external circumstances, and traditions known to the users of those terms." Finally, there are the scores of rhetoricians who more or less equate the ethics of rhetoric with listening, curiosity, and mutuality, what we might label, however broadly, the "rhetoric of respect" (Booth 1974; Couture 1998; Crowley 2006; Ratcliffe 2005; Young 1992). For these latter theorists, ethical rhetoric is dependent on the underlying aims of the speaker or writer, that is, are they trying to foster identification, promote altruism, or exhibit care, for instance, or are they trying to silence an interlocutor, demean an opponent, or render an insult?

In sum, for many contemporary theorists, rhetoric is first and foremost a resource or set of tools that is neither good nor bad in itself. The ethics rhetoric reflects—whatever might make it "good" in a given instance—can be located in relation to the particular value systems in which those rhetorical actions play out. According to this logic, the relationship between rhetoric and ethics is bilateral; each informs but does not necessarily depend on the other. Consequently, it's difficult to inquire about the ethics *of* rhetoric without slipping into reasoning about ethics *and* rhetoric.

To think more concretely about this slippage, is it possible to develop an ethical framework within which rhetoric can be assessed without recourse to independent, situationally grounded systems of value? Can there be an ethics of rhetoric that is internal to rhetoric itself, what James Porter in this volume calls a search for "an ethic *inside* rhetoric," one that could help us consider what makes rhetoric good apart from the ideologies already at work in rhetorical situations? To do so would require identifying, as much as possible, the general aims we ascribe to rhetoric as both a theoretical and practical concept, even though many teachers of writing probably agree with Candace Spigelman (2001, 324) who notes that "an ethical approach to composition is problematized by a postmodern understanding of the anti-foundational nature of any system of values." To be clear, I'm not interested in the possibility of reaching into the ether to locate Platonic forms from which to define a set of supra-ethical standards for judging discourse. Nor am I interested in throwing out the demands of situational ethics, moral traditions, religious commitments, or anything else that informs how we make and evaluate everyday decisions. Rather, my curiosity stems in large part from Sharon Crowley's (2006, 30) observation that one of the chief problems affecting much of today's public discourse is a lack of concern for framing propositions in ways that allow for stasis amid disagreement, the common ground needed to facilitate further exchange instead of foreclosing it.[1] But it also stems from a related question: How can we promote the qualities of civil exchange that Crowley laments when at present the ecologies of our public discourse have seemingly become resistant to, if not incompatible with, such deliberative ideals?[2]

One potential remedy is found in exploring the connections between rhetoric and virtue in the Aristotelian corpus.[3] For instance, Aristotle positions both rhetoric and virtue as sites of apprenticeship in which students learn that to excel in either requires studying the examples of those who have a demonstrated capacity for such things, whether rhetorical acumen or virtuous character. But they are also related insofar as both rhetoric and virtue are most fully realized in contexts where a decision must be made in the face of competing choices, and this because both rhetoric and virtue are indeterminate—they are founded not on a set of abstract prescriptions but on the simple fact that what is good and expedient is always context-dependent. What ought to be done "in particular circumstances can never, for Aristotle, be fully codified in human speech or writing as a series of abstract antecedently specified rules" (Abizadeh 2002, 268). Herein is where rhetoric and virtue most overlap because to choose the right or most expedient course of action in most situations requires the ability for good deliberation, which for Aristotle, according to M. F. Burnyeat (1980, 83), "is a process whereby practical thought articulates a general good that we wish for and focuses on a particular action it is in our power to do, thereby producing in us a desire to do this thing." In other words, good deliberation involves locating the available means for achieving a "general good," something most people in similar situations would agree is desirable, and, just as important, *wanting* to achieve that outcome.[4] This kind of deliberation requires a continual assessment of the shifting ground under "the good and the expedient, the ideal and the possible," thinking that muddies distinctions between what is right and what is effective since the best outcome in such matters "depends on choosing good ends and appropriate means to achieve them" (Self 1997, 133, 139). In both the *Rhetoric* and the *Nicomachean Ethics* (1999), Aristotle uses the same concept for describing the trait required for such deliberation: the virtue of *phronesis*.

Often translated as "prudence" or "practical wisdom," *phronesis* is a reasoned capacity for demonstrating excellent character and sound judgment in practical matters. The rhetorician John Gage (2005, 35) defines *phronesis* as "an overarching virtue," one that allows us to make "practical decisions based on the good, in particular situations, in the absence of absolute knowledge." While virtue ethicists today categorize *phronesis* as an intellectual virtue, for Aristotle it has a clear moral dimension because, according to him, prudence is apparent only to the good person; that is, one must be habitually disposed to appreciate this disposition in the first place. As he explains, "We fulfill our function [to live excellently] insofar as we have prudence and virtue of character for virtue makes the goal correct, and prudence makes the things promoting the goal correct." Therefore, he reasons, "we cannot be prudent without being good" (Aristotle 1999, Book VI, 12 1144a–b). But how exactly does one identify practical wisdom? Other intellectual virtues, things like episteme (scientific knowledge) or *techne* (craft knowledge), are more or less recognizable in situations where one might expect to see them, say, in a medical doctor's office or in the studio of a portrait artist. But what makes *phronesis* similarly recognizable? Aristotle seems to imply that asking such a question misses the point of that in which practical wisdom consists, which is the promotion of the good life. Or as he explains it, "Prudence is a state grasping the truth, involving reason, concerned with action about things that are good or bad for a human being. For production [e.g., *techne*] has its end in something other than itself, but action does not, since its end is acting well itself" (Aristotle 1999, Book VI, 5 1140b).

Here is another opening for recognizing the link between rhetoric and virtue because to ask about what counts as a practically wise course of action without first studying the particular situation in question assumes what moral philosophers of the deontological persuasion believe, namely, that we are beholden to standards of behavior that exist above and beyond the particularities of circumstance. But Aristotle did not think this way. As J. O. Urmson (1980, 162) puts it:

> If one were to ask Aristotle how to decide how to act on particular occasions, his initial answer would be that one must do so by bringing to bear the intellectual excellence of practical wisdom. If we then ask in what wisdom consists, we shall get a long answer about its involving, among other things, planning ability, experience, ability to appreciate the situation, an executive ability (*deinotes*). There is no simple decision procedure for the wise man to use. How could there be when there are so many variables?

Such a list of variables around which practical wisdom must be negotiated falls squarely in the realm of the rhetorical, the spaces in and out of which we must consider the available means of persuasion. "We cannot remove the deliberating agent from ethics," Arash Abizadeh (2002, 270) reminds us; "judgment is required," and hence the importance of *phronesis*. But as with rhetorical skill, practical wisdom is not a silver bullet. The *phronimos*, or prudent person, can and should be able to anticipate outcomes by weighing available choices, but she certainly can't predict them with complete accuracy. How could she when, to echo Urmson, there are so many variables at work in our everyday affairs?

But just as we shouldn't assume that a practically wise course of action can be flawlessly identified ahead of the action itself, we should also not assume that *phronesis* or any other of the virtues we might invoke to define "good" rhetoric, for that matter, are completely relative.[5] For Aristotle, virtue (*arete*) is only realized when one locates the mean between states of excess and deficiency. So, for instance, a self-absorbed person might indecorously brag about his goodwill to others, while the self-effacing person might deny it. But when a person acts in a way that is neither self-absorbed nor self-effacing but somewhere in the middle, we might say they are exhibiting the virtue of magnanimity. When it comes to the standards we might use to assess ethical rhetoric, then, even though we cannot and should not expect to be able to define such rhetoric ahead of the actual situation, this doesn't mean that attempting to establish such standards is a fool's errand, especially if we turn to the virtue ethical tradition for outlining what those standards might be.[6]

The turn to Aristotelian virtue ethics as a resource for teachers of rhetoric and composition has most recently been taken up by John Duffy in a series of essays that explore the consequences of recognizing how the teaching of writing presupposes the teaching of ethics. In his contribution to *Naming What We Know*, for instance, Duffy (2015, 31) notes that writers constantly make ethical choices "because every time we write for another person, we propose a relationship with other human beings." In "The Good Writer," Duffy (2017, 231) follows up this observation by proposing "rhetorical virtues," his term for understanding how virtues such as honesty and generosity get manifested discursively by writers interested in promoting these dispositions with their rhetoric.[7] While I don't have the space to comment on the full range of virtues that might align with Duffy's project, I do want to use the remainder of this chapter to consider *phronesis* as a rhetorical virtue because when we survey the virtues Aristotle explicates in the *Nicomachean Ethics* (1999), not only is *phronesis* the one that appears most elusive, it's also the one Aristotle seems to position as the most important. As Daniel C. Russell (2013, 13) reminds us, most virtue ethicists "have believed that we are defined by our capacity for practical reasoning, both in thinking about what to do and in acting with emotions that can be intelligently trained." In other words, whatever qualities we might use to identify ethical rhetoric, *phronesis* is the one that allows us to recognize and, in turn, foster all the other virtues. But this gets us back to the question I posed earlier: How *does* one identify practical wisdom? In this case, what does practical wisdom "practically" entail if we want to understand it as a rhetorical virtue in the teaching of writing?

I can imagine two primary qualities we might ascribe to rhetoric that is practically wise. The first is that such rhetoric displays decorum, which is to say practically wise rhetoric *is appropriate for the situation at hand.* While decorum sometimes gets associated with genteel behavior, as a rhetorical concept it speaks more generally to the habits and expectations we come to associate with how various types of generic (i.e., recurrent) situations play out. How audience members comport themselves at a child's piano recital, a high school marching band competition, or a Super Bowl halftime concert will be very different from one instance to the next, even though all three examples fall under the general category of a music performance. Accordingly, decorous rhetoric is rhetoric that "fits" with the rhetorical situation.[8] This aligns with Gage's (2005, 35, original emphasis) understanding of *phronesis* as the capacity "that enables people who we consider (for the most part) to be ethical arguers to know, not *what* arguments to make, but *when* a particular *kind* of rhetorical act is appropriate and when it isn't." This leads to the second quality I propose for identifying practically wise rhetoric, and that is its capacity to foster *the continuation of interaction and exchange.* By this I mean that practically wise rhetoric has an invitational quality that anticipates the potential for further discourse.

I will tackle these two ideas one at a time.

At their most basic level, virtues speak to qualities of attitude. As Julia Annas (2001, 8, original emphasis) notes about Aristotle's conception of virtue more generally, "It is *active*: to have it is to be disposed to act in certain ways," so *phronesis* can't and shouldn't be equated with specific behaviors; it should instead be understood as a *disposition to act* toward particular ends. But to what ends? As I noted earlier, Aristotle (1999, Book VI, 5 1140a) explains that *phronesis* is what allows us to make decisions that support "living well in general." The Greek term here is *eudaimonia*, which both virtue ethicists and rhetoricians have historically translated as "happiness" or "human flourishing" or even more specifically, achieving one's full potential. As J. L. Ackrill (1980, 24, original emphasis) suggests, "There can be plenty of disagreement as to what form of life *is eudaimonia*, but no disagreement that *eudaimonia* is what we all want." In this way, *eudaimonia* as a virtue ethical concept is not that different from the "happiness" concept in speech-act theory, the belief that when one's words are appropriately deployed in a rhetorical situation, they meet certain felicity conditions that make intelligible the potential for rhetorical action in that context. In the *Rhetoric*, Aristotle notes that *eudaimonia* is speaking without qualification, for "all forms of exhortation and dissuasion are concerned with this and things that contribute, or are opposed, to it; for one should do things that provide happiness or one of its parts or that make it greater rather than less, and not do things that destroy it or impede it or effect its opposites" (Kennedy 1991, 57). To make sense of this claim from a rhetorical perspective, we might say that what makes rhetoric good is the extent to which it results in "happy" consequences—rhetoric that achieves its ends without qualification—without an excess of misunderstanding. Practically wise rhetoric must therefore be fitting; it reflects a rhetor's awareness of her audience, the time and place of her words, and what historically have been the expectations for rhetors in similar circumstances.

To suggest that practically wise rhetoric adheres to decorum speaks to the conditions from which an audience assesses credibility, especially to the extent they are willing to listen, engage, and be persuaded by a rhetor. Indeed, consider what Aristotle (1999, Book VI, 9 1142b) says in his discussion of *phronesis* in the *Nicomachean Ethics*, that "good deliberation is correctness that accords with what is beneficial, about the right thing, in the right way, and at the right time." To exhibit practical wisdom therefore requires, first and foremost, enough training and experience to be able to identify the mores and customs at work in rhetorical situations, what counts as "right" for those circumstances. A practically wise rhetor, we might say, is rhetorically attuned and virtuously disposed to the contingencies of circumstance, ready to adjust his or her words as a conversation, debate, or other discourse plays out in ways that are appropriate for that place and time.

So when it comes to the decorous demands of *phronesis*, the student of rhetoric learns to reflect on and learn from his rhetorical practice, which on a basic level means there is virtue in helping students internalize not only the idea that practical wisdom (however we might talk about it) develops with experience but also that they are more likely to develop this capacity by treating rhetorical engagements, especially ones that involve conflict, in ways that leave room for such practical wisdom to manifest itself. This leads to my second recommendation for understanding *phronesis* as a rhetorical virtue, namely, that when the possibility for continued interaction and exchange is exhausted, so, too, is the potential for rhetorical flourishing in the Aristotelian sense of *eudaimonia*. While I'm hesitant to linger on and inadvertently reify the proposal that rhetoric has an ultimate end, I do think that rhetorical flourishing from a virtue ethical standpoint is rooted in the continuation of discourse. If the virtue of *phronesis* requires rhetors to balance what is good with what is expedient, in other words, the "expedient" might in this sense mean not only rising to the demands of particular exigencies but doing so in ways that don't foreclose the possibility of further exchange.

To develop the claim that practically wise rhetoric aims for the continuation of interaction and exchange, I believe there is value in considering what the early twentieth-century sociologist George Herbert Mead argues is the emergent quality of social ethics. His is a philosophy based on an ecological understanding of the way all ethics naturally evolve, one that anticipates in important ways the material rhetorics now gaining popularity in humanities studies.[9] Organisms and environments are mutually determinative; every adaptation on the part of the organism results in a new (or at least changed) environment, and every change in the environment requires a similar adaptation on the part of the organism. Here is how Mead (1964, 83) puts it in his characteristic idiom: "The growth of moral consciousness must be coterminous with that of the moral situation. The moral life lies in the interaction of these two; the situation rises up in the accusation of the moral personality which is unequal to it, and the personality rises to the situation only by a process which reconstructs the situation as profoundly as it reconstructs the self." While abstract, when Mead uses the term *moral*, he has in mind something more expansive than codes of conduct about right and wrong; he is speaking to the entire range of forces that bear upon our actions. In this way, Mead (1964, 84) declares, "There is nothing which may not be a condition or an element of conduct, and moral consciousness reaches its climax in the estimation of every possible content of the individual and his situation." What he offers here is a pragmatic understanding of ethical behavior as an emergent quality of our interactions, one that arises *within* and *not before* our mutual engagements with one another. The motive for moral action, he says, "does not arise from the relations of antecedently given ends of activities"; rather, "the motive is the recognition of the ends as it arises in consciousness," and thus "the moral interpretation of our experience must be found within the experience itself" (Mead 1964, 85–86). While it might be tempting to label this claim a defense of relativism—after all, he's saying that morality is an emergent quality of localized actions—it points more accurately to a casuistic model of moral reasoning in which the determination between right and wrong is less important than the determination of what constitutes the best possible outcome for all the parties involved in a given situation, which, to bring this back to the virtue ethical approach I'm using to understand the ethics of rhetoric, suggests a *eudaimonic* kind of open-ended flourishing.

So how is the notion that *phronesis* is actualized through the continuation of interaction and exchange supported by Mead's philosophy of language? The closest answer to this question comes when Mead (1964, 331) equates "thought with the solution of problems." Specifically, he argues that the problem underlying all of our interactions all of the time is the continuation of the common world. While it is easy to chalk up differences between one another as difference in worldview, Mead (1963, 34) reminds us that "there lies before them [us] a common world" and "this common world is continually breaking down. Problems arise in it and demand solution." When applied to his general ethics of experience, Mead is suggesting that discourse that is good, in general, is discourse that continues the common world, the shared world that not only makes our experiences with one another possible but makes the *potentiality for further experience* possible as well.[10] To be sure, this ethic does not trump or render unimportant our moral commitments. As Mead (1964, 342) puts it, "This criterion of truth does not then transcend experience, but simply regards the conditions of ongoing experience which has become problematic through the inhibitions of the natural processes of men." When we identify the primary ethic at work in Mead's philosophy of language as the continuation of the common world, to say that one of rhetoric's general ethics should therefore be that our interactions with one another should not foreclose the potential for further discourse, all this means is that while we cannot predict the specific demands our future interactions will engage, we can anticipate that to the extent that we allow our current interactions to limit these further exchanges, we are in essence restricting what will be the available means of persuasion for shaping the mutual conditions that will define our shared future.[11]

I don't expect this outline of *phronesis* as a rhetorical virtue to spark immediate pedagogical uptakes. After all, what I've offered here is a speculative rendering of how to imagine the rhetorical potential of what is perhaps the most abstract of Aristotle's virtues. With that said, by way of conclusion I will share one example of how I recently witnessed a student begin to come to terms with the practical wisdom of rhetoric as it concerned a heated classroom debate in which he found himself a potential instigator. A couple of semesters ago, while teaching a first-year writing course, I had students produce rhetorical analyses of two photos related to the Black Lives Matter campaign. The first photo showed two African American women standing in the middle of a street during a protest. One of the women is holding a sign with the BLM hashtag written on it, and the other is holding a sign that reads "Is My Son Next?" The second photo showed a piece of graffiti next to what looks to be a basketball court in a park. The text of the graffiti reads "Black Lives Matter," but overtop the "Black" someone wrote the word "ALL" in bright-red paint. I asked students to identify the different claims conveyed in each image and to then consider the rhetorical tactics they suggest.

During the ensuing discussion about the photos, several students pointed out and elaborated on how the second image, the one depicting the claim that "all" lives matter, could be interpreted as an attempt to silence minority voices. One student, whom I'll call Chris, was visibly agitated. When I asked if he wanted to share his thoughts, Chris offered an impassioned defense of the latter claim. "But all lives *should* matter," he kept saying, followed by the assertion that "he shouldn't have to feel like a racist for saying this." The atmosphere in the classroom quickly turned tense; it was obvious that several of the other students wanted to respond but didn't. From my vantage, I could see that Chris was sincere, namely, that he didn't want to be viewed as racist for believing that the "All Lives Matter" claim is just as important as the "Black Lives Matter" one, but what he wasn't seeing is that his articulation of this belief was overpowering the voices of some of his classmates. After class ended, Chris approached me to ask if he was "wrong" for saying what he did. In response, I asked what he thought of his remarks. He reiterated his belief that all lives matter but said he didn't understand why no one responded to him. Rather than attempt an answer, I encouraged Chris to pose this question in the next class meeting, suggesting that he think about different ways of framing his question, especially ways that don't sound oppositional to the concerns raised by Black Lives Matter.

To be honest, I don't recall the details of that subsequent class meeting. I do remember that Chris brought up the previous discussion and that other students responded, but I don't remember much more. What stands out to me as someone interested in the ethics of rhetoric, however, is that short conversation Chris initiated with me. At the time, I wasn't thinking about the ideas I've shared in this chapter; in fact, when I encouraged Chris to reengage his classmates, I wasn't thinking about this course of action as an "ethical" response to a stymied exchange. All I knew is that the only way to resolve this discursive conflict was to engage in further discourse. But reflecting on that experience now, I recognize Chris's dilemma as an example of rhetoric that aspired to but failed to be practically wise. As for the question of decorum, Chris's words were appropriate for the conversation. That is, he adhered to the conventions of a classroom discussion: he didn't talk over his classmates, he was on topic, and his contribution was intended to spark further discussion. What he didn't recognize, however, is how his comments actually put a cap on the discussion. Chalk it up to the exasperated tone of his delivery or that he failed to acknowledge the legitimate aims of the Black Lives Matter movement or that he overemphasized his personal desire not be viewed as racist (and thus prioritizing, at least seemingly, his own feelings over the plight of African Americans unfairly targeted by law enforcement)—whatever it was, his remarks failed to leave room for the continuation of the common world, so to speak, embodied by the members of this particular writing course.

The fact that this example is the one that came to mind as I was writing an earlier draft of this chapter doesn't surprise me, at least not as far as my thinking about the pedagogical applications of *phronesis* is concerned. That is, I wonder if practical wisdom isn't most identifiable when it is absent, when what we are left with is misunderstanding, which according to I. A. Richards (1936), rhetoric exists to remedy. Of course, this makes sense only insofar as we recognize that as with all the virtues, *phronesis* is an emergent capacity that develops with experience, with trial and error, with others showing us when and how we've missed the mark. Perhaps, then, *phronesis* manifests most concretely in moments that resemble those of *esprit de l'escalier*, after-the-fact recognitions of missed opportunity. When it comes to what we might call ethical rhetoric, then, I suggest that what practical wisdom demands of us is a willingness to treat our argumentative encounters with one another as the contingent opportunities they are. Moreover, when we are equipped with the knowledge that virtue is what develops with experience and not prior to it, we are more likely to embrace the prudence necessary to harness that virtue by treating rhetorical encounters in ways that leave room for such practical wisdom to suggest itself.

NOTES

1.   While the overall scope of their respective arguments is quite different, Crowley's concern for the state of public discourse is similar to the concern MacIntyre

(2007) articulates in the beginning of his seminal *After Virtue*, namely, that humanity has no common moral language with which to communicate ethical concerns.

2. While I agree with Christy Friend (1999, 16) that calling attention to the "mean-spiritedness" that inheres in much of our public discourse is "so commonplace as to be a rhetorical trope, obligatory for anyone who writes on ethical issues for academic and public forums alike," I do think that since the election of Donald Trump there have been some compelling arguments that public discourse has undergone a structural shift in ways that render the values associated with deliberative rhetoric quaint, even anachronistic. For example, Scott Sundvall argues that Trump's discourse (and, by extension, much of the talk prompted by Trump's discourse, especially on social media) is more *electrate* than *literate* in Gregory Ulmer's use of these terms. "Literacy is still a vital component of intellectual development," explains Sundvall (2017), but "the post-truth era has already arrived, a Third Sophistic in need of sobering reanalysis, and using the apparatus logic of the past (literacy) to combat the rhetoric of the present (electracy) will win few battles." For more on the idea of electracy, see Ulmer (2004).

3. I've made an earlier argument for this in "Rhetoric, Virtue, and the Necessity of Invention" (2009).

4. Lois Self (1997, 136) explains this idea by noting how in both the *Rhetoric* and the *Nicomachean Ethics* what counts as "the good" is whatever is most sought after by everyone, and as a result, "rule by consent rather than force makes requisite the virtue of practical wisdom and the art of rhetoric."

5. In fact and as this chapter attempts to do, I believe we can position *phronesis* as a virtue that holds across contexts, what Martha Nussbaum (2000, 448) might explain as a non-relative ethical capacity informed by "general rules" but reliant on a "keen awareness of particulars."

6. As should be clear, I don't conflate virtue ethics with the stuff of "character education," the popular neo-conservative approach to the teaching of ethics that Friend (1999, 19) nicely summarizes as "static properties to be stored in and conveyed through culturally shared texts."

7. For the record, I don't think Duffy's approach to virtue ethics and rhetorical education necessarily falls under the "rhetoric of respect" rubric I mentioned at the beginning of this chapter. There are two reasons for this. First, Duffy doesn't define "good" rhetoric according to any one virtue or set of virtues. Instead, he offers virtue ethics as a framework for assessing what good rhetoric might look like and do in particular situations. Second, Duffy doesn't confine his treatment of virtue to qualities that would necessarily foster positive forms of identification. "Righteous anger can also be a virtue," he notes, "called upon in the right moment, for the right audience, for the right purpose" (Duffy 2015–16, 6).

8. I'm using "rhetorical situation" in a general sense, which is to say I agree with Scott Consigny (1994, 178) who reminds us that a rhetorical situation always "involves particularities of persons, actions, and agencies in a certain place and time," constraints that can't be ignored if we want our rhetoric to be effective.

9. One of the most accessible summaries of how this material turn is at work in rhetoric and composition studies is Micciche (2014).

10. In a recent article, Craig Rood (2017, 314) theorizes "Rhetorical Closure," a concept he offers to help us understand "communication that attempts to stop further communication." While I don't have the space to comment on how this might be useful for understanding *phronesis* as a rhetorical virtue, I will point out that Rood considers this concept as descriptive, not evaluative. That is, he leaves open the question of when rhetorical closure might or might not be ethical.

11.   As I read early versions of the chapters in this volume, I noticed that this concern
      for the reciprocal continuation of interaction and exchange resonates with Bo
      Wang's discussion of the methodological relations between the Confucian notions
      of *ren* and *shu*, wherein the *shu* denotes a concern for reciprocal mutuality that
      promotes the quality of flourishing associated with *ren*.

REFERENCES

Abizadeh, Arash. 2002. "The Passions of the Wise: *Phronesis*, Rhetoric, and Aristotle's Passionate Practical Deliberation." *Review of Metaphysics* 56: 267–96.

Ackrill, J. L. 1980. "Aristotle on *Eudaimonia*." In *Essays on Aristotle's Ethics*, ed. Amélie Oksenberg Rorty, 15–33. Berkeley: University of California Press.

Annas, Julia. 2011. *Intelligent Virtue*. Oxford, UK: Oxford University Press.

Aristotle. 1999. *Nicomachean Ethics*. 2nd ed. Trans. Terence Irwin. Indianapolis, IN: Hackett.

Booth, Wayne C. 1974. *Modern Dogma and the Rhetoric of Assent*. Chicago: University of Chicago Press.

Burke, Kenneth. 1969. *A Rhetoric of Motives*. Berkeley: University of California Press.

Burnyeat, M. F. 1980. "Aristotle on Learning to Be Good." In *Essays on Aristotle's Ethics*, ed. Amélie Oksenberg Rorty, 69–92. Berkeley: University of California Press.

Butler, Judith. 2013. "The Sensibility of Critique: Response to Asad and Mahmood." In *Is Critique Secular? Blasphemy, Injury, and Free Speech*, ed. Talal Asad, Wendy Brown, Judith Butler, and Saba Mahmood, 95–130. New York: Fordham University Press.

Consigny, Scott. 1974. "Rhetoric and Its Situations." *Philosophy and Rhetoric* 7 (3): 175–86.

Couture, Barbara. 1998. *Toward a Phenomenological Rhetoric: Writing, Profession, and Altruism*. Carbondale: Southern Illinois University Press.

Crowley, Sharon. 2006. *Toward a Civil Discourse: Rhetoric and Fundamentalism*. Pittsburgh, PA: University of Pittsburgh Press.

Dewey, John. 2012 [1927]. *The Public and Its Problems: An Essay in Political Inquiry*. Ed. Melvin L. Rogers. University Park: Pennsylvania State University Press.

Duffy, John. 2015. "Writing Involves Making Ethical Choices." In *Naming What We Know: Threshold Concepts in Writing Studies*, ed. Linda Adler-Kassner and Elizabeth Wardle, 31–32. Logan: Utah State University Press.

Duffy, John. 2015–16. "Reconsidering Virtue." *Journal of the Assembly for Expanded Perspectives on Learning* 21: 3–8.

Duffy, John. 2017. "The Good Writer: Virtue Ethics and the Teaching of Writing." *College English* 79 (3): 229–50.

Duffy, William. 2009. "Rhetoric, Virtue, and the Necessity of Invention." In *The Responsibilities of Rhetoric*, ed. Michelle Smith and Barbara Warnick, 37–43. Long Grove, IL: Waveland.

Friend, Christy. 1999. "Resisting Virtue: Rhetoric, Writing Pedagogy, and Popular Moral Discourse." *Composition Forum* 10 (1): 16–29.

Gage, John. 2005. "In Pursuit of Rhetorical Virtue." *Lore* 5 (1): 29–37.

Gage, John. 2011. "Introduction." In *The Promise of Reason: Studies in the New Rhetoric*, ed. John T. Gage, 1–7. Carbondale: Southern Illinois University Press.

Habermas, Jurgen. 1991. *The Structural Transformation of the Public Sphere: An Inquiry into the Category of Bourgeois Society*. Cambridge, MA: MIT Press.

Kennedy, George A. 1991. *Aristotle on Rhetoric: A Theory of Civic Discourse*. New York: Oxford University Press.

MacIntyre, Alasdair. 2007. *After Virtue: A Study in Moral Theory*. 3rd ed. Notre Dame, IN: University of Notre Dame Press.

McKeon, Richard. 1987. *Rhetoric: Essays in Invention and Discovery*. Ed. Mark Backman. Woodbridge, CT: Ox Bow.

Mead, George Herbert. 1964. *Selected Writings*. Ed. Andrew J. Reck. Indianapolis, IN: Bobbs Merrill.

Micciche, Laura. 2014. "Writing Material." *College English* 76 (6): 488–505.

Nussbaum, Martha. 2000. "Non-Relative Virtues: An Aristotelian Approach." In *Ethics: Classical Western Texts in Feminist and Multicultural Perspectives*, ed. James P. Sterba, 439–57. New York: Oxford University Press.

Perelman, Chaim, and Lucie Olbrechts-Tyteca. 2001. "From *The New Rhetoric*." In *The Rhetorical Tradition: Readings from Classical Times to the Present*, ed. Patricia Bizzell and Bruce Herzberg, 1375–78. 2nd ed. Boston: Bedford/St. Martin's.

Ratcliffe, Krista. 2005. *Rhetorical Listening: Identification, Gender, Whiteness*. Carbondale: Southern Illinois University Press.

Richard, I. A. 1936. *The Philosophy of Rhetoric*. New York: Oxford University Press.

Rood, Craig. 2017. "Rhetorical Closure." *Rhetoric Society Quarterly* 47 (4): 313–34.

Russell, Daniel C. 2013. "Virtue Ethics, Happiness, and the Good Life." In *The Cambridge Companion to Virtue Ethics*, ed. Daniel C. Russell, 7–28. Cambridge, UK: Cambridge University Press.

Self, Lois S. 1997. "Rhetoric and *Phronesis*: The Aristotelian Ideal." *Philosophy and Rhetoric* 12 (2): 130–45.

Spigelman, Candace. 2001. "What Role Virtue?" *JAC: A Journal of Rhetoric, Culture, and Politics* 21 (2): 321–48.

Sundvall, Scott. 2017. "The First 100 Days of an Electrate President: Post-Truth, Alternative Facts, and Fake News in the Third Sophistic." *Textshop Experiments* 3. http://textshopexperiments.org/textshop03/first-100-days-of-an-electrate-president.

Ulmer, Gregory. 2004. *Teletheory*. 2nd ed. New York: Atropos.

Urmson, J. O. 1980. "Aristotle's Doctrine of the Mean." In *Essays on Aristotle's Ethics*, ed. Amélie Oksenberg Rorty, 157–70. Berkeley: University of California Press.

Warner, Michael. 2002. *Publics and Counterpublics*. Cambridge, MA: Zone Books.

Weaver, Richard. 1985 [1953]. *The Ethics of Rhetoric*. Davis, CA: Hermagoras.

Young, Richard. 1992. "Rogerian Argument and the Context of Situation: Taking a Closer Look." In *Rogerian Perspectives: Collaborative Rhetoric for Oral and Written Communication*, ed. Nathaniel Teich, 109–21. Norwood, NJ: Ablex.

Zarefsky, David. 1979. "The Great Society as a Rhetorical Problem." *Quarterly Journal of Speech* 65 (1979): 364–78.

3
REIMAGINING THE ETHICS OF STYLE

Lois Agnew

We live in a world that desperately needs ethics. We also live in a world that desperately needs greater appreciation for the power of language. Although many of us might assume that there is an obvious connection between the two, we also have ample evidence that this is not a perspective that everyone shares. The argument becomes even more complicated when rhetorical history becomes part of the mix. Certainly, there are good reasons for people in the field of rhetoric and writing studies to be wary of placing too much emphasis on Western rhetorical history, particularly if that interest leads to a nostalgia for a classical ideal that was never really ideal.

But it is complexity and imperfection that makes Western rhetorical history such a valuable resource in conversations about rhetoric and ethics today. Rhetorical history offers varied models for thinking through why it's so important to bring rhetoric and ethics together and how the relationship between the two can be enacted and sustained. Rhetorical history also reminds us that as passionately and as long as people have debated the question of what the union of rhetoric and ethics entails, they've never quite settled on "the right answer." This recognition can promote a nuanced approach to contemporary discussions of how to teach and practice an ethical rhetoric, as well as encourage a productive humility in our efforts to respond to questions that have remained unresolved for centuries.

Rhetorical history offers a number of models for theorizing and teaching ethical rhetoric, and I'm particularly interested here in exploring style's central role in ancient conversations about ethical communication, as well as examining the historical forces that have persistently complicated this perspective. Much of Western rhetorical history has been guided by the classical view that the choices people make about language are an integral part of their message and one of the primary means through which ethos is established. However, this perspective has

DOI: 10.7330/9781607329978.c003

gradually been eclipsed as a consequence of tensions in the way style has been conceived within and beyond our discipline. A historical perspective offers insight into the regrettable detachment of language from ethics, points toward the role of our discipline in enabling that separation, and offers a path forward for reasserting the vital link among ethics, rhetoric, and language. Engagement with rhetorical history illuminates some of the factors that have interfered with efforts to assert the central role of style in sustaining the vital relationship between rhetoric and ethics, and it also offers an opportunity to explore how renewed attention to style might support the enactment of our field's commitment to the development of an ethical rhetoric today.

THE DILEMMA OF AN ETHICS OF STYLE IN WESTERN RHETORICAL HISTORY

Plato's representation of style as both a corrupting influence and the means for achieving rhetoric's ethical purpose foregrounds a tension that has surrounded efforts to define the relationships among style, rhetoric, and ethics for centuries. In *Gorgias*, Plato (2001a, 123) cautions against skillful use of language that is "set on gratifying the citizens" rather than engagement in a dialectical process that focuses strictly on the pursuit of truth. However, in *Phaedrus*, written more than a decade after *Gorgias*, Plato (2001b) depicts attention to style as a major element of the approach to artful rhetoric that supports the search for truth. In this dialogue, ethical persuasion originates with the rhetor's knowledge of the soul of the person who is being addressed. This step is followed by careful attention to diction that will support the speaker's ability to share the truth with a particular audience:

> He must now make a practical application of a certain kind of speech in a certain way to persuade his hearer to a certain action or belief—when he has acquired all this, and has added thereto a knowledge of the times for speaking and for keeping silence, and has also distinguished the favorable occasions for brief speech or pitiful speech or intensity and all the classes of speech which he has learned, then, and not till then, will his art be fully and completely finished. (Plato 2001b, 163–64)

The juxtaposition of Plato's suspicion that skillful language use may threaten rhetoric's ethical commitment with his explication of style as integral to the pursuit of artful persuasion brings into focus the conundrum that has challenged efforts to articulate the relationships among style, rhetoric, and ethics for many centuries: on one hand, style can provide the basis for mesmerizing and misleading audiences; on the other hand, style embodies the speaker's ethical commitments and facilitates the relationships with others that are crucial to rhetoric's mission.

The unresolved tensions that infuse Plato's writings about rhetoric are to some extent offset by Isocrates's confidence that language plays an integral role in cultivating public and private virtue. His system of rhetorical education instantiates a number of classical concepts concerning language's role in supporting intellectual discipline and fostering social relationships. Isocrates's rhetorical vision features a mythical account of civilization's origin in language that proves influential in subsequent classical and early modern rhetorical theories. This myth portrays language as uniquely empowering humanity through "the power to persuade each other and to make clear to each other that whatever we desire, not only have we escaped the life of wild beasts, but we have come together and founded cities and made laws and invented arts" (Isocrates 1929, 254). Because Isocrates sees language as the foundation for fully realizing the human potential of shared understanding and social harmony, he perceives the outcome of instruction attentive to the skillful use of language as an intricate network of interrelated achievements. While he makes no definite promises concerning the capacity of rhetoric to promote an ethical disposition, he insists that rhetorical education is the most likely path to the development of personal and civic virtue:

> I consider that the kind of art which can implant honesty and justice in depraved natures has never existed and does not now exist, and that people who profess that power will grow weary and cease from their vain pretensions before such an education is ever found. But I do hold that people can become better and worthier if they conceive an ambition to speak well, if they become possessed of the desire to be able to persuade their hearers, and, finally, if they set their hearts on seizing the advantage—I do not mean "advantage" in the sense given to that word by the empty-minded, but advantage in the true meaning of that term. (Isocrates 1929, 274–75)

Isocrates stresses the value of rhetorical education in cultivating judgment; although inborn talent with language is valuable, innate ability with language does not ensure the reflection that is crucial to the development of an ethical perspective. He criticizes those who maintain an abstract appreciation for language without maintaining a commitment to an educational enterprise that requires students to connect their rhetorical practice to real social concerns. Isocrates's stated goal is to provide instruction and practical application to ensure that people achieve their full potential as rhetors and citizens, an approach that includes consistent attention to style:

I marvel at men who felicitate those who are eloquent by nature on being blessed with a noble gift, and yet rail at those who wish to become eloquent, on the ground that they desire an immoral and debasing education . . . it is well that in all activities, and most of all in the art of speaking, credit is won, not by gifts of fortune, but by efforts of study. For men who have been gifted with eloquence by nature and by fortune are governed in what they say by chance, and not by any standard of what is best, whereas those who have gained this power by the study of philosophy and by the exercise of reason never speak without weighing their words, and so are less often in error as to a course of action. (Isocrates 1929, 291–92)

Isocrates's lofty confidence in the power of style is grounded in practical application to civic life, which means that his idea of rhetoric is neither purely theoretical nor strictly instrumental. Werner Jaeger notes that for Isocrates, "artistically disciplined Form" represents "the middle way between highflown theory and vulgar penny-chasing technical adroitness." (1994 [1943], 133) Isocrates sees rhetoric not as a system of rigid rules but as a discipline that requires students to use their own talents and ingenuity in fashioning discourse that has "the qualities of fitness for the occasion, propriety of style, and originality of treatment." Thus Isocratean oratory constitutes not merely the means to the end of achieving judgment but an "imaginative literary creation" (Jaeger 1994 [1943], 134) that serves as the foundation for forming community; students become good citizens through an educational process that fosters the intellectual power they develop through artistic discipline that both promotes intellectual agility and strengthens their relationships with other people.

Cicero's *De inventione* (1949) carries forward Isocrates's account of language as the divine gift that brought civilization into being. Cicero (1949, I, ii) describes rhetoric's introduction into society as the result of the recognition of "the power latent in man and the wide field offered by his mind for great achievements if one could develop this power and improve it by instruction." Because language has been given to humans as the primary vehicle for creating strong social relationships, attention to skill with language is intrinsically an ethical endeavor. Eloquence serves as a vital force in the process through which people "learn to keep faith and observe justice and become accustomed to obey others voluntarily and believe not only that they must work for the common good but even sacrifice life itself" (Cicero 1949, I, ii). Cicero therefore sustains Isocrates's view of style's importance in cultivating the qualities central to an ethical sensibility. For Cicero as for Isocrates, attention to style fosters intellectual discipline, civic responsibility, and social awareness, which collectively strengthen the individual's capacity for virtue.

This link means that language fully embodies character; as he explains in *De oratore*, "Such influence, indeed, is produced by a certain feeling and art in speaking, that the speech seems to represent, as it were, the character of the speaker; for, by adopting a peculiar mode of thought and expression, united with action that is gentle and indicative of amiableness, such an effect is produced that the speaker seems to be a man of probity, integrity, and virtue" (Cicero 1970, II, xliii). In *De officiis* (1947, I, xxxv), Cicero depicts his vision of the comprehensive relationship among language, character, and social engagement as synthesized in the concept of propriety, which "shows itself also in every deed, in every word, even in every movement and attitude of the body. And in outward, visible propriety there are three elements—beauty, tact, and taste . . . in these three elements is included also our concern for the good opinion of those with whom and amongst whom we live."

The Isocratean and Ciceronian view of style as the manifestation of individual character and as central to the formation of strong social relationships resonates across centuries of Western rhetoric's development. The assumption that language has a fundamental role in the formation of a healthy society appears for many ancient and early modern theorists to connect naturally with the idea that both intellectual growth and social relationships are achieved through attention to style. Yet in spite of Cicero's profound influence on the evolution of Western rhetorical history, various developments within and beyond the academy have altered perceptions concerning the value of style in a student's educational program. In some instances, this was the result of new iterations of Plato's suspicion that rhetoric threatens the pursuit of truth. Although prominent Renaissance rhetoricians such as Thomas Wilson upheld the importance of style in fulfilling rhetoric's ethical function (see Agnew 1998b), anxieties about excessive attention to the fine points of language use are also present in dominant strains of rhetorical history during the same period. One of these strains understands stylistic considerations to be entirely distinct from the content of the message, a position that refigures Plato's concern that linguistic flourishes potentially distract audiences from the essence of what they need to understand. As James Porter has aptly argued in this volume, this view achieved new force during the sixteenth century through the Ramistic division between rhetoric and logic, a position that challenged the premise that rhetoric's central function "is to do good work in the world, to provide value or benefit for somebody, to change the world from its current state to some better state." The Ramistic view not only undermined our disciplinary claim to intellectual substance through institutionalizing the view of rhetoric as a mechanical process entirely distinct from art, but it also discounted the intricacies of language choice as integral to the process of ethical decision-making. This view has contributed to the diminished reputation of our field over time and has also supported the dangerous assumption that ethics can be removed from the realm of language entirely: that the words we select are somehow independent of our efforts to pursue good and meaningful relationships with others and to cultivate a social life in which people are able to work together productively.

A related historical challenge comes through the writings of seventeenth-century scientists whose challenge to the dynamic interaction between style and ethics came about through their insistence that language should be reduced to the seamless transmission of content achieved through empirical investigation. Thomas Sprat's 1667 discussion of the formation of the Royal Society defines the goal of language as accurate representation and sharply criticizes ancient writers who departed from reporting facts in a manner "that impos'd their <u>imaginations</u> on us, as the only <u>Truths</u>" (1959, 117). In a similar vein, John Locke offers an influential critique of the historical emphasis on stylistic refinement, which he considered an obstacle to the straightforward representation of an individual's experience of reality. In Locke's (1975, 497, 508) view, excessive indulgence in experimentation with language supports an approach of "tossing Words to and fro" that ultimately makes words "a perfect cheat." Thus, words are most effective when they perfectly capture impressions the individual has acquired independently of engagement with others and then transmit those ideas to others in the most simple and straightforward manner possible.

On the other hand, threats to ethical style also came from replacing the social responsiveness of rhetoric with excessive enthusiasm for aesthetics detached from the immediate concerns that had previously been crucial elements of rhetorical contexts. Eighteenth-century belletristic rhetoricians such as Adam Smith and Hugh Blair reinforced the notion of style as the means to pursue intellectual agility and social relationships, but the belletristic emphasis on the morally purifying exercise of aesthetic judgment reveals the strengths and hazards of connecting style and ethics. The notion that an ethical style includes responsiveness to others can hold positive educational benefits, but it can also define morality as unquestioned conformity to elitist cultural standards.

It is important to recognize that the writings of eighteenth-century British theorists whose work was central to the development of composition in the United States reflect a strong appreciation for the ethical potential of rhetoric. Stephen J. McKenna (2006, 78) argues that Adam

Smith sees communication as the necessary precursor to ethics, for "just as humans cannot become fully developed moral agents without communicating with others, so must they have some practical knowledge of communication before they can have theoretical knowledge of ethics." Hugh Blair also references ethics throughout his *Lectures on Rhetoric and Belles Lettres.* His well-known emphasis on aesthetic criticism features the argument that "the exercise of taste is, in its native tendency, moral and purifying" (Blair 2005, I, 9), while his view of style carries forward the emphasis on language use as a manifestation of the individual's mental discipline and social relationships. Blair (2005, X, 99) argues that style provides a window into "an author's manner of thinking" and notes that perspicuity "is a degree of positive beauty," as it establishes a positive relationship with audience members who see the author's accessible style as evidence of concern for them: "We are pleased with an author, we consider him as deserving praise, who frees us from all fatigue of searching for his meaning" (2005, X, 100). Although Blair's cultural context leads to a philosophical orientation and vocabulary that are quite distinct from those found in Isocrates and Cicero, he sustains the classical assumption that a focus on language promotes virtue through fostering productive social interactions.

In Blair's view, the relationship among aesthetic appreciation, style, and ethics includes the assumption that the standards of style inevitably shape and reflect the surrounding culture. Although Blair (2005, II, 16) maintains that "the Tastes of men may differ very considerably as to their object, and yet none of them be wrong," he believes that the potentially uplifting character of taste lies in its capacity to train the individual to be more attentive to the evolving standards of the community (Agnew 1998a). This is where the strengths and hazards of the connection between style and ethics can be found. On one hand, for speakers or writers to pursue styles that are responsive and sensitive to others can be seen as a valuable ethical commitment; on the other hand, the corollary to this view often leads to the assumption that stylistic propriety is determined by narrowly defined guidelines that reflect the preferences and interests of the dominant order—a community that imposes its standards on speakers rather than being engaged in the dynamic interaction that is a necessary component of an expansive understanding of rhetoric's ethical function. It is little wonder that this is the case since authorized participation in civic discourse has been confined to such a small proportion of the population through most of Western rhetorical history.

Blair's (2005, 19) insistence that "taste is far from being an arbitrary principle, which is subject to the fancy of every individual" usefully underscores the notion that standards of language use are socially situated and require negotiation, but his claim that "what interests the imagination, and touches the heart, pleases all ages and all nations" reflects not an inclusive vision but an assumption that those ages and nations qualified to make judgments are those whose authority and shared cultural capital can lead to ready agreement about those standards that are pleasing. Although Blair (2005, 212) criticizes contemporary writers (such as Lord Shaftesbury) whose excessive refinement causes them to deviate from a desirable simplicity of style, his adaptation of the civilization myth found in the work of Isocrates and Cicero places an emphasis on the progress that distinguishes language use in refined societies from the more figurative styles found in "the first and rude periods of Society" (2005, 61), features of language use that he imagines to be characteristic of people in locations outside of his own sphere. For example, Blair (2005, 61) claims that "the Iroquois and Illinois carry on their treaties and public transactions with bolder metaphors, and greater pomp of style, than we use in our poetical productions." Although Blair's notion of style and taste is based in the ideal of social negotiation, he assumes that such negotiations should ultimately yield to the judgment of civilized society and is dismissive of those "primitives" whose stylistic range departs from what he considers to be rhetorically desirable.

This narrowing process was evident in the eighteenth-century public sphere, which instantiated an ideal of civility distinct from the classical model of deliberative debate, a model that continues to influence our understanding of public discourse. In his incisive study of the tension between eighteenth-century polite society and the lingering ideal of ancient oratory, Adam Potkay (1994, 227) concludes that the standard of politeness continues to define the style found in contemporary journals, which "keep alive the ideal (and to a greater or lesser degree the reality) of polite community roughly as Hume envisioned it—that is, a social world of quiet readers that includes professional writers, politicians, university professors, moderate clergy, and members of the other professions and the business community." One problem with reclaiming our disciplinary heritage in asserting the ethical potential of style is that we have also inherited the eighteenth-century fusion of style with the ideal of polite society, a link that has frequently been deployed for the purpose of maintaining power structures that preserve the status quo, restrict access to full civic participation, and consequently create barriers to those pursuing social justice.

The push and pull between language's capacity to inspire creativity, social relationships, and the development of an ethical sensibility, on one hand, and the tendency to confine and control language, on the other, have a persistent presence in rhetorical history. Although Locke's effort to protect scientific knowledge from the corruption of language is quite distinct from the belletristic view that aesthetic judgment leads to superior refinement, the two converge in a view of language that distances individuals from the civic commitments that were considered to be the ideal outlet for classical eloquence. Thomas P. Miller (1977) argues that over time, English studies in the dissenting academies "became less engaged with fostering social critique and assumed a more belletristic emphasis that was oriented to personal refinement rather than public controversies." Miller's (1977, 166) view that "from the outset, the paradigm of rhetoric and belles lettres emphasized polite taste and deemphasized rhetoric's traditional concern for civic discourse" points toward one way our field's historical commitment to style as the vehicle for ethical rhetoric has been derailed. The influence of belletrism on the development of composition has had a lasting impact on rhetorical education, as previous views of style grounded in a responsive awareness of audience and context are often replaced by universalized standards of clarity and correctness. Consequently, the legacies the field of rhetoric and composition has inherited from belletrism include both a narrow view of style based on acontextual standards of idealized language and the determination to reject that heritage by refusing to attend to matters of style at all. Certainly, critics of writing instruction that is excessively preoccupied with aesthetics are justified in resisting a retreat into an era in which style was codified as an entry point for refinement, idealized usage standards divorced from audience and context, and a privileged detachment from civic concerns. At the same time, this position eliminates the potential to benefit from important insights about the ways attention to language use can foster ethical awareness and facility in responding effectively to important civic issues.

Stylistic Dilemmas

In spite of the powerful classical arguments for the role of style in cultivating individual discipline, reflecting the rhetor's sensitivity to audience and context, and promoting civic virtue, the potential that style might detract from the audience's understanding, that language skill might be deployed in ways that are unethical, and that the cultivation of style might further the standards of the dominant social order are all good reasons to question the value of style as a mechanism for fulfilling rhetoric's ethical mission. The push toward universalized standards has often reinforced a disembodied and elitist understanding of the ideal that not only discourages the rhetorical engagement of those whose language use is deemed to be inferior but also implicitly questions the moral worth of people whose prose is deemed inadequate based on narrow standards accessible to the small percentage of the population whose training puts them in touch with the transcendent and elusive qualities that are associated with the ideal. This pattern has all too often supported long-standing patterns that restrict civic discourse to those who speak and write in certain ways. Nancy Welch (2012, 35) argues that efforts to calm public protest during the 2011 Nuclear Regulatory Commission briefing about the Indian Point nuclear power plant functioned not as "the open demand of an informed and passionate public but the concealed goal of a private industry and its quasi-governmental defenders aiming to shut down audible protest—and to do so in the name of civility." Welch's (2012, 36, original emphasis) examination of the protestors' insistent challenge to authority serves as a point of entry for the study of incivility as a strategy that can "*make* rhetorical space in which more views could be heard." Welch's caution about the use of civility as a weapon to silence dissent is an important reminder that classical notions of decorum in style and delivery, particularly as they are filtered through the lens of eighteenth-century standards of politeness, demand a cautious approach to any effort to restore the historical connection among rhetoric, ethics, and style.

At the same time, recent trends in political discourse reflect the hazards of entirely rejecting the notion of style as an ethical enterprise, particularly when that rejection is deployed by those who have the power to control the state of public discourse. The political right's determined refusal to adhere to what have been cast as the oppressive standards of "political correctness" has undoubtedly licensed those who have privately harbored hateful attitudes to make them publicly visible in a way that threatens the flourishing and even the safety of members of any number of marginalized populations. Although the ideal of polite society that has been embedded in the idealized Western public sphere since the Enlightenment is undoubtedly problematic and has served as the basis for oppressive language standards, the brash insensitivity of Donald Trump leaves many people longing for a return to at least some version of the civility we have lost, particularly as it has become clear that uncivil language in the hands of the powerful can often fuel unjust policies and violent actions.

The classical understanding of style as necessarily enacting the individual's responsibility to the community stands in stark opposition to the careless treatment of language that often characterizes contemporary political discourse. The release of a tape containing then-presidential candidate Trump's lewd remarks about women prompted a range of responses. Although a number of people expressed outrage over the clip, many of Trump's supporters apparently accepted his defense of the incident as an example of "locker-room banter." His insistence during the second presidential debate that these are "just words, folks, just words" laid a foundation for an administration that has persistently pressed to widen the gap between language and reality. In suggesting that it is possible to separate the manner of representation from all other concerns, our current political moment has advanced a radical revision of earlier understandings of the relationship between style and substance that has had ripple effects in the way people communicate across contexts. The insistence of many Trump supporters that in spite of what the president might say "that's not who he is" (K. Conway, quoted in Heim 2017) implicitly argues that the words we choose can be entirely detached from the reality of who we are. Rick Santorum's recent defense of Trump's handling of the Russia investigation summarizes the state we appear to be in (quoted in Baragona 2019): "The president doesn't tell the truth about a lot of things fairly consistently," so the "fact that he's not telling the truth about Russia fairly consistently, at least in the eyes of people around here, why is that any different?" The fact that White House officials are known for language use that is vague, inconsistent, and removed from the material concerns that have historically held rhetoricians accountable illustrates the hazard of moving too far from historical ideals concerning the role of style in establishing an ethical sense that individuals enact through sensitive engagement with others and a demonstrated responsiveness to diverse perspectives and broad civic concerns.

Rhetorical history illuminates the tangled views of language that have brought us to this point and can offer an approach to ethical style that creates middle ground between a class-based politeness that obscures difference and a complete rejection of civility that ultimately eliminates the possibility of shared accountability and understanding. A historical perspective offers an alternative to the notion that authentic style can be determined by an individual entirely removed from the interests of those to whom the communication must be addressed, but it also affords a recognition of flaws that have persistently interfered with efforts to achieve the civic vitality the classical tradition promises. On one hand, the understanding that appropriate language use is socially constructed can become a vehicle for constraining style to suit narrow external interests. On the other hand, the view of style as purely a matter of personal expression can emphasize individual autonomy at the expense of the accountability to others that is central to achieving an ethical position and realizing the full potential of style. The middle ground between these extremes can lead to a vision of style and culture as engaged in a dynamic relationship, as rhetoric ideally ensures "that by the judgment and wisdom of the perfect orator, not only his own honor, but that of many other individuals, and the welfare of the whole state, are principally upheld" (Cicero 1970, I, viii) but that will also maintain the agility to allow for productive resistance to standardization that ultimately stifles style's ethical function—in other words, restoring to style its full potential as a rhetorical tool.

Revitalizing Style

To reclaim historical notions of style as central to the cultivation of an ethical sensibility complements recent conversations that extend style beyond the limits of syntax. Andrea Olinger (2016, 125) emphasizes the integral relationship among writer, audience, and context in defining style as the "dynamic co-construction of typified indexical meanings (people, practices, situations, texts) perceived in a single sign or cluster of signs and influenced by participants' language ideologies." For Olinger (2016, 124, 126), the study of style requires moving beyond the strict parameters of language use to attend to "the social meanings associated with their use"; she emphasizes the co-construction of style as a fluid act defined by "action, activity, process." Paul Butler (2008, 3) also emphasizes context and fluidity in defining style "as the deployment of rhetorical resources, in written discourse, to create and express meaning." Butler (2008, 4) challenges the reductive view that attention to style should focus strictly on sentence-level edits aimed at pursuing clarity, insisting that style requires an awareness that language choices are embedded in purpose, responsive to context, and instrumental in shaping readers' responses. In fact, Butler's (2008, 4) rhetorical emphasis includes the recognition that there is no way to interpret style and meaning independent of context and audience; his rejection of a linguistically oriented approach to text is based on his conviction that "what makes meaning is contextual and dependent on such 'extralinguistic' factors as the reader and his or her responses to the text."

Barry Brummett also argues for the importance of style in the rhetorical construction of identities and meaning. Brummett (2008, 118) argues that "texts are primary sites for the construction of identity and social affiliation. In a performative world of unstable communities and identities, people create texts to say who they are and to call out to others." The recognition of style's vital function in "cultivating identity and social affiliation" and the conception of style as "calling out to others" highlight the role of language in countering the ethical problems created by the modern tendency to detach the individual's single-minded judgment from the engagement with others that is a necessary element of true virtue. The classical perspectives of Isocrates and Cicero establish an approach to style that emphasizes the social nature of all language use, an insight that is in keeping with the emphasis on the centrality of the social in the writings of contemporary virtue ethicists. Alasdair MacIntyre (1981, 201) describes virtue as emerging within the contexts of narratives, for the human is "a story-telling animal." MacIntyre (1981, 204) emphasizes the fact that each person's story must contain a degree of unity but cannot be self-contained, as it requires intersection with the communities of which he or she is a member: "We all approach our own circumstances as bearers of a particular social identity." MacIntyre's treatment of the role of narrative in the formation of personal and collective virtue offers an opportunity to explore style as an integral feature of the stories we tell. The individual's ability to tell the stories that need to be told is grounded in language use that embodies his or her social identities and experiences, and the language used, in turn, calls forth a community that acquires new insight through every aspect of the exchange. James Baldwin's (1998, 781, original emphasis) argument against the refusal of white society to acknowledge Black English as a language includes the recognition that it is ludicrous "to penalize black people for having created a language that permits the nation its only glimpse of reality, a language without which the nation would be even more *whipped* than it is." History points toward style as a central element in the rhetorical exchange that protects the integrity and vitality of all communities and the impoverishment that comes from reducing style to a formula that prohibits the new insights that offer a "glimpse of reality" that is only available through the rich diversity that language offers.

The recognition that style is grounded in the social serves as a counter to the modern emphasis on individualism. It is not purely a coincidence that the value placed on individualism has coincided with the decline of both concerted attention to style and robust discussions of civic virtue. MacIntyre (1981, 146–53) locates the enervation of virtue in the Enlightenment shift to a view of morality grounded in subjectivity, a departure from Aristotle's emphasis on *eudaimonia*, human flourishing made possible by *phronesis*, practical wisdom that requires a commitment to the essential questions that affect human life. In MacIntyre's (1981, 153) view, engagement with others demands negotiation and encounters with difference; he cites Australian philosopher John Anderson in arguing that "it is through conflict and sometimes only through conflict that we learn what our ends and purposes are." Julia Annas (2011, 8–10, 55) also emphasizes virtue not as a static quality but as active and developing, emerging through the formation of a "shared community of activity and attitude." In Annas's (2011, 13–15) view, virtue can therefore be seen as the cultivation of habitual ways of responding effectively to new and unexpected situations. This notion of virtue resonates with the historical cultivation of style as a dynamic use of language responsive to the demands of particular rhetorical contexts, which gains strength through encounters with difference and conflicting forms of expression. Will Duffy's (this volume) insight that *phronesis* challenges the philosophical view that "we are beholden to standards of behavior that exist above and beyond the particularities of circumstance" can be complemented through renewed attention to our field's historical emphasis on style, which offers a significant resource in supporting the rhetor's ability to develop an appropriate and ethical response to important issues that arise in particular times and places but also supports an ethical disposition that informs the individual's way of engaging with people across contexts.

The ethical force of style can only be achieved through critically reflecting on how language functions in the cultivation of identities and communities, an understanding reflected in the Conference on College Composition and Communication (2012) Strategic Governance Vision Statement: "We will advocate for a broad definition of *writing* (including composition, digital production, and diverse language practices) that emphasizes its value as a human activity that empowers individuals and communities to shape their worlds." Language that "empowers individuals and communities to shape their worlds" is fostered in courses that neither ignore style nor teach style as defined by grammatical convention. Instead, we need to teach style as a rhetorical resource through which people share their experiences and establish meaningful social relationships. Teaching style should encourage students to consider carefully the language choices they make, engage creatively with diverse audiences, adopt a playful approach to language that considers multiple possibilities for matching style to purpose and context, and understand language as integral to communicative acts that shape the way others understand the world. This critical engagement with style should help students understand what James Baldwin (1998, 780–81) means in writing that "language, incontestably, reveals the speaker. Language, also, far more dubiously, is meant to define the other . . . language is also a political instrument, means, and proof of power." Teaching style as an ethical enterprise means confronting the many dimensions of how language works and even becoming aware of the hazards of connecting style with ethics in the first place.

In addition to the capacity of style to engage rhetors and audiences in meaningful encounters that take place across contexts, the notion of style as fluid, emergent in "action, activity, process" (Olinger 2016, 126), provides the basis for considering that style's ethical function resides in part in its capacity to create new possibilities through challenging reductive views of language. MacIntyre (1981, 205, original emphasis) stresses that community affiliations should not be seen as a limitation that prevents needed change from taking place: "The fact that the self has to find its moral identity in and through its memberships in communities . . . does not entail that the self has to accept the moral *limitations* of the particularity of those forms of community." Because speakers and writers draw from a range of linguistic resources that are dynamic and shaped through encounters with others, style not only reflects existing social conditions but also serves as a vehicle for establishing new forms of personal and social engagement. Brummett (2008, 119) notes that "it is in the connection to imaginary communities that the political dimensions of a rhetoric of style can be seen." An awareness of style as embedded in the formation of the shared pursuit of imagined possibilities sharply contrasts with Sprat's (1959, 117) insistence on a plain style that emphasizes factual reporting over ancient writings "that impos'd their imaginations on us, as the only Truths." MacIntyre (1981, 200) describes the pursuit of such imagined possibilities as central to virtue: "We live out our lives, both individually and in our relationships with each other, in the light of certain conceptions of a possible shared future, a future in which certain possibilities beckon us forward and others repel us, some seem already foreclosed and others perhaps inevitable." The key to reclaiming the ethical capacity of language lies in exploring style as supporting the virtue of imagined possibilities rather than as a formulaic use of language dictated by standards that are static and inevitable.

Those who seek to reclaim civic action as the central focus of our field's vitality may see the aesthetic dimensions of language as part of the baggage from the past that we must now reject. Although Miller (1977, 284) accurately notes that the sublimation of belletristic rhetoric to literary criticism ultimately "removed individuals from the perspective of the political agent that had been assumed by rhetoricians," a different approach to style is possible. This vision of an ethical style must be fluid, responsive to the unique communicative needs of rhetors and audiences, and not bound by options that "seem already foreclosed and . . . perhaps inevitable" (MacIntyre 1981, 200). The revitalization of ethical style offers new opportunities to explore the capacity of language to imagine selves that do not yet exist and to engage in the imaginative enterprise through which "rhetoric calls into being audiences, publics, and communities" (Brummett 2008, 121). Engagement with rhetorical history tells us that these lofty goals will never be perfectly realized, but it also creates a path for usefully exploring a new vision of style as ethical action—one that substitutes earlier stylistic values such as erudition, refinement, and autonomy with a wider array of ethical dispositions, such as flexibility, respect, candor, sensitivity, compassion, and imagination.

REFERENCES

Agnew, Lois. 1998a. "The Civic Function of Taste: A Re-Assessment of Hugh Blair's Rhetorical Theory." *Rhetoric Society Quarterly* 28 (2): 25–36.

Agnew, Lois. 1998b. "Rhetorical Style and the Formation of Character: Ciceronian *Ethos* in Thomas Wilson's *Arte of Rhetorique.*" *Rhetoric Review* 17 (1): 93–106.

Annas, Julia. 2011. *Intelligent Virtue.* Oxford, UK: Oxford University Press.

Baldwin, James. 1998. "If Black English Isn't a Language, Then Tell Me, What Is?" In *James Baldwin Collected Essays*, ed. Toni Morrison, 780–83. New York: Library of America.

Baragona, Justin. 2019. "Rick Santorum: Trump Lies All the Time, So Why Are Russia Lies 'Any Different'?" *Daily Beast*, February 17. https://www.thedailybeast.com/rick-santor um-trump-lies-all-the-time-so-why-are-russia-lies-any-different.

Blair, Hugh. *Lectures on Rhetoric and Belles Lettres.* 2005. Ed. and with an introduction by Linda Ferreira-Buckley and S. Michael Halloran. Carbondale: Southern Illinois University Press.

Brummett, Barry. 2008. *A Rhetoric of Style.* Carbondale: Southern Illinois University Press.

Butler, Paul. 2008. *Out of Style: Reanimating Stylistic Study in Composition and Rhetoric.* Logan: Utah State University Press.

Cicero, Marcus Tullius. 1947. *De officiis.* Trans. Walter Miller. Cambridge, MA: Harvard University Press.

Cicero, Marcus Tullius. 1949. *De inventione.* Trans. Harry Mortimer Hubbell. Cambridge, MA: Harvard University Press.

Cicero, Marcus Tullius. 1970. *On Oratory and Orators.* Trans. and ed. John Selby Watson, introduction by Ralph A. Micken, foreword by David Potter, preface by Richard Leo Enos. Carbondale: Southern Illinois University Press, 1970.

Conference on College Composition and Communication. "Strategic Governance Vision Statement, November 2012." 2012. http://cccc.ncte.org/cccc/about.

Heim, Joe. 2017. "'They Never Saw This Coming': A Q&A with Kellyanne Conway." *Washington Post*, January 26. https://www.washingtonpost.com/lifestyle/magazine/ they-never-saw-this-coming-a-qanda-with-kellyanne-conway-on-trumps-victory/2017/ 01/26/2bf64c10-da96-11e6-9a36-1d296534b31e_story.html?noredirect=on&utm_term =.782b93532b16.

Isocrates. 1929. *Antidosis.* Trans. George Norlin. In *Isocrates: Volume II*, 185–365. Cambridge, MA: Harvard University Press.

Jaeger, Werner. 1994 [1943]. "The Rhetoric of Isocrates and Its Cultural Ideal." In *Landmark Essays on Classical Greek Rhetoric*, ed. Edward Schiappa, 119–41. Davis, CA: Hermagoras.

Locke, John. 1975 [1689]. *An Essay Concerning Human Understanding.* Ed. and with an introduction by Peter H. Nidditch. Oxford, UK: Clarendon.

MacIntyre, Alasdair. 1981. *After Virtue: A Study in Moral Theory.* Notre Dame, IN: University of Notre Dame Press.

McKenna, Stephen J. 2006. *Adam Smith: The Rhetoric of Propriety.* Albany: State University of New York Press.

Miller, Thomas P. 1977. *The Formation of College English: Rhetoric and Belles Lettres in the British Cultural Provinces.* Pittsburgh, PA: University of Pittsburgh Press.

Olinger, Andrea. 2016. "A Sociocultural Approach to Style." *Rhetoric Review* 36 (2): 121–34.

Plato. 2001a. *Gorgias.* Trans. Walter R.M. Lamb. In *The Rhetorical Tradition: Readings from Classical Times to the Present*, ed. Patricia Bizzell and Bruce Herzberg, 87–138. Boston: Bedford/St. Martins.

Plato. 2001b. *Phaedrus.* Trans. Harold N. Fowler. In *The Rhetorical Tradition: Readings from Classical Times to the Present*, ed. Patricia Bizzell and Bruce Herzberg, 138–68. Boston: Bedford/St. Martins.

Potkay, Adam. 1994. *The Fate of Eloquence in the Age of Hume.* Ithaca, NY: Cornell University Press.

Sprat, Thomas. 1959 [1667]. *History of the Royal Society.* St. Louis, MO: Washington University Studies.

Welch, Nancy. 2012. "Informed, Passionate, and Disorderly: Unruly Rhetoric in a New Gilded Age." *Community Literacy Journal* 7 (1): 33–51.

4

REN, RECIPROCITY, AND THE ART OF COMMUNICATION
Conversing with Confucius in the Present

Bo Wang

As the discipline of rhetoric and writing studies increasingly confronts issues related to the deterioration of public discourse in the post-truth era and to cultivating citizens who can speak and write ethically in both local and global contexts, a cross-cultural study of the relationship between rhetoric and ethics might offer some valuable insights. In this chapter, I turn to Confucius (551–479 BC) for contemplation on our current discussions about the role of ethics in rhetorical theory, practice, pedagogy, and history.[1] My aim is to explore how Confucius views the self, human relationships, speech, and ritual practices and how that view can inform and complicate our understanding of the ethical dimension of rhetorical theory, practice, and pedagogy. What draws me to a re-reading of Confucian rhetoric—by which I mean Confucian theory and practices of communication—is less a matter of what it is or what it should be than that of how it could and should serve our purpose in the present.

Confucian rhetoric has been attracting growing attention in the fields of comparative philosophy and rhetoric in the United States. Some scholars have defined the scope of a Confucian rhetorical paradigm. For example, David L. Hall and Roger T. Ames (1987) observe that Confucius's modes of communication include language, ritual action, and music, which are performative activities that constitute human feelings, attitudes, and their relationships. Yameng Liu (2004) points out that semantics, speech, rituals, ceremonies, the legal system, and human dispositions and behaviors are all ingredients of Confucian rhetorical practices. Other scholars have tried to understand the Confucian view in terms of Greco-Roman rhetoric. George A. Kennedy (1998) notes that Confucius stressed the need to adapt a speech to an audience and to form a reciprocal relationship between speaker and audience. Still others have identified specific concepts and modes in the *Analects* (2017) in

DOI: 10.7330/9781607329978.c004

the Chinese cultural context in hopes of gaining a better understanding of both Chinese and Greco-Roman traditions. Arabella Lyon (2004), for instance, speculates that Confucian remonstration (*jian* 谏) and silence reveal an implicit model of deliberation that works to create a respectful society. Whereas Xiaoye You (2006) finds some affinities between Confucian ritualization and epideictic rhetoric, Haixia W. Lan (2017) discovers that both Aristotle and Confucius see rhetoric as a mode of thinking essential to the human understanding of the truths of things. And for Xing Lu (1998), Confucius's perspective of naming (*ming* 名) and speech (*yan* 言) is strongly characterized by ethical concerns for the reconstruction of an orderly society capable of moral living. These perspectives together allow us to see both the breadth and nature of Confucian rhetoric; the work of Hall and Ames, Lu, Lyon, You, and Lan in particular sheds light on Confucius's view of the role and function of rhetoric. To further develop this line of inquiry, I focus on the relationship between Confucian rhetoric and virtue cultivation—an area that warrants more discussion, in my view.

Specifically, I argue that the *Analects* (2017) can be read as a virtue-oriented rhetoric.[2] Confucius's emphasis on the constitutive role of the art of communication in cultivating the moral self and forming reciprocal human relationships to achieve communal, social harmony can offer an alternative vision for imagining the relationship of ethics to rhetorical theory, practice, and pedagogy in our time.[3] I examine the *Analects* and relevant commentaries to provide the grounds for understanding and reconstructing Confucius's thinking. I use what LuMing Mao (2010, 334) calls "the art of recontextualization" to identify concepts from the original Chinese text and bring them into dialogue with euroamerican terms. That is, I situate my interpretation of the *Analects* in both Confucius's cultural context and the scholarly conversations about Confucius's view on ethics and rhetoric. I seek to understand these concepts and their relationship by recourse to issues originating within contemporary rhetorical studies, issues Confucius may well have not explicitly entertained. Although this approach requires cross-cultural anachronistic references (in Hall and Ames's sense of the phrase), the recontextualized analysis, I hope, can enable "plural local terms" to converse with each other across miles and centuries (Wang 2015, 249).[4]

REN 仁: THE UNIFYING REFERENT FOR CONFUCIAN VIRTUE

To provide some context and parameters for my claims about Confucian rhetoric and its relationship to virtue cultivation, I discuss briefly the major ethical concepts related to my analysis. By "Confucian virtue" I mean an acquired quality or a cultivated disposition that contributes to human development rather than the moral strength of a human will that fulfills one's rationally defined duty. Confucius's notion of virtue resonates more or less with ancient Western views such as Aristotle's but differs markedly from the Enlightenment positions such as Kant's. The term *ren* 仁 appears to be the unifying referent for self-transformation in virtue cultivation—an overarching theme in the *Analects*. For various commentators, *ren* seems to be a rich, complex, and sometimes obscure concept; but most have agreed that Confucius transformed *ren* from a particular virtue (translated as "benevolence") into general virtue. *Ren* as the all-inclusive virtue and a spiritual condition has various English translations, including "moral life" (Gu 1898), "goodness" (Waley 1938), "humanity" (Chan 1963; Tu 1985), "cohumanity" (Boodberg 1953), and "the authoritative conduct" (Ames and Rosemont 1998). This sense of *ren* is made clear in Confucius's (Ames and Rosemont 1998, 17.6, 204) response to a question about *ren*: "A person who is able to carry into practice five attitudes in the world can be considered authoritative (*ren* 仁) . . . Deference, tolerance, making good on one's word (*xin* 信), diligence, and generosity. If you are deferential, you will not suffer insult; if tolerant, you will win over the many; if you make good on your word, others will rely upon you; if diligent, you will get results; if generous, you will have the status to employ others effectively." At another time, Confucius (Yang 2017, 6.30, 93, my translation) elaborates on *ren*: "The exemplary person, desiring to establish oneself, establishes others; desiring to promote oneself, promotes others. The ability to take what is near to one as an analogy may be called the way of *ren*."[5] In these remarks, *ren* is closely linked to human relationships and implies that self-cultivation is a painstaking process of becoming. It is through social relationships, regulated by *li* 礼 (authenticated norms of conduct, rituals), that we become human. By making constant efforts to act morally toward others, one is making oneself a person with *ren*. In its deepest sense, Confucius's *ren* "is to take someone into one's sphere of concern, and in so doing, make him an integral aspect of one's own person" (Hall and Ames 1987, 121). Put differently, the concern for the good of others makes the exemplary person irreducibly communal and relational.

Despite the complexity of its meaning, it is safe to say that *ren* is a referent of Confucius's ideal for living a moral life in society.[6] What seems central to Confucius's ethical theory is the idea that a moral person is one who incorporates others' interests as one's own and conducts oneself in a manner that addresses the general good. Indeed, *shu*

恕 (reciprocity, reciprocal care, altruism) illuminates the communal and relational sense of *ren*.[7] The meaning of *shu* is clearly stated in Confucius's (Ames and Rosemont 1998, 15.24, 189) golden rule: Zigong asked, "Is there one expression that can be acted upon until the end of one's days?" The Master replied, "There is *shu* 恕: do not impose on others what you yourself do not want." For Confucius, the exemplary person certainly has responsibilities to serve the community and the state, but the minimal moral standard is to not impose one's own way on others. As Tu Wei-ming (1985, 26) rightly points out, the Confucian golden rule, deliberatively stated in a negative form, implies "a consideration for the integrity of the other" and "a recognition that one can never fully comprehend another to the same extent and in the same degree as one can comprehend oneself." If *ren* signifies the highest level of moral cultivation, *shu* provides a specific methodology for achieving *ren* in the sense that extending oneself to the other to determine appropriate conduct can help one form reciprocal relationships with others (Lau 1983, xiii–xiv). Such a methodology requires that one constantly try to empathize with other human beings as an integral part of one's own effort to become *ren*. It is this sense of reciprocity and community that is essential for moral self-development in Confucius's vision. *Ren*, however, does not necessarily mean self-effacing; nor does it mean that the Confucian self lacks agency. Enacting traditional cultural values in one's own context and cultivating virtue are predicated on both individual agency and interdependent relationships with others. Caring about others is intimately bound up with caring about oneself, for such moral actions can benefit one's self-development (Yang 2017, 12.24, 187). In that sense, the highest level of a moral life is reflexive, "incorporating in one's own person the entire field of self-other concerns" (Hall and Ames 1987, 122). Such an orientation illuminates Confucius's virtue-oriented rhetoric—a rhetoric grounded in thick relations with a sense of shared humanity and constituted by rituals, language, music, and other symbolic acts.

LI 礼 AND *YAN* 言: THE CONFUCIAN ART OF COMMUNICATION

As indicated in the *Analects*, rituals, language, and music seem to have been the major modes of communication in Confucius's time. These communicative practices are all of a kind, serving to cultivate virtues and restore the Way. *Li* 礼, translated as rites, rituals, ritual action, ritual propriety, authentic norms of conduct, is a primary means to live a virtuous life in the Confucian tradition. In *Liji* 礼记 (Book of Rites), *li* refers to two types of rituals: ceremonial rituals, which include a series of important Confucian rites performed at various levels of society, such as family rites of weddings, mourning, and sacrificing and state rites of visiting the emperor and offering sacrifices to Heaven; and minute rituals, which signify everyday small behavior patterns such as various quasi-ceremonial manners, etiquettes, and customs (Legge 1967).[8] These rituals are governed by a system of ritual rules created by ancient Chinese sages that allows certain natural objects and human behaviors to bear symbolic meanings in proper contexts. For example, doing such and such things in such and such ways constitutes offering sacrifices to ancestors reverently or getting married properly. In the *Analects*, Confucius expanded the sense of the word *li* from its original meaning of religious ceremonial to standards of proper behavior in a social and ethical context, envisioning society itself on the model of *li*.[9] Confucius sees the rituals created by the ancient sages as essential practices to accomplish an authentic way of human life. He stresses the importance of personal responsibility and engagement in performing rituals rather than simply following the *li* blindly. Observing the *li* with a sense of personal investment allows one to contribute creatively to the tradition. In this chapter I use *li* to refer to rituals as well as authenticated norms of conduct, depending on the context in the *Analects*.

The communicative function of the Confucian rituals (*li* 礼) has been recognized in recent scholarship. In their discussions of *li*, commentators have invoked "communicative medium" and "rhetorical process," for it is through *li* conceived as a communicative medium or rhetorical process that the Confucian Way can be achieved. For David Hall and Roger Ames (1987, 284), rituals serve as a communicative medium to promote "aesthetic order" and bring harmony (*he* 和) between self and others. The realization of interpersonal and social harmony is the effect of submitting to appropriate models of aesthetic sensibility as constituted by rituals, language, and music. According to Hall and Ames (1987, 88), rituals are formalized structures that allow a person to interpret the accumulated meaning of a tradition and to further strengthen it by his or her contribution of novel meaning and value. In that sense, they uncover Confucius's assumptions about how rituals can be put to work as a heuristic, a method or system of rhetorical invention for deriving meaning and value as well as reforming one's inherited tradition in response to the contingencies and processive nature of the tradition.[10] Hall and Ames's insight on the Confucian rituals as a medium and heuristic is important, for it illuminates what it means to observe and practice the rituals in Confucian culture. This insight also allows us to see the centrality of communication in virtue cultivation. Hall and Ames's evocation of "attunement," though, seems to suggest that music rather than ritual is a paradigm for understanding the nature of communication in the Confucian tradition—an interpretation that may have downplayed the importance of *li* in Confucian rhetorical practices.

Xiaoye You puts his finger on the pivotal role of rituals in the Confucian rhetorical tradition by looking to the concept of *li*. You proposes conceiving ritualization as a primary feature of Confucian rhetoric. Synthesizing theories of ritual in symbolic anthropology and sociology, You points out that as multimodal configurations of symbols endorsed by a collective, ritual works dialectically between the social bond and structure, homogeneity and differentiation, equality and inequality. As such, You (2006, 431) observes, ritual symbols have potential for social transformations. Echoing Hall and Ames's interpretation of Confucian rituals as an inventional heuristic, You (2006, 431) views *li* as a "time-honored form of cultural communication" and ritual performance as acts of rhetorical invention that enable participants to carry on shared cultural values and enact positive social changes. You then gives his full account of the Confucian ritualization as a rhetorical process of transforming the self and others into devoted practitioners of the rites. Further, You (2006, 440) explains that Confucian rhetoric values balanced use of all symbolic forms, and words need to be connected with other symbolic acts to exert their power in ritualization. What You is saying is that in Confucian culture, language carries strong ritualizing power to the extent that it is used in coordination with other symbolic acts to convey human connectedness. You (2006, 432), however, goes on to claim that the *Analects* is not a rhetoric on verbal persuasion but rather "a rhetoric on ritualization as the ultimate goal of communication." This claim may have overlooked virtue cultivation as a primary goal of communication in Confucian rhetoric; in other words, the *Analects* emphasizes ritualization precisely because it plays an essential role in virtue cultivation. To be fair to You (2006, 433), in his analysis of the Confucian rituals he acknowledges that ritualization helps the participants develop their understanding of the moral standards, yet it is not clear why ritual practices are necessary for developing an understanding of those standards—a question I return to later.

Interestingly, Hall and Ames's and You's accounts about *li* allow us to see indirectly how language is perceived in Confucian rhetoric. They seem to agree that language, like rituals and music, is a medium, a kind of symbolic act used in Confucius's world, though You characterizes speech as a type of rhetorical practice within the larger framework of ritualization. Speech may be shadowed by an emphasis on *li* in the *Analects* but nonetheless deserves a brief examination here because Confucius's view of speech may shed light on the relationship between the Confucian art of communication and virtue cultivation. In his conversations with disciples, Confucius used *yan* 言 (speech, talk) to discuss oral speech and eloquence.[11] Many Confucian dialogues show his rather cautious attitude toward *yan*. For instance, when he was asked about *junzi* 君子, the exemplary persons, Confucius (Ames and Rosemont 1998, 2.14, 79) said, "They first accomplish what they are going to say, and only then say it." Such doubtful remarks about *yan* have been interpreted by some as a Confucian denouncement against eloquence (Xu 2004). Others have argued that Confucian silence is valued as a tool for building social relationships (Lyon 2004, 137). These scholars eschew any suggestion of a more positive view of eloquence in part because they realize, rightly, that to attribute such a view to Confucius, however inchoate, runs the risk of attributing to him a position that may be alien to Confucian culture. However, their interpretations miss the nuances of Confucius's view of speech—a view more subtle than it appears to be.

From the *Analects* we can see that Confucius developed a sophisticated moral perspective of *yan*. As Xing Lu (1998, 164) observes, Confucius conceived various categories of *yan* such as *de yan* 德言 (virtuous speech), *xin yan* 信言 (trustworthy speech), *shen yan* 慎言 (cautious speech), and *ya yan* 雅言 (correct speech). Confucius indeed cautioned his contemporaries against glib speech; however, he recognized the value of eloquence as well as the impact of language on human perceptions and actions. His suspicion of glib talk is not so much a denouncement of eloquence as a concern about the danger of speaking falsehoods and half-truths. Confucius lived in an era of social upheaval in which the traditional values of the Zhou dynasty (1046–256 BC) were challenged and neglected. Seeing a world of turmoil, disorder, and social degradation, he regarded this state of affairs as the consequence of the inappropriate use of language and neglect of rituals. For Confucius, eloquence can serve the general good if employed by a virtuous person for a noble purpose. When his disciple Zizhang inquired about proper conduct, the Master replied: "Be conscientious and sincere in what you say; be earnest and respectful in what you do" (Yang 2017, 15.6, 230, my translation). On a different occasion, Confucius commented on virtue and speech, saying "a person of virtue is sure to speak eloquently, but a person who speaks eloquently is not necessarily virtuous" (Lau 1983, 14.4, 143). His remarks about speaking sincerely and making good on one's words appear again and again in the *Analects*. Confucius's notion of *yan* is thus closely linked with the qualities of the exemplary person or with the principles by which a moral person conducts himself. Conducting oneself in a way that earns the trust and cooperation of others by corresponding one's words with actions to promote the general good is the way of *junzi*. From the Confucian perspective, appropriate speech is a manifestation of the exemplary person.

The significance of speaking appropriately is most obvious in Confucius's discussions of *zheng ming* 正名 (the rectification of names).[12] This concept reflects his view on the essential role *ming* 名 (naming) plays in shaping interpersonal and social relationships. When Confucius was asked a question about the priority of administering a state, he said: "Certainly, it would be to make sure that names are used correctly . . . When names are not correct, speech will not be appropriate; when speech is not appropriate, tasks will not be accomplished; when tasks cannot be accomplished, the performing of rituals and the playing of music do not flourish; when the performing of rituals and the playing of music do not flourish, the application of punishments will not justify the crimes; when the application of punishments does not justify the crimes, the people will not know what to do" (Yang 2017, 13.3, 189, my translation). Confucius proposes *zheng ming* as an important way of restoring the Dao (order), governing a state, developing harmonious human relationships, and building a stable society. For Confucius, a name corresponds with a concept and a reality. If names are not used properly, misperceptions of the world may arise, which can consequently lead to social chaos. However, to say that Confucius's *zheng ming* puts an emphasis on human relationships and social order is not to say that the Confucian mind does not care about the facts of matter. The Confucian way of naming involves both theory-like and practice-like elements. The rectification of names, as May Sim (2007, 76) notes, "serves authoritative practice but it also serves truth," whose goal is a rightness "that is at one and the same time a harmony with other people in an order of social relations and a harmony with nonhuman nature under the order of heaven."

LI 礼 AND *YAN* 言 IN VIRTUE CULTIVATION

The work of Hall and Ames, You, and Lu gives us a glimpse into the function of the Confucian art of communication. Their analyses of *li* and *yan* open up space for further inquiry into the following questions: What kind of role do *li* and *yan* play in achieving *ren*? Why are rituals and the appropriate use of language necessary for virtue cultivation in Confucian culture? To tackle these questions, we need to look at Confucius's notion of humanity. As a philosopher and rhetorician, Confucius was largely concerned with how to become a cultivated, knowledgeable, and morally good person.[13] The basic assumption about human in the *Analects* is that an individual is a being born into the world and especially into society with the potential to be cultivated into a true human being; in other words, people are close to one another in nature, but their customs and habits set them apart. What this means is that human nature is something innate, but it is malleable and will become distinctive as people grow up in different social environments. Human development is compared to "cutting, filing, chiseling and polishing" the raw material into an ideal vessel (Yang 2017, 1.15, 12)—that is, one becomes "human" through learning and cultivation. Moral virtue is precarious and difficult to achieve for the individual and society. By implication, self-development and moral cultivation require lifelong making and remaking of the self in alignment with *ren*. When his favorite disciple Yan Hui inquired about *ren*, Confucius replied, "Through self-discipline and observing *li* 礼 one becomes a person with *ren* (Yang 2017, 12.1, 174, my translation) . . . Becoming a person with *ren* is self-originating—how could it originate with others" (Ames and Rosemont 1998, 12.1, 152). Yan Hui went on to ask him what becoming *ren* entails, and the Master said, "Do not look at anything that violates the observance of ritual propriety; do not listen to anything that violates the observance of ritual propriety; do not speak about anything that violates the observance of ritual propriety; do not do anything that violates the observance of ritual propriety" (Ames and Rosemont 1998, 12.1, 152). For Confucius, *li* is meaningful because it is the means to live a moral life, providing specific norms and standards of proper behavior for common folk as well as the sage king. To become "human" or civilized is to "establish human relationships, relationships of an essentially symbolic kind, defined by tradition and convention and rooted in respect and obligation" (Fingarette 1972, 76). In that sense, the practices of *li* and *yan* involve a continual process of symbolic exchange through the sharing of communal values between the self and other selves in society.

As mentioned earlier, on the point of how to become morally virtuous, Confucius's understanding of virtue is in consonance with Aristotle's—one acquires the virtues through habituation.[14] However, on the issue of the specific methods to learn and acquire the virtues, Aristotle seems to fall short of providing a means for a person to cultivate ethos. In Book 2 of *Nicomachean Ethics*, Aristotle (2011, 27) compares learning the virtues with learning the arts, noting that we learn the arts and virtues by doing them: "By doing just things we become just; moderate things, moderate; and courageous things, courageous." For Confucius, such a statement would be misleading; if one is not yet virtuous, what methods can help one move from doing a seemingly virtuous deed halfheartedly or unwillingly to doing such a deed wholeheartedly? The Aristotelian Thomist philosopher Alasdair MacIntyre (2004, 157) wisely notes: "For in saying that we become just by performing just actions and courageous by performing courageous actions, Aristotle omitted to point out that the just actions of those who are not yet just . . . are precisely actions in which the outward behavior is one thing and the inner motivation quite another . . . So the outward appearance of justice does not express the agent's inner attitude. And it is not only that the agent's inner attitude has to be transformed, but also that it has to be transformed in such a way as to close the gap between inner and outer." It is precisely the merging of the inner feelings, attitudes, and thoughts and the outer movements, gestures, and speeches that is at the core of virtue cultivation. *Ren* is "fundamentally an integrative process"—the transformation of self from the "small man" (*xiao ren* 小人), preoccupied with selfish advantage, toward "the sensibilities of the profoundly relational person" who can empathize with others (*shu* 恕) and become larger than self (Hall and Ames 1987, 115). In Confucius's view, it is important for such exemplary persons to provide models for the development of others. Confucius's account of *li* and *yan* can complement Aristotle's all too brief account of ethos (habit) and the method of its cultivation, for it provides rich resources for such a process of integration that is necessary in the achievement of *ren*.[15]

Confucius recognizes that rituals are the most important practices for children as well as adults to learn in order to become virtuous. Virtue cultivation entails learning not only abstract moral concepts but also rituals, language, music, and other symbolic practices that allow one to build reciprocal and harmonious relationships with others in society. Ritual practices are of paramount importance in virtue learning and acquisition.[16] Moral concepts can provide the rationale for why one should observe the rituals in a given situation, but they cannot replace the rituals in virtue cultivation. Take the virtue of filial piety (*xiao* 孝), for example. Confucius (Ames and Rosemont 1998, 2.7, 77) requires one to apply the notion of *jing* 敬 (reverence) to treating one's parents: "Those today who are filial are considered so because they are able to provide for their parents. But even dogs and horses are given that much care. If you do not respect your parents, what is the difference?" However, one cannot attain the virtue of filial piety by only following the abstract principle; one has to be exposed to and practice the appropriate rituals to know what filial conduct entails. Confucius (Yang 2017, 2.5, 17, my translation) emphasized, "When your parents are living, serve them according to *li*; when they die, bury them and offer sacrifices to them according to *li*." To be filial to one's parents, one should observe the rituals to treat them with respect. As this example shows, the balanced and dialectic process of learning the notion of *jing* and practicing the serving, burying, and sacrificing rituals allows one to understand why one needs to observe the rituals and what it means to treat one's parents with respect. It is Confucius's belief that if one can acquire such virtues through ritual practices with one's family members, one can exercise the virtues with others in various domains in larger society.[17]

The appropriate use of *yan* is equally important in virtue cultivation in Confucian culture. Language, as "a medium" (to use Hall and Ames's words), is essential in the articulation and realization of cultural values and norms. Self-development entails *si* 思 (thinking) and *xue* 学 (learning)—which involve a process of "interpersonal communications and transactions" whereby the emerging person pursues integration of personal social environs and cultural values through "the expression of one's own appropriateness" (Hall and Ames 1987, 83). For instance, the Confucian virtue of *xin* 信 (trustworthiness, living up to one's word) is crucial in interpersonal communications because personal articulation requires the participation of others. For Confucius, *xin yan* 信言 (trustworthy speech) must be practiced to attain the virtue of *xin* and establish reciprocal and trustworthy relationships with others. In his view, living up to one's word (*xin* 信) allows one to be close to being appropriate (Yang 2017, 1.13, 11). Indeed, Confucius taught his disciples that "speech must be trust-worthy, action must be followed through" (Lau 1983, 13.20, 123). To become a person with *ren*, one should not only understand the notion of *xin* but also use speech in such a way as to speak honestly and make one's words correspond with one's action in everyday life.

Confucius's special attention to the appropriate use of language in virtue cultivation is also demonstrated through his notion of *zheng ming* 正名 (the rectification of names). In the Confucian sense, each name defines a person or a thing and is the essence or concept of that to which the name refers. Naming, in the social sphere, is about defining a relationship between self and others. When the Duke of Qi asked Confucius about governing effectively, Confucius replied, "Let the ruler be ruler, the minister minister; let the father be father, and the son son" (Fung 1952, 12.11, 60). The names and titles (ruler, minister, father, son) define the moral obligations one should accept or fulfill in accordance with the meanings these names convey; the names also carry a sense of certain specific virtues one is expected to exercise. For example, in Chinese culture, children should be taught how to properly address other individuals, especially their family members. One should call one's elder sister *jiejie* 姐姐 rather than her given name to show respect (gong 恭) and use the pronoun *nin* 您 rather than *ni* 你 (you) to address one's parents, grandparents, and elders to show reverence (*jing* 敬). Through the proper use of names and speech in interactions with members of one's family and community, the specific virtues such as *gong, jing*, and *xiao* 孝 can be cultivated and integrated into one's character. For Confucius, a person is with *ren* precisely because she is able to say and do the right thing at the right time for the right feelings. Words, as You might indicate, when used in connection with other symbolic acts in observing *li*, become significant in shaping human relationships.

Such emphasis on the effect of observing *li* and using *yan* appropriately in the realization of *ren* would suggest that communicating and virtue learning and acquiring cannot be separate activities because ritual practices, language, and other symbolic acts are, in fact, the modes of virtue cultivation. Communicative practices illustrated by Confucius in the *Analects* involve the process of becoming *ren* as both cause and consequence. The act of communicating and the act of cultivating *ren* are symbiotic; the Confucian art of communication is ethics writ large. Virtue cultivation at all levels is accomplished through various communicative practices—be it listening, speaking, writing, singing, dancing, or performing rituals. Thus in Confucius's virtue-oriented rhetoric, the art of communication plays a *constitutive* role in cultivating the moral self and building reciprocal relationships with others for the good of society. To say that Confucius developed profound insights into the function of communication in the essentially relational fabric of ethical life is not to say that he has no failings in his thought. In his ethical vision, which is necessarily a product of its own social and cultural milieu, there is an implicit assumption of *homo aequalis*—an assumption that ignores the hierarchical and stratified social and political structures in Confucian society. Although he makes the appropriate action and virtue cultivation accessible to many people regardless of their socioeconomic backgrounds, paradoxically, he views *junzi* as a man, relegating women to the inner chamber of domestic space. Despite these limitations, we can learn from Confucius and make his view on the relationship of ethics to rhetoric useful and intelligible.

IN CONVERSATION WITH CONFUCIUS

Confucius's view on communication and virtue cultivation might offer an alternative model for envisioning the relationship between ethics and rhetorical theory and pedagogy. His discussion of *ren*, *li*, and *yan* could complicate our understanding of the function of communication, complementing Plato's philosophical rhetoric. Whereas Plato insisted that transcendent truth exists and is accessible to human beings through analytic, objective, and dialectical discourse, Confucius believed that self-development and ethical social engagement are facilitated and realized through symbolic exchanges. For Plato, to influence the soul, the philosopher-rhetor must define his terms carefully; he must analyze and synthesize before he can speak well. His assumption about rhetoric seems to be that the primary role of language is in describing the world and communicating ideas and beliefs about the world. The use of language and persuasion is good to the extent that it is used to seek knowledge and truth.[18] For Confucius, to achieve *ren*, a *junzi* should observe rituals and use language and other symbolic practices appropriately. He must listen to and evoke responses from others deferentially; he must make his words correspond with his action. The realization of his interpretation of the world and especially of society depends on his effectiveness in leading others to ritualize and transform themselves. The primary role of communication is in cultivating moral virtues to achieve communal, social harmony. Speech is of value insofar as the speaker acts according to *li* and uses it to realize *ren*. Confucius could help Plato expand his curriculum of ethics by including *li* as both social morality and rhetorical art.[19] With its critical attention to *zheng ming* 正名, Confucius's virtue-oriented rhetoric might provide us with a different mode of rhetorical criticism with which to read contemporary public discourse in the era of "alternative facts."

If communicative practices (rituals, language, music, and other symbolic acts) are considered constitutive of virtue cultivation, they are then concerned directly with human relationships and with how humans should address, treat, and interact with one another. Consequently, the primary goal of communication is to nurture the good of human relationships rather than to win an argument. This deeply moral perspective of rhetoric has significant implications for rhetorical education and pedagogy in our own time. A rhetorical education based on Confucius's vision would integrate moral education into the curriculum in the sense that speaking, writing, and communicating in various modes are themselves moral practices and decisions. Speaking and writing and the realization of *ren* are mutually entailing. Resonating with John Duffy's concept of "rhetorical virtues," Confucius's virtue-oriented rhetoric would embrace the idea that communicative practices reflect the quality, attitudes, and disposition of an exemplary person. Confucius would agree with Duffy's eloquent statement that "writing involves proposing a relationship with others" (2017, 241). As situated communicative-moral practices, *li* and *yan* call for the right words at the right time in the right way for the right feelings. They involve interpreting and communicating with others the narratives of communities, cultural values, and traditions from which they are developed. Confucius's understanding of *li* and *yan* as the primary means of virtue cultivation could enrich "rhetorical virtues" and help us recognize that "discursive practices of virtue" are the expression as well as the *process* of cultivating honesty, *xin* 信, accountability, courage, generosity, *jing* 敬, *shu* 恕, and other virtuous qualities (Duffy 2017, 235). Confucius's *zheng ming* emphasizes that naming involves defining a relationship between self and others; following Confucius, we can call students' attention to the moral implications and social consequences of naming in everyday communicative practices whether one uses a pen, a computer, or a Twitter account. Confucians are especially sensitive to interpersonal and social harmony and have an acute sense of how *li* and *yan* create aesthetic order in the communicative process. We can learn from the Confucian sensibility by encouraging students to see rhetoric as a process of listening, empathizing, understanding, and putting oneself in the other's position.

Finally, the Confucian perspective might also provide an alternative to the rhetoric of autonomy and possessive individualism in the Western liberal tradition. In a time when "the center cannot hold" (Yeats 2000, 64), when the rhetoric of individual freedom, property rights, and development is used to implement policies that relentlessly dismantle social security systems, privatize public infrastructure, cause environmental damage, and increase poverty in non-Western countries as well as many Western countries, we can learn from Confucius that human beings are members of families and communities and are inheritors of traditions; they have moral obligations to one another and for the general good. The centrality of *shu* 恕 (reciprocity) in the Confucian framework could give us an alternative language to speak about our moral and political concerns cross-culturally. With his conviction that *shu* (do not impose on others what you yourself do not want) provides a methodology for achieving *ren*, Confucius could help us understand that it is unethical to believe that our values—or values developed in any single culture—are universal and that we can therefore feel justified to force those values on everyone else by economic and military threat. Confucius's deeply relational and communal *junzi* 君子 who communicates well might set up a role model of a different kind for students as they learn how to speak and write ethically in both a local and a global context in the twenty-first century.

Confucius's virtue-oriented rhetoric offers *one* alternative vision for seeing ethics' relationship to rhetorical theory, practice, and pedagogy in our time. Let the conversation continue.

NOTES

1. The name Confucius is a Latinization of Kong Fu Zi 孔夫子, meaning Master Kong; his given name is Qiu 丘 and his cognomen is Zhongni 仲尼. According to *Shiji* 史记 (Historical Records), Confucius was born in 551 BC in the state of Lu. Confucius served as an official in Lu, traveled across many states of China, and later returned to Lu, where he spent the last three years of his life studying literature and teaching his disciples.
2. The *Analects* (Lunyu 论语 [2017]), a text that recorded Confucius's thought, was compiled by Confucius's disciples after his death. A living document, the *Analects* has been interpreted and reinterpreted through centuries. With the revival of the study of classical Chinese language and culture in the past few decades, contemporary Chinese scholars have contributed to the conversation. For recent commentaries on the *Analects*, see Qian Mu's *Lunyu xin jie* [A new interpretation of the *Analects*, 2012], Li Zehou's *Reading the Analects Today* (2006), Qian Xun's *Lunyu* [The *Analects* with annotations and interpretations, 2017], and Chen Lai's *Confucius, Mencius, and Xunzi* (2017).
3. I use "the art of communication" to refer to Confucius's entire repertoire of communicative modes, including rituals, speech, music, and other symbolic acts. In this chapter, I focus on rituals and speech.
4. In their study of Confucius, Hall and Ames (1987, 1–9) use "cross-cultural anachronism" as a comparative method to bring together two hermeneutical foci constituted by the cultural sensibilities of classical China and the West, thinking through Confucius but also engaging his thought from the perspective of the present. For more detailed discussions on comparative and historiographic methodology, see Rorty (1984); Mao (2003); Garrett (2013); Hum and Lyon (2009); Wang (2013); Mao and Wang (2015, 239–74).
5. There are several English translations of the *Analects*. For the quoted passages, I chose the most faithful version from the available published translations. When I find the rendition inadequate, I provide my own translation. For the primary text of the *Analects* that has the original version in classical Chinese language along with annotations or translations in the modern Chinese language, I consulted and used Yang Bojun's *Lunyu yizhu* [The *Analects* with translations and annotations, 2017].
6. Tu Wei-ming offers insightful analyses of the Confucian concept of *ren* in "The Creative Tension between *Jen* and *Li*" (1979, 5–16) and "*Jen* as a Living Metaphor in the Confucian Analects" (1985, 81–92). His interpretation has informed my understanding of Confucian ethics.
7. The Chinese philosopher Fung Yu-Lan (1952) notes that Confucius uses the concepts *zhong* 忠 (conscientiousness to others) and *shu* 恕 (altruism) to illuminate *ren*. To practice *zhong* and *shu* genuinely is to practice *ren* genuinely. There are other important cognate concepts in Confucius's moral philosophy that help form the

conceptual domain of his notion of virtue, such as *zhongyong* 中庸 (The Doctrine of the Mean, moderation, mean-in-action), *xin* 信 (trustworthiness), *yi* 义 (righteousness), *yong* 勇 (courage), *shen* 慎 (prudence), *gong* 恭 (courtesy, respect), *jing* 敬 (reverence), and *xiao* 孝 (filial piety).

8. According to *Liji* 礼记 (Book of Rites), the Confucian society in ancient times had practiced approximately 300 ceremonial rituals and 3,000 minute rituals (*Liji: Liqi* 礼记: 礼器; Legge 1967, I, 404).

9. Herbert Finagrette provides a thoughtful account of the Confucian *li* in *Confucius: The Secular as Sacred* (1972).

10. For an interesting comparative study of *li* and *topoi*, see Haixia Lan's (2017) discussion on the rhetorical inventiveness of *li* and *yue* 乐 (music) in the *Analects*.

11. In the *Analects*, on most occasions *yan* 言 is used to refer to oral speech in both formal and informal settings. *Yan* has been translated as speech; here, speech means the expression of thoughts in spoken words, exchange of spoken words, or something that is spoken.

12. It was reported that Confucius compiled *Shi Jing* 诗经 (Book of Songs), *Shu* 书 (Book of History), and *Liji* 礼记 (Book of Rites). In this literacy context, Confucius recognized *zheng ming* as of utmost importance in both speaking and writing.

13. Some comparative philosophers refrained from using Aristotle's first philosophy to study Confucius's moral philosophy (e.g., Hall and Ames); others have integrated metaphysics into their reconstruction of Confucian ethics (e.g., Tu, Sim).

14. See Book 2 of Aristotle's *Nicomachean Ethics* (2011), 26–33.

15. For a detailed comparative analysis of *li* and ethos, see Yu (2007).

16. The social linguist and literacy scholar James Paul Gee's distinction between "learning" and "acquisition" might be helpful for us to understand the process of virtue cultivation in Confucian culture. Learning is a process that involves "attaining, along with the matter being taught, some degree of (conscious) meta-knowledge about the matter." Acquisition, in contrast, is "a process of acquiring something subconsciously by exposure to models and a process of trial and error" (Gee 2001, 539). Becoming a person with *ren* necessitates learning abstract moral concepts as well as being exposed to and practicing the rituals and appropriate use of speech.

17. In Confucius's view, virtue cultivation begins with one's interactions with family members. If one cannot teach one's own family to observe *li* in the spirit of *ren*, one cannot teach others or govern the state. For a more detailed discussion on Confucius's ethical, educational, and political programs, see Zhu Xi's (1991) annotations on *Da Xue* 大学 (The Great Learning).

18. See Plato's *Phaedrus* (1995). Richard L. Weaver offers a thoughtful analysis of Plato's view on ethics and rhetoric in his excellent essay "The Phaedrus and the Nature of Rhetoric" (Weaver 1953, 3-26).

19. Plato explains in detail his educational program for philosopher kings in chapter 8 of the *Republic* (1993).

REFERENCES

Ames, Roger T., and Henry Rosemont Jr., trans. 1998. *The Analects of Confucius: A Philosophical Translation.* New York: Random House.

Aristotle. 2011. *Aristotle's Nicomachean Ethics.* Trans. Robert C. Bartlett and Susan D. Collins. Chicago: University of Chicago Press.

Boodberg, Peter. 1953. "The Semasiology of Some Primary Confucian Concepts." *Philosophy East and West* 2 (1953): 317–32.

Chan, Wing-Tsit. 1963. *A Sourcebook in Chinese Philosophy*. Princeton, NJ: Princeton University Press.

Chen, Lai. 2017. *Confucius, Mencius, and Xunzi.* Beijing: SDX Joint Publishing Company.

Duffy, John. 2017. "The Good Writer: Virtue Ethics and the Teaching of Writing." *College English* 79 (3): 229–50.

Fingarette, Herbert. 1972. *Confucius: The Secular as Sacred.* New York: Harper and Row.

Fung, Yu-Lan. 1952. *A History of Chinese Philosophy*, vol. I: *The Period of the Philosophers.* Trans. Derk Bodde. Princeton, NJ: Princeton University Press.

Garrett, Mary. 2013. "Tied to a Tree: Culture and Self-Reflexivity." *Rhetoric Society Quarterly* 43 (3): 243–55.

Gee, James Paul. 2001. "Literacy, Discourse, and Linguistics: Introduction and What Is Literacy?" In *Literacy: A Critical Sourcebook*, ed. Ellen Cushman, Eugene R. Kintgen, Barry M. Kroll, and Mike Rose, 525–44. Boston: Bedford/St. Martins.

Gu, Hongming. 1898. *The Discourses and Sayings of Confucius.* Ed. Jingtao Wang. Reprinted, 2017. Beijing: Zhonghua Book Company.

Hall, David L., and Roger T. Ames. 1987. *Thinking through Confucius.* Albany: State University of New York Press.

Hum, Sue, and Arabella Lyon. 2009. "Recent Advances in Comparative Rhetoric." In *The Sage Handbook of Rhetorical Studies*, ed. Andrea A. Lunsford, Kirt H. Wilson, and Rosa A. Eberly, 153–65. Thousand Oaks, CA: Sage.

Kennedy, George A. 1998. *Comparative Rhetoric: An Historical and Cross-Cultural Introduction.* Oxford, UK: Oxford University Press.

Lan, Haixia W. 2017. *Aristotle and Confucius on Rhetoric and Truth: The Form and the Way.* London, UK: Routledge.

Lau, D. C. 1983. *Confucius: The Analects.* Chinese Classics: Chinese-English Series. Hong Kong: Chinese University Press.

Legge, James. 1967. "Translator's Introduction." *Li Chi: Book of Rites*, vols. I and II. 1-60. New York: University Books.

Li, Zehou. 2006. *Reading the Analects Today.* Beijing: SDX Joint Publishing Company.

Liu, Yameng. 2004. "Nothing Can Be Accomplished if the Speech Does Not Sound Agreeable: Rhetoric and the Invention of Classical Chinese Discourse." In *Rhetoric Before and Beyond the Greeks*, ed. Carol S. Lipson and Roberta A. Binkley, 147–64. Albany: State University of New York Press.

Lu, Xing. 1998. *Rhetoric in Ancient China, Fifth to Third Century BCE: A Comparison with Classical Greek Rhetoric.* Columbia: University of South Carolina Press.

Lyon, Arabella. 2004. "Confucian Silence and Remonstration: A Basis for Deliberation?" In *Rhetoric Before and Beyond the Greeks*, ed. Carol S. Lipson and Roberta A. Binkley, 131–45. Albany: State University of New York Press.

MacIntyre, Alasdair. 2004. "Once More on Confucian and Aristotelian Conceptions of the Virtues." In *Chinese Philosophy in an Era of Globalization*, ed. Robin R. Wang, 151–62. Albany: State University of New York Press.

Mao, LuMing. 2003. "Reflective Encounters: Illustrating Comparative Rhetoric." *Style* 37 (Winter): 401–25.

Mao, LuMing. 2010. "Searching for the Way: Between the Whats and Wheres of Chinese Rhetoric." *College English* 72 (4): 329–49.

Mao, LuMing, and Bo Wang, eds. 2015. "Symposium: Manifesting a Future for Comparative Rhetoric." *Rhetoric Review* 34 (3): 239–74.

Plato. 1993. *Republic.* Trans. Robin Waterfield. Oxford, UK: Oxford University Press.

Plato. 1995. *Phaedrus.* Trans. Alexander Nehamas and Paul Woodruff. Indianapolis, IN: Hackett.

Qian, Mu. 2012. *Lunyu xin jie* [A new interpretation of the *Analects*]. Beijing: SDX Joint Publishing Company.

Qian, Xun. 2017. *Lunyu* [The *Analects* with annotations and interpretations]. Beijing: National Library of China Press.

Rorty, Richard. 1984. "The Historiography of Philosophy: Four Genres." In *Philosophy in History: Essays on the Historiography of Philosophy*, ed. Richard Rorty, J. B. Schennwind, and Quentin Skinner, 49–75. London: Cambridge University Press.

Sim, May. 2007. *Remastering Morals with Aristotle and Confucius*. London: Cambridge University Press.

Tu, Wei-ming. 1979. *Humanity and Self-Cultivation: Essays in Confucian Thought*. Berkeley, CA: Asian Humanities Press.

Tu, Wei-ming. 1985. *Confucian Thought: Selfhood as Creative Transformation*. Albany: State University of New York Press.

Waley, Arthur. 1938. *The Analects of Confucius*. New York: Random House.

Wang, Bo. 2013. "Comparative Rhetoric, Postcolonial Studies, and Transnational Feminisms: A Geopolitical Approach." *Rhetoric Society Quarterly* 43 (3): 226–42.

Wang, Bo. 2015. "Transrhetorical Practice." In *Symposium: Manifesting a Future for Comparative Rhetoric*, ed. LuMing Mao and Bo Wang. *Rhetoric Review* 34 (3): 246–49.

Weaver, Richard M. 1953. *The Ethics of Rhetoric*. Chicago: Henry Regnery.

Xu, George. 2004. "The Use of Eloquence: The Confucian Perspective." In *Rhetoric Before and Beyond the Greeks*, ed. Carol S. Lipson and Roberta A. Binkley, 115–29. Albany: State University of New York Press.

Yang, Bojun. 2017. *Lunyu yizhu* [The *Analects* with translations and annotations]. Beijing: Zhonghua Book Company.

Yeats, W. B. 2000. *W. B. Yeats: Poems Selected by Seamus Heaney*. London: Faber and Faber.

You, Xiaoye. 2006. "The Way, Multimodality of Ritual Symbols, and Social Change: Reading Confucius's *Analects* as a Rhetoric." *Rhetoric Society Quarterly* 36 (4): 425–48.

Yu, Jiyuan. 2007. *The Ethics of Confucius and Aristotle: Mirrors of Virtue*. London: Routledge.

Zhu, Xi. 1991. *Si shu zhangju jizhu* [Collected annotations on the four Confucian classics]. Jinan, China: Qilu shushe.

5

TRANSNATIONAL PERSPECTIVES ON ETHICS

Rasha Diab

> *The self is not a thing, a substrate, but the protagonist of a life's tale.*
> *The conception of selves who can be individuated prior to their moral*
> *ends is incoherent.*
>
> —Seyla Benhabib
>
> *Under conditions of the veil of ignorance, the other disappears.*
>
> —Seyla Benhabib
>
> *Knowing at the limits of justice is at once a kind of knowing and*
> *doing; it is a praxis, one that unsettles what has become but offers*
> *no guidance for what has yet to become. Knowing the limits of*
> *justice, nonetheless, is an ethical-political praxis; it acknowledges*
> *all the effects and implications as well as the presuppositions*
> *informing our accounts of existing with/in one another.*
> *Knowing at the limits of justice, as an ethicopolitical praxis,*
> *requires ontoepistemological accounts that begin and end with*
> *relationality (affectability)—that do no more than to anticipate*
> *what is to be announced, perhaps, a horizon of radical exteriority,*
> *where knowing demands affection, intention, and attention.[1]*
>
> —Denise Ferreira da Silva

When I began writing this chapter, I wanted to ward off a romanticized version of transnationalism wherein we center and celebrate its potential (i.e., transnational identifications or mobility) while cropping out its relational dynamics and consequences. Generally defined as migration and "multiple ties and interactions linking people or institutions across the borders of nation-states," transnationalism is a complex phenomenon (Vertovec 1999, 447). These ties, interactions, and mobility abound with possibility for some but are fraught with easy to ignore risk for many, as scholarship in rhetoric and writing studies and other disciplines makes clear.

DOI: 10.7330/9781607329978.c005

Because I was haunted by Seyla Benhabib's (1992, 162) reference in the epigraph to the "veil of ignorance" and how it hides the transnational other, I wanted to revisit pressing ethical-political dilemmas of (trans)nationalism and border crossing. Rather than seeking or pretending to offer a full answer to the question "what does a transnational perspective on ethics bring to rhetoric and writing studies," I seek to provoke further discussion of the *(trans)national* in a world that prides itself on the compression of time and space, border crossing, transnational identification, and a global community. Their celebration can crop out global capitalist forces; histories and legacies of colonialism, racism, nationalism, and other-isms; and the immobility and precarity facing many around the world. Throughout the chapter, what is cropped out or centered helps me reflect on relationality and the rhetoric of moral consideration.

In this excursion, I join rhetoric and writing scholars who invite us to revisit how we think about ethical imperatives (of rhetoric and writing studies) in an increasingly transnational world.[2] Across borders, visions for the moral subject are (re)negotiated; texts and cultural artefacts are produced, appropriated, circulated, and engaged; rhetoric and writing instruction and rhetorical analytics are promoted; discursive spaces are created and foreclosed. In all these rhetorical interactions, the border is at the epicenter symbolizing (state) power, hope, risk, and a potential togetherness.

Yet to many, the border is an elusive presence. Even if unseen, borders author(ize) national doxa, which has far-reaching consequences on perceptions of and ethical obligations to others.[3] The border—symbolically and materially—author(ize)s because it names who *we, the people*, are (not) and determines whether we belong (i.e., have the right to political membership and legal entitlements); in addition, as it sets the terms of engagement with those on the other side of the border, it can name who is morally relevant (e.g., visitor versus infiltrator). Border crossing, too, brings to the fore national doxa and (potentially competing) moral views.

Like an elephant in the room, borders are at the center of numerous ethical dilemmas: for example, a commitment to universal human rights principles and the protection of state sovereignty often collide.[4] We glimpse this dilemma when (1) rhetoric constituting a national self clashes with the epistemic, linguistic, and cultural rights of the migrant other (e.g., English-only policy versus multilingual or translingual policy) and (2) when national rhetoric conflates cultural/linguistic membership with political membership as manifest in an assumed linguistic/cultural deficit or liability and the desirability of gate-keeping linguistic and cultural practices, which are assumed to foster conditions for a harmonious, good life. We have a glimpse of this dilemma (3) when rhetoric prioritizing national security deflects attention away from a refugee's security needs. Then a refugee is represented only as a security liability (Nyers 2003).

As I explore what a transnational perspective on ethics has to offer, I revisit the iconic image of Aylan Kurdi's refugee body that went viral in 2015. Far away, Aylan lies face-down, washed up dead on a beach in Bodrum, Turkey. He is joined by Rihan (his mother) and Galib (his brother). All were snatched by death in a rough sea. Aylan is survived by Abdullah Kurdi (his father), whose only hope in 2015 was to repatriate their bodies to be buried in Kobani, Syria. Aylan had traveled with his family—all severed from Syria. They fled war that ravished a land they once called home and sought Kos, a Greek island. They hoped to reunite with an aunt who had lived in Vancouver, Canada, for twenty years. The boat capsized. Abdullah Kurdi tried to hold on to Rihan, Aylan, and Galib, only to swim back and forth between drowned bodies.

At the time, different photos of Aylan circulated. In two, a Turkish police officer towers over Aylan's body and takes notes or lifts Aylan. Other photos focus on Aylan's body with his face down. Photos center either on his partially visible face or the back of his head.[5] The one that went viral is of Aylan's body lying face-down on a sandy beach. His face is partially visible.

The photo confronts us *again*—even if momentarily—with the fact that the transnational phenomenon is no longer *just* the abstracted movement of bodies, bodies of knowledge, technologies, and capital across national borders. As it centers Aylan's body, the photo becomes viral in transnational, networked discursive spaces; in these spaces, it represents and crops out. Both rhetorical acts allow this iconic image to communicate and shape a sphere of moral consideration.

Like many others, albeit untold, Aylan's story as (un)captured by the photo has the potential to hold a space for reflection on the shadow side of transnationalism, the migrant, responsibilities to distant others, and bearing witness. The immediate response to the photo can help us identify a transnational literacy. Zooming in on what the photo centers and crops out, I explore whether/how the photo holds the space for what Denise Ferreira da Silva (2013, 44) refers to as "an ethicopolitical praxis . . . that begin[s] and end[s] with relationality" and what Rebecca Dingo (2013) deems a transnational literacy.

In the epigraph at the beginning of this chapter, da Silva names relationality as an antidote. She explains that "knowing at the limits of justice, as an ethicopolitical praxis, requires ontoepistemological accounts that begin and end with relationality (affectability) . . . where knowing demands affection, intention, and attention" (da Silva 2013, 44). The *trans* points toward knowing at the jurisdictional limits of justice, which, in turn, directs our attention to the juridical/jurisdictional powers of the *nation-state* and the imaginaries these powers anchor: a trace of these powers is seen in the juridical description *illegal*, which differs from the humanitarian description *refugee/asylee.*[6] In the sections that follow, starting with the assumption that *transnational* implies expanded spheres of interactions but not necessarily relations based on recognition, immanent value, interdependence, and dynamic flow of rights and obligations, I first define the terms *transnational* and *relational ethics* as grounded in a relational worldview. Then I revisit the (after)life of Aylan's photo and what the photo's circulation tragically illuminates, and I tap into ethical questions foregrounded by the transnational movement of bodies, bodies of knowledge, technologies, and capital across national borders.

CENTERING TRANSNATIONALISM

I center *transnational* as a provocation to revisit the intersections of rhetoric and ethics. As a complex phenomenon, transnationalism is generally defined as the movement of people, ideas, goods, services—mainly because of globalization and the spread of neo-liberal economies and governmentality—across international borders. Transnationalism is not just movement, interaction processes, an expansive landscape that can be seen as a backdrop, for it is also the consequences and uneven effects of globalization. For rhetoric and writing studies, transnationalism helps us study "how globalization has influenced the movement of people and the production of texts, culture, and knowledge across borders so that the strict distinctions among nations and national practices can become blurred" (Dingo 2012, 8). As an analytical term, *transnationalism* becomes an interpretive lens that can help us realize some of our epistemic imperatives, including knowing others and knowing ourselves. As Jacqueline Jones Royster (2003, 148) explains, "Highlighting landscaping as an interpretive process underscores the extent to which interpretive enterprises are contingent more generally on perception and more specifically on the limitations of perception." Concomitantly, feminist transnational scholars (1) shed light on how globalization (as manifest in transnational corporations, migration, and enhanced communication technologies) has enabled cross-border "connectivities," or networks of economic, social, political, and cultural exchange and flow, and (2) shed light on "how increasing global capitalism can create conditions of economic exploitation for some women [and vulnerable populations] and possibilities for others" (Dingo 2012, 9).

Transnational feminist scholars study these connectivities to shed light on "vectors of power (often present within textual production through representational practices) that impact categories of identity, state sovereignty, and the markers of citizenship" (Dingo 2012, 9). As these categories indicate, transnationalism covers mobility and connectivity and uncovers national doxa—or state-centric logics—that negotiate/determine movement of actors or circulation of epistemic, social, political, and economic goods, artefacts, values, and processes/activities beyond the jurisdictional boundaries of one nation-state and into other nation-state(s).

As an interpretive framework, transnationalism is multifaceted. It

- Emphasizes cross-border, local-global networks;[7]
- Recognizes "state-centric narratives and territorially defined national borders" and the material, "symbolic[,] and imaginary geographies through which we attempt to make sense of our increasingly transnational world" (Mitchell 2003, 74; Jackson, Crang, and Dwyer 2004, 3);
- Recognizes non-state actors;
- Alerts us to the long, sometimes subtle reach of economic forces (e.g., capital flow, the market mechanism's impact on non-market domains), cultural forces (e.g., consumer culture informing texts and subjectivities), technologies (e.g., YouTube channels and drones), performances of (em)power(ment), and values that author(ize) an *ought to be* (e.g., the neo-liberal values of individual responsibility, self-management, self-improvement, self-sufficiency, and efficiency);[8]
- Nuances our awareness of different scales of interaction: "The crossing of scales (body, local, national, regional, international) is constitutive of transnationalism" (Ratcliffe, Laurie, and Andolina 240 quoted in Mayhew 2015);
- Explicates how these scales of interaction can set up the stage for activities, processes, emotional landscapes, and relational logics that defy national borders.

As such, transnational studies invites a transnational analytic and models a transnational literacy that (1) challenge the impulse to center (national) boundaries and (2) emphasize local-global connections, relations, and (assumed) fluidity. More important, transnational studies resets the terms for analytical responsibility: "The term 'transnationalism' with the emphasis on the *trans* allows this type of relational theorizing . . . in a number of different arenas—from examinations of the interactions and literal back-and-forth movement of goods, people, and ideas across national borders, to the theoretical suppleness of poststructuralist thought across containing and linear narratives and disciplinary confines" (Mitchell 2003, 74). With the emphasis on the *national*, transnational studies asks us to pay attention to how the flow/ movement inscribes/resists power and how flow/movement is policed, celebrated, or used to limit/energize ethicopolitical deliberations: with increased migration, there is a potential surge in nationalist discourses and (re)centering of a locally flavored nationalist and "racial grammar and lexicon" (da Silva 2013, 57).

These ethicopolitical deliberations often evoke descriptors (e.g., citizen and infiltrator/alien, global citizen/community). The web of relations made possible by globalization is complex. We assume that telecommunications, the compression of time and space, and reliance on digital public spheres eliminate distance and bridge gaps: "However, distance in this case is not simply a spatial phenomenon, it has a specifically moral component that emerges through intensified globalization and creates a category of a distant and invisible other" (MacDonald 2002, 65). Kenneth MacDonald (2002, 65–66, emphasis added) continues to explain that

> the technologies of globalization that annihilate socio-spatial distance insert us into webs of relationships with individuals and communities that are unknown to us in any corporeal way. Despite a general sense of expanding knowledge of the world, distant people and places are known to us vicariously as an agglomeration of representations brought to us through interpretive popular media, or sporadic touristic contact . . . *Distant others seem to remain outside of an immediate sphere of moral consideration* . . . This duty fails, some authors suggest, because of a radically outdated notion of the significance of physical or ideological proximity to moral consideration.

MacDonald's insight into the distant other and corporeal recognition dovetails with Benhabib's (1992) "generalized" versus "concrete" other and da Silva's (2013) reference to affectability in the epigraph. Because their terms signal an interest in relationality and the sphere of moral consideration, I revisit relational ethics, compare it to personal and social ethics, and reflect on why/how relational ethics attends to the sphere of moral consideration.

CENTERING RELATIONS, CENTERING RELATIONAL ETHICS

Relation is the focal point of relational ethics. However, relational ethics as described below is not just the external manifestation of personal ethics. Generally, ethics invests in excellence (proactive investment) and rectification (responsive investment). Personal excellence or virtues (personal ethics) focuses on the moral agent.[9] Personal ethics—assuming its cultivation has an outward, positive effect—impacts the interaction between and among individuals. This outward reach, often referred to as *social ethics*, prepares us to deal with others justly and with care.

However, the move from personal to social ethics is not automatic. As they strive for an *ought to be*, ethical ideals and endeavors hinge on relations for development, testing, and actualization. Moreover, the actualization of an ethical position for its in/extrinsic value hinges on perceptions of the self and perceptions of the other, and so does actualization of a self's interests or narratives, which might collide/converge with ethical considerations. Furthermore, the term *social ethics* assumes a social life, so what if there is none? What if the other is distant/distanced, disembodied, invisible and our relation to them suspended or barred by borders?

A transnational context complicates social ethics not just because it brings to the fore a distant, general other but also because this distant other is addressed from/through a habitus.[10] Nevertheless, in a transnational world, this rhetorical situation seems invisible. As noted earlier, communication technologies and circulation simulate patterns of sociality across borders while obfuscating how "distant people and places are known to us vicariously as an agglomeration of representations" (MacDonald 2002, 65–66). Using Benhabib's dictum, this is typically an abstracted, disembedded, disembodied, and generalized other, which, as MacDonald (2002, 65–66) explains, "remain[s] outside of an immediate sphere of moral consideration." Moreover, as different nationals relate with one another, in addition to individual actors we face an imagined collective self, its (dis/owned) history, its affective landscapes and material/symbolic attachments to a nation-state and those deemed other. Within this imaginary, the self's ethical obligations, rights, and actions are determined/negotiated. This collective self is an embodied self with deep-rooted emotions, narratives, and attachments and culturally sedimented discursive habits/habitus of identifying with/against others.

In this context, in addition to personal and social ethics, the term *relational ethics* is illuminating. In general, relational ethics hinges on the principles of radical (not instrumental) interdependence, immanent value, and transcendence.[11] What makes relational ethics different from social ethics is that it is more than just the external manifestation of personal ethics in social life.[12] Rather, relational ethics is a manifestation of a moral philosophy, a relational worldview, and an interdependent, relational self.[13] Elsewhere I explain that "a relational worldview emphasizes the dynamic and nonpolarized/nonpolarizing relation between people and seeks to balance autonomy and interdependence" (2016, 183). Interdependence is key to understanding the relational value system that underwrites the relational worldview: "By relational values we mean a way of being, knowing, understanding, feeling, and acting in relationship to other humans, plants, animals, and the natural world, as interrelated and spirit-filled" (Verbos and Humphries 2014, 2).[14] It is this worldview that counters the excesses of the self proactively and reactively (i.e., excellence and rectification), for "individuals are seen as both separate and connected, both individuated and similar. They are viewed as being to some degree autonomous, self-aware, and self-interested but also to some degree connected, sensitive, and responsive to others" (Kuttner 2010, 931–32).[15] It is this view that makes relations "the fulcrum for ethical action (how to be, how to act)" (Pollard 2015, 364). As such, relations hold the space for and spell out the imperatives of ethicopolitical praxis. For this reason, relational ethics mandates that everyone is recognized as having immanent value or, to use Benhabib's (1992, 159) language, as a concrete other, "an individual with a concrete history, identity and an affective-emotional constitution."

I draw here on the familiar dictum of knowing the other and their immanent value, recognizing interdependence as well as demonstrating respect, responsibility, and responsiveness. Without a relational worldview, this dictum responds (i.e., rectification) to an ever-present history of objectification that asserts power asymmetry, denies immanent value, and deems conditional the duty to recognize and respect. A relational worldview, however, starts and ends with relationality (i.e., a fluid interdependence of proactive excellence and rectification); therefore, there is no *other*. Knowing the (br)*other* or sister in a relational worldview is embodied, proximal knowing that defies border logics because *all* life depends on it.

In response to "the challenge of transnational non-existence of associational ties," numerous scholars shed light on traditions of relational moral philosophy, such as Anyiam-Osigwe's African moral philosophy of extended, nonrestrictive family/kinship. According to Anyiam-Osigwe, "The value of relationality emphasizes the *ontological connection* of all human persons across the morally arbitrary state boundaries, showing that relations among persons in the global society ought to be morally grounded, regardless of natural barriers" (quoted in Badru 2017, 79, emphasis added). From a relational perspective, "T[ransnational]

E[thics] advances a system of moral connection and consideration between the self and the other across national boundaries, that is, beyond the traditional statist account of ethical thinking and practice" (Badru 2017, 81). Putting the ethical imperatives of relational ethics and transnational analytics and literacy together, I now revisit Aylan Kurdi's photo.

CROPPED OUT: FROM KOBANI TO BODRUM AND BACK

Against the backdrop of an un(der)recognized, destabilized Middle East, a prolonged, multiparty war in Syria, and alarming refugee crises, Aylan Kurdi's photo circulated. Many considered it a commendable moment of transnational identification in which the link between Aylan's washed-up body on the one hand and the regional crises and the global-south refugee problem on the other was/could be obvious. The micro-macro connection is the main tenet of a transnational literacy/analytic (Dingo 2013). Iconic images like Aylan's have the potential to nudge us to see the different scales of the migrant/refugee question as a humanitarian crisis (i.e., as it maps on the human body of refugees, region, and globe). But rhetorical scholarship teaches us that iconic representations and the immediate emotional response indicate neither systematic nor long-term investments (Reeves 2013). I return to this rhetorical moment not because it is troubling but because it can help us trouble our understanding of the sphere of moral consideration in a transnational world.

Against the backdrop of the Syrian war, the photo testifies to the plight of war, desperate migration away from home, and the risks of crossing the borders of Turkey and Greece—neighboring countries typically known as tourist destinations. Aylan's photo had the potential to hold the space for ethicopolitical reflections: for bearing witness and attending to affectability—embodied emotion and relating to a concrete other. Was this potential realized? To respond to this question, I turn next to three deflections (i.e., cropped-out matters) that sometimes come up in rhetorical responses to/analyses/coverage of Aylan's photo. Each explores how/why/whether Aylan entered the sphere of moral consideration.

First, Aylan's face is partially visible. The "face" of the other is crucial for intentionally attending to and recognizing them; their presence becomes an ethical claim that constitutes—even if momentarily—a sphere of moral consideration.[16] Some noted that *though* Aylan's face is partially visible, the photo did attract global attention.[17] Some wondered if people identified with Aylan *because* his face is partially visible: "We don't quite see his face, you see the side of his face *so you can project onto him the face of someone you know.* You cannot distance yourself as easily" (Cole 2017, emphasis added).[18] Similarly, Angela Naimou (2016, 229) alerts us to *whom* we actually identified with: "The corpse of toddler Alan Kurdi . . . becomes a galvanizing image whose affective power was repeatedly described as arising from his pale complexion (he could be any European refugee), his death pose (like a toddler asleep in a crib), and the new shoes he was wearing—like the shoes of any European or American toddler." His face becomes dissociated from the after images of war victims and destitute refugees.

Second, Aylan traveled with others. My earlier summative narrative attends to his mother and brother, who also drowned that day; they are less visible. What the photo represents calls attention to what/why it deflects.[19] If/when we imagine the family members together, we bear witness to a family in the throes of war, war profiteers, and human traffickers. If/when we imagine the family, we center their severed connections with what to them became survival familial associations as well as their re-association with the "infiltrator/terrorist":

> Less visible but no less suggestive of the social texture refugees carry with them are the relatives many have already living in Europe, the United States, or Australia, familial ties that take on the urgency of a lifeline for the displaced but are often cut or knotted by the bureaucratic arm of immigration systems. Such was the case with Alan, whose aunt in Canada had been trying to sponsor her brothers, too slowly and imperfectly, through legal channels . . . These aspirations, appearances, devices, and objects speak powerfully to the affective experience and images of neoliberal citizenship and social life even when one is rendered a stateless refugee. Such familiar remnants of social life alter the imagined distance not only between "refugee" and "citizen" but also between "refugee" and "terrorist." The November 2015 attacks in Paris have spurred a widespread conflation of these two latter designations in particular. The distance between these various categories of personhood becomes increasingly difficult to ascertain. (Naimou 2016, 229)

Some might dismiss Naimou's attempt to underline this dangerous conflation, which is backed by a concern about one's border. However, Tima Kurdi (Aylan's aunt) similarly showed us the associational rhetoric that is cropped out and the associational rhetoric superimposed on the image of the refugee. She explained, in December of the same year, that people were not forgetting *just* her family's suffering but that of many others. She also clarified, "They're not terrorists. They're human beings . . . They had businesses. They had jobs. They owned a house. They sent their kids to school. They're like every single one of us in the West" (*National Post* 2015).[20]

Third, the outpouring emotional response of compassion—an indication that someone has entered the sphere of moral consideration—has mobilized many publics and resulted in interventions. To a great extent, these interventions point to what can be done (i.e., positive acts of rectification)—unfortunately, not for Aylan but for living others in a similar predicament. Many noted the public response and surge of donations to the Red Cross campaigns for Syrian refugees and the Refugees Welcome campaigns (nongovernmental actors' response), Naguib Sawiris's proposed voluntary commitment to buy an island and re-territorialize and shelter refugees (Egyptian billionaire's philanthropic initiative), and Angela Merkel's declaration (Germany's governmental response) that a refugee program will take 800,000 refugees (Cole 2017; De Andrés, Aldás, and García-Matilla 2016). These interventions help many. And, more important, they manifest charitable, rescue rhetoric. The problem with rescue rhetoric is that it is a trace of the victim-survivor-hero narrative; its main investment is immediate intervention, which is not necessarily invested in long-term solutions. This rescue narrative is comforting because it distances us from complicity, positions us in a giving relation to others, and brings us a step closer to rectification. We must guard against being interpellated as the charitable person who rescues/helps rescue another. This self is interpellated when we read "affective and emotional stories about other women's [or vulnerable populations'] oppression" (Dingo 2013, 531). The rescue narrative also distances us from a fuller form of solidarity and recognition of negative intervention toward rectification (e.g., abstaining from actions that impede the end of war in Syria or actions that set up the international community to tolerate gross humanitarian abuses and not develop a culture of common destiny).[21] A fuller form of solidarity would find the aforementioned measures a helpful beginning, a starting point enriched with compassion, but one that cannot end with donations or the acceptance of refugee/asylee petitions.

A relational worldview makes us too uneasy to ignore. Since "under conditions of the veil of ignorance, the other disappears" (Benhabib 1992), relational ethics mandates solidarity, which "involves commitment, and work, as well as the recognition that even if we do not have the same feelings, or the same lives, or the same bodies, we do live on common ground" (Ahmed 2014, 189). In a relational world, the ethical imperative of a community of common ground and shared destiny—including acts of solidarity—is pursued not for the benefit of another but is the daily work of self-love and self-nurturance. Across often emotionally charged communication nodes, Aylan was momentarily grieved for, but there were no consistent transformative articulations of (actionable) commitment to end this plight. In 2020, this lack of commitment continues to be the case. Many continue to surface ashore or migrate in caravans across borders, and nationalistic rhetoric intensifies, impacting local politics, international relations, and transnational possibilities. Tragic moments like Aylan's ask us to answer these questions: How do we resist aestheticizing border crossing or disseminating images of dead bodies while cropping them out of sight when alive? How do we recognize the other *before* and not just *after* the calamity? How do we relate with others across nations and borders?

NOTES

1. da Silva (2013, 44) seems to equate relationality with affectability, or embodied emotion, which helps us recognize and include an other in our spheres of attention, intention, and ethical consideration.

2. For more on the global and transnational turn, see Dingo, Riedner, and Wingard (2013); Hesford (2006); Hesford and Schell (2008).

3. Drawing on classical rhetoric and Pierre Bourdieu, I define national doxa as assumed, enthymematic arguments that shape, for example, perceptions of national self/other, affective landscapes (e.g., patriotic sentiments), and discursive interactions (e.g., hostile to or welcoming of strangers). National doxa (re)set the terms of national institutions, boundaries, national membership, and terms of engagement. For more, see Deer (2008).

4. For more on this tension, see Benhabib (2004).

5. See Kjeldsen (2017); Mortensen (2017).

6. Drawing on Samera Esmeir's work (2006, 1544), I point to this distinction, which is necessary to any uptake of "relationality . . . where knowing demands affection, intention, and attention" (da Silva 2013, 44). Esmeir (2006, 1544) calls our attention to the risks of "juridical humanity": "There exists an association between modern law, specifically international human rights law, and the human . . . This relation carries with it a force of constitution. Human rights law, like modern law more generally, aspires to name, define, call into being, redeem the human (Asad) . . . I am concerned with law's ambition to transform humanity into a juridical status, which precedes, rather than follows and describes, all humans. I call the conflation of the human and its assigned legal status an instance of juridicalization and the resulting humanity a 'juridical humanity.'"

7. To illustrate, transnational feminists underline the production, circulation, and reception of texts across borders. See, for example, Dingo (2012); Grewal (2005). Using the network metaphor, they "examine how texts are written, dispersed, and circulated, how they persuade, and how they might impact audiences who reside in different geopolitical locations." They invite feminist transnational rhetoricians to complement their study of nation-bound rhetorics with the study of "how arguments are transnationally networked and how neoliberal economics and neocolonial power relationships are often exigencies for particular arguments and representations" (Dingo 2012, 16, 15).

8.   The global-south border accents not only "juridical humanity" (see note 6 above) but also neo-liberal "economic humanity/liability." Relating Esmeir's (2006, 1544) critique to a different domain, a case can be made concerning the border, which can also be said to generate an "economic humanity" that "precedes rather than follows and describes, all humans." Dingo (2012, 10) explains, "Today neoliberalism . . . refers not only to market-centric policies, free trade, and the spread of global capitalism but also to how individuals ought to act . . . The ideology of neoliberalism trickles into our everyday lived experiences . . . and manifests within particular values: entrepreneurship, competition, individual choice, self-interest, and self-empowerment . . . Neoliberal policies then extend capitalist market logic—that is, competition, free trade, and business—to all institutions, including social welfare" in a nation. Pathologizing any "deviance," neo-liberal rhetoric locates problems in the individual, who is deemed an economic liability, within and across national borders and deflects attention away from dis/enabling systems and structures.

9.   See John Duffy's and William Duffy's discussions of virtue ethics in this volume; for more on the limitations of Aristotle's virtue ethics, see Badru (2017, 81).

10. Benhabib (1992) critiques the Western conception of justice as premised on an abstracted, disembedded, disembodied, and "generalized other."

11. Because of space limitations, I briefly address interdependence and immanent value, which are necessary precursors to including someone in one's sphere of moral consideration. The negative counterparts for claims to interdependence and immanent value are claims asserting liability and deficit as inherent qualities of the othered. Relationality is the positive counterpart to an expanded understanding of objectification. For more, see, for example, Buber (1937).

12. Relational ethics is often linked to feminist ethics or care ethics. However, relational ethics predates these scholarly endeavors, as is abundantly evident in the knowledges and moral praxis of numerous indigenous African, Asian, and Native American peoples. For more, see Metz and Miller (2016).

13. Christians (2011, 3) explains why worldviews cannot be dismissed: "Theories of morality do not arise from an objectivist rationalism, but from our fundamental beliefs about the world. Worldviews are the gyroscope around which our thinking and experience revolve. They are the home of our ultimate commitments at the core of our being. Worldviews give meaning to our consciousness. They represent a set of basic beliefs about human destiny. Presuppositions are therefore sine qua non in rethinking moral theory."

14. For more on interdependence and interconnectedness, see Royster and Kirsch, this volume.

15. The relational worldview counters the excesses of the organic and individualistic worldviews. The organic worldview—as Kuttner (2010, 931, 942) explains—centers on "community survival or welfare," and an individual—as Diab (2016, 183) explains—"is expected to both prioritize the needs of the collective and develop an ethic of devotion, sacrifice, and service." In contrast, according to Kuttner (2010, 931), the individualistic worldview centers on "a vision of the individual as a separate being, autonomous and unconnected," and the imperative is to satisfy their needs, which are typically elevated at the expense of others. For more on the differences among organic, individualistic, and relational worldviews, see Bush and Folger (2005); Kuttner (2010).

16. The ethical claim of the face of the other is repeatedly addressed by Levinas (1969, 50): "For the presence before a face, my orientation toward the Other, can lose the avidity proper to the gaze only by turning into generosity, incapable of approaching the other with empty hands." Levinas's *face* converges with Benhabib's *concrete other*.

Both seek to counter the exclusion or denial of the other. Relational ethics starts not with exclusion but with the other's immanent value and presence.

17. While noting the problems of "compassion fade" and failure to "scale up," Slovic, Västfjäll, Erlandsson, and Gregory (2017) studied Google searches of "Syria" and "Aylan" before and after the photo's circulation and compared responses to statistical accounts of refugee deaths versus the photo.

18. These are the words of Paul Slovic, the lead scholar of the study cited in note 17.

19. Aylan's photo went viral in September 2015. We often forget that in this case, nine other bodies were found in the Aegean strait between Turkey and Kos. To add yet another layer of deflection, by September there were 442,400 migrants from many "refugee-producing countries, led by Syria," Afghanistan, and Kosovo. And "nearly 3,000 people have died or gone missing trying to cross the Mediterranean this year [2015]" (Redmond 2015).

20. Her appeal seeks to counter the recession of the humanitarian recognition of the other as it contends with a "juridical humanity," which Naimou points to in the block quotation and which Esmeir alerts us to. See note 6.

21. For more on negative and positive transnational justice, see Badru (2017).

REFERENCES

Ahmed, Sarah. 2014. *The Cultural Politics of Emotion*. Edinburgh, UK: Edinburgh University Press.

Badru, Ronald Olufemi. 2017. "Transnational Ethics, Justice, and Anyim Osigwe's Philosophy of the Family." In *Themes, Issues, and Problems in African Philosophy*, ed. Isaac E. Ukpokolo, 77–96. Cham, Switzerland: Springer International.

Benhabib, Seyla. 1992. "The Generalized and the Concrete Other: The Kohlberg Gilligan Controversy and Feminist Theory." In *Situating the Self: Gender, Community, and Postmodernism in Contemporary Ethics*, 148–77. New York: Routledge.

Benhabib, Seyla. 2004. *The Rights of Others: Aliens, Residents, and Citizens*. New York: Cambridge University Press.

Buber, Martin. 1937. *I and Thou*. Trans. Ronald George Smith. Edinburgh, UK: T. & T. Clark.

Bush, Robert A. Baruch, and Joseph P. Folger. 2005. *The Promise of Mediation: The Transformative Approach to Conflict*. San Francisco: Jossey-Bass.

Christians, Clifford. 2011. "Primordial Issues in Communication Ethics." In *The Handbook of Global Communication and Media Ethics*, ed. Robert S. Fortner and P. Mark Fackler, 1–19. 2 vols. Somerset, UK: John Wiley.

Cole, Diane. 2017. "Study: What Was the Impact of the Syrian Boy?" National Public Radio, January 13. https://www.npr.org/sections/goatsandsoda/2017/01/13/509650251/study-what-was-the-impact-of-the-iconic-photo-of-the-syrian-boy/.

da Silva, Denise Ferreira. 2013. "To Be Announced: Radical Praxis or Knowing (at) the Limits of Justice." *Social Text* 31 (1): 43–62.

De Andrés, Susana, Eloísa Nos Aldás, and Agustín García-Matilla. 2016. "The Transformative Image, the Power of a Photograph for Social Change: The Death of Aylan." *Comunicar* 24 (47): 29–37.

Deer, Cécile. 2008. "Doxa." In *Pierre Bourdieu: Key Concepts*, ed. Michael Grenfell, 114–25. Stocksfield, UK: Acumen.

Diab, Rasha. 2016. *Shades of Ṣulḥ: The Rhetorics of Arab-Islamic Reconciliation*. Pittsburgh, PA: University of Pittsburgh Press.

Dingo, Rebecca. 2012. *Networking Arguments: Rhetoric, Transnational Feminism, and Public Policy Writing*. Pittsburgh, PA: University of Pittsburgh Press.

Dingo, Rebecca. 2013. "Networking the Macro and Micro: Toward Transnational Literacy Practices." *Journal of Advanced Composition* 33 (3–4): 529–52.

Dingo, Rebecca, Rachel Riedner, and Jennifer Wingard. 2013. "Transnational Feminisms." Special issue, *Journal of Advanced Composition* 33 (3–4).

Esmeir, Samera. 2006. "On Making Dehumanization Possible." *Publications of the Modern Language Association* 121 (5): 1544–51.

Grewal, Inderpal. 2005. *Transnational America: Feminisms, Diasporas, Neoliberalisms.* Durham, NC: Duke University Press.

Hesford, Wendy S. 2006. "Global Turns and Cautions in Rhetoric and Composition Studies." *Publications of the Modern Language Association* 121 (3): 787–801.

Hesford, Wendy S., and Eileen E. Schell. 2008. "Introduction: Configurations of Transnationality: Locating Feminist Rhetorics." *College English* 70 (5): 461–70.

Jackson, Peter, Philip Crang, and Claire Dwyer. 2004. "Introduction: The Spaces of Transnationality." In *Transnational Spaces*, ed. Peter Jackson, Philip Crang, and Claire Dwyer, 1–23. London: Routledge.

Kjeldsen, Jens E. 2017. "The Rhetorical and Argumentative Potentials of Press Photography." In *Multimodal Argumentation and Rhetoric in Media Genres*, ed. Assimakis Tseronis and Charles Forceville, 51–80. Amsterdam: John Benjamins.

Kuttner, Ran. 2010. "From Adversity to Relationality: A Buddhist-Oriented View of Integrative Negotiation and Mediation." *Ohio State Journal on Dispute Resolution* 25 (4): 931–74.

Levinas, Emmanuel. 1969. *Totality and Infinity.* Trans. Alphonso Lingis. Pittsburgh, PA: Duquesne University Press.

MacDonald, Kenneth. 2002. "Epistemic Violence: The Body, Globalization, and the Dilemma of Rights." *Transnational Law and Contemporary Problems* 12 (1): 65–87.

Mayhew, Susan. 2015. "Transnational Relations Theory." In *A Dictionary of Geography.* 5th ed. Oxford, UK: Oxford University Press.

Metz, Thaddeus, and Sarah Clark Miller. 2016. "Relational Ethics." In *The International Encyclopedia of Ethics*, ed. Hugh LaFollette, 1–10. Oxford, UK: John Wiley.

Mitchell, Katharyne. 2003. "Cultural Geographies of Transnationality." In *Handbook of Cultural Geography*, ed. Kay Andersen, Mona Domosh, Steve Pile, and Nigel Thrift, 74–87. London: Sage.

Mortensen, Mette. 2017. "Constructing, Confirming, and Contesting Icons: The Alan Kurdi Imagery Appropriated by #humanitywashedashore, Ai Weiwei, and Charlie Hebdo." *Media, Culture, and Society* 39 (8): 1142–61.

Naimou, Angela. 2016. "Double Vision: Refugee Crises and the Afterimages of Endless War." *College Literature* 43 (1): 226–33.

National Post. 2015. "Alan Kurdi's Aunt on Canada's Response to the Refugee Crisis: I Want the World to Remember That Picture." National Post, December 26, http://nationalpost.com/news/canada/alan-kurdis-aunt-on-canadas-response-to-the-refugee-crisis-i-want-the-world-to-remember-that-picture/.

Nyers, Peter. 2003. "Abject Cosmopolitanism: The Politics of Protection in the Anti-Deportation Movement." *Third World Quarterly* 24 (6): 1069–93.

Pollard, Cheryl L. 2015. "What Is the Right Thing to Do: Use of a Relational Ethic Framework to Guide Clinical Decision-Making." *International Journal of Caring Sciences* 8 (2): 362–68.

Redmond, Ron. 2015. "Another Weekend Tragedy Marks the Mediterranean with up to 40 Refugees Dead." UNHCR, September 20. http://www.unhcr.org/en-us/news/latest/2015/9/55ff19226/weekend-tragedy-marks-mediterranean-40-refugeesdead.html/.

Reeves, Joshua. 2013. "Suspended Identification: *Atopos* and the Work of Public Memory." *Philosophy and Rhetoric* 64 (3): 306–27.

Royster, Jacqueline Jones. 2003. "Disciplinary Landscaping, or Contemporary Challenges in the History of Rhetoric." *Philosophy and Rhetoric* 36 (2): 148–67.

Slovic, Paul, Daniel Västfjäll, Arvid Erlandsson, and Robin Gregory. 2017. "Iconic Photographs and the Ebb and Flow of Empathic Response to Humanitarian Disasters." *Proceedings of the National Academy of Sciences* 114 (4): 640–44.

Verbos, Amy Klemm, and Maria Humphries. 2014. "A Native American Relational Ethics: An Indigenous Perspective on Teaching Human Responsibility." *Journal of Business Ethics* 23 (1): 1–9.

Vertovec, Steven. 1999. "Conceiving and Researching Transnationalism." *Ethnic and Racial Studies* 22 (2): 447–62.

Wielsch, Dan. 2013. "Relational Justice." *Law and Contemporary Problems* 76 (2): 191–211.

6
ETHICS AND TRANSLINGUAL WRITING

Xiaoye You

The intricate relationship between rhetoric and ethics is a perennial subject among Eastern and Western thinkers. For instance, Daoists emphasized the danger of language in causing social disturbance and language's inability to represent *dao,* or the Way the universe, including humans, operates (*Dao Jing* 2003). While Confucius had more faith in language's ability to resolve social issues, when annotating the *Book of Change* he also suggested using language with caution lest social turmoil would ensue ("乱之所生也，则言语以为阶") (Yang and Zhang 2011, 581). Looking to the West, we see similar tensions in how ancient thinkers perceived the role of rhetoric in public life. Intending to lead students to a meaningful and fulfilling kind of life and to educate them about truth and beauty, Plato entrusted the power of philosophy and disparaged rhetoric as cookery. Although he employed written words to construct philosophical dialogues, Plato cast doubts on writing, portraying it as a roadblock in one's pursuit of truth. He did so in *Phaedrus* by telling a story of an Egyptian king who rejected writing as a harmful invention (Plato 2003). While concurring with Plato on the inability of rhetoric to lead one to truth, Aristotle (2006) believed in its power in securing happiness, or a fulfilling life, through training and participation in public discourse.

Dealing with rhetoric and ethics, these thinkers' works have captured cultural and language difference prominent in their times. In his annotation of the *Book of Change* (Yang and Zhang 2011), Confucius highlights the complementary relationship among words, images, and trigrams. He explains that language could not fully capture the meaning of the universe, thus it was inadequate for guiding human action. Therefore the sage invented imagistic symbols and trigrams and blended them with words in the book ("圣人立象以尽意，设卦以尽情僞，系辞焉以尽其言，变而通之以尽利，鼓之舞之以尽神") (Yang and Zhang 2011, 599).

DOI: 10.7330/9781607329978.c006

Plato's use of the Egyptian king story can be attributed to the mobility of people and cultural products between Greece and its North African colonies in Plato's times. When discussing ways of achieving happiness, Aristotle (2006, 59) enumerates things viewed honorable in Asiatic states: "Among barbarians such things as proskynesis and rights of precedence and gifts . . . are in honor in each society." Speaking of style, he emphasizes the native, natural use of words, hence not the deviations heard in foreigners' speech: "A word in its prevailing and native meaning and metaphor are alone useful in the *lexis* of prose" (Aristotle 2006, 199). Examples like these suggest that cultural and language difference shaped these thinkers' thoughts in rhetoric.

Nevertheless, these thinkers held different attitudes toward language and cultural difference, thus positioning them as well as their students within the dominant society in remarkably distinct ways. Aristotle studied rhetoric as practiced in Athenian society and taught students how to shape public discourse as participating citizens. He positioned his students as members of the elite class and underscored the undesirability of sounding like an outsider. Language and cultural difference ought to be contained, if not eliminated. Like Aristotle, Diogenes was a foreigner to the Athenian city-state. However, joining the state was never his intent. Of him it is said, "Asked where he came from, he answered: 'I am a citizen of the world (kosmopolitês)'" (Laertius 1972, passage 63). Articulating a groundbreaking concept, Diogenes challenged the basis of social identity in Greece at that time, which would have been either the individual city-state or Greek society as a whole. Setting his goals on unsettling accepted wisdom and social conventions, he mocked various people he ran into, including philosophers like Plato and politicians like Alexander the Great. He also mocked the practice of rhetoricians, accusing them of paying lip service and focusing on gaining fame. He called rhetoricians and all who talked of reputation "thrice human," meaning thereby "thrice wretched." He went so far as to distract audiences attending Anaximenes the rhetorician's lectures by producing salt fish. He viewed good rhetoric as focusing on satirizing and tearing down sophisticated social conventions, including the city-state system.

Along with the high-profile places language and cultural difference occupied in these thinkers' works, their writing, for the most part, is translingual. Some spoke multiple languages or dialects, which were drawn on as resources in their composing process. Although they used one language that was "native" and "natural" to their community of readers, it contained words and expressions from outside the community. Some also used multiple languages or even multiple representational systems in texts like the *Book of Change*. Despite the fact that writing has been historically translingual, rhetoricians do not seem to have paid much attention to this feature until recent years. In the first half of this chapter, I attempt to explore this historical reticence. Drawing on past and present examples, I suggest that the state tends to put pressure on writers in their language choices, pushing them to choose the script system authorized by the powerful. However, negotiating with or breaking away from the authorized system is a common practice in everyday language use and is even more critical for those who have to cross language and cultural boundaries to survive or prosper. In the chapter's second half, I survey recent discussions of ethical treatment of language and cultural difference in the teaching of writing and suggest cosmopolitanism as a complement to the social justice imperative.

TRANSLINGUAL WRITING AND MONOLINGUAL STATE

The formation of a state always involves constructing "walls"—geographic, cultural, ethnic, and racial. It was the case with ancient nations, such as the Athenian city-state and Qin China (221–206 BCE). The Great Walls were built to demarcate the geographic and cultural borders between the agrarian Han and the northern pastoral nomadic tribes. The Qin government issued standards for almost every aspect of life, including measurements and language, such as script size and shape and the length of chariot axles. The ultimate purpose was to identify those who conformed to the standards as "us" and those who didn't as "them." Deeply intertwined with European colonialism, the formation of modern nations has very much followed the same path for building "walls." Native peoples were often described as "them," as barbarians, savages, degraded races that needed to be salvaged by the civilized colonizers. Modern nations came into being always in response to those with whom the subjects identified, the privileged colonizer or the wretched colonized. This national subject formation was always accompanied by both real and imagined boundaries. As part of an "imagined community" (Anderson 1991), national subjects are indoctrinated by a bounded perspective toward language and nation, or monolingualism. In the monolingual frame, it is assumed that one communicates with members of an "imagined community," sharing a national language and a national culture; other languages are considered ethnic or foreign and are best kept at home or in the classroom (Dicker 2003).

However, historically, writing has always been a translingual practice. One almost always lives in a multilingual or multidialectal context, interacting with speakers of such. Although a script may seem "native" or "natural" to a particular group, the script system has gradually sedimented in currents of interaction and exchange among different groups, tribes, and communities. For instance, Old English developed from a set of dialects originally spoken by Germanic tribes known as the Angles, Saxons, and Jutes. The vocabulary of Middle English was deeply shaped by Norman French. As British colonizers marched to different parts of the world, English was further transformed by its expanding users, taking on local expressions and meanings. The same happened when Qin China unified the script system shortly after 221 BCE. While the government managed to eliminate competing script systems by burning books collected from the states it conquered, it also absorbed elements from these systems. These interactions and exchanges between peoples and between states left distinct cultural meanings in the words and expressions of a script system like palimpsest. They have become so naturalized that even native speakers may be insensitive to their historical meanings.

What alerts native speakers to the translingual nature of writing tends to come from their encounter with texts by someone coming from the outside. They will sense a difference: while the script looks familiar, there are subtle differences in expression and meaning. The foreigner's script may or may not contain foreign-sounding words, but the use of certain words and expressions as well as textual organizations may intrigue or puzzle native speakers (Kachru 1990; Kaplan 1966; Martin 1896). They may see their own writing as monolingual and the foreigner's as multilingual. Therefore, what constitutes multilingual can be a subjective matter. It depends on how one feels about both the script and the writer, as well as whether there are traces of foreign expressions and structures.

Whether viewed as monolingual or multilingual, writing often matters tremendously to the writer and his or her community. A foreigner has to compose in a language "not of his or her own" because of compelling reasons. He or she has to toil for years to master the written form. The acquisition of this foreign tongue was historically connected to colonialism, migration, religious work, and trade. The spread of Chinese in East and Southeast Asia, for instance, was such a case. People learned its written form because it brought them cultural and economic capital crucial for their life-world. In the process, they could transform this foreign import into their own. The spread of classical Chinese in Japan, for instance, took place largely through migration and travel. Brought in by Chinese and Korean immigrants in the fifth century CE, it became

Japan's first major writing system. Over time, its users appropriated it along with imported Chinese texts for their practical and imaginative purposes. When the oldest extant chronicle in Japan, *Kojiki*, was composed in the eighth century, Confucian and local historiographic methods were fused; and the practice of writing with Japanese syntax while using kanji (Chinese characters), partially as phonograms, was firmly established (Seeley 1991). The engagement with Chinese texts enabled the Japanese literati to exercise more control over their lives and transcend their geographic and cultural borders.

At the personal level, this "foreign" script matters to the writer, too. The script may be the only means for an individual to communicate with a target community, to live among them physically or imaginatively, to mark the writer's multivalent connections with the community despite his or her official status as an "outsider," or simply to gain access to social or cultural capital connected to the language. The "foreign" script highlights this undeletable cross-cultural bond between the individual and the native speaker community. In China, there are age-old online English-language bulletin boards. They are places where young professionals use English for a variety of personal aims, which may be related to or distant from those of native speakers. In one such forum that I initially introduced in You (2016), many young professionals have internalized English in their lives, making it part of what defines them. For instance, a female migrant worker nicknamed "Sunshine" used English to describe her life after moving to Shanghai. Her writing has captured her diasporic consciousness, the feelings and emotions connected to working away from her hometown and her extended family (You 2016, 69):

> Sitting in front of the newly-bought desk by my host, I hoped to tackle everything with the new Korean ballpoint pen every day in Shanghai. Shanghai is the most attractive city in China, different from Guangzhou. When walking along the neat street against the cool autumn wind, I felt good: It is Shanghai; I'm here now. She is like an elegant lady, peaceful but open minded which is opposite to Guangzhou, an impetuous boy, energetic but impolite. However, there still many interesting things [that] happened since the day I stepped out of the train and on the land that Annbaby, a pop writer in China, described.
>
> At 5:20 a.m., August 28, 2002, I arrived. ("流年 [Fleeting years]" post no. 2)

Sunshine depicts her feelings upon her arrival in Shanghai. Her use of similes ("elegant lady" versus "an impetuous boy") vividly captures two cities' characters in the eyes of a young migrant worker. Permeating the text are outpourings of delight ("I felt good"), excitement ("I hope to tackle everything"), and enchantment ("many interesting things" and the pop writer "Annbaby"). Having just arrived in a new city, Sunshine hopes to "tackle everything" with her "Korean ballpoint pen," which signifies both her multilingual repertoire and writing's pivotal role in her diasporic life.

Translinguality matters to native speakers as well, especially those marginalized in their community or nation. In the United States, the best-known examples probably come from the African American community. Geneva Smitherman (1985, 1999, 2000) has identified linguistic and rhetorical features of African American Vernacular English (AAVE) distinct from those of Standard Written English. These features are commonly captured in writing, ostensibly in fictions depicting working-class people, such as those in the works of Alice Walker (1982), Toni Morrison (2004), and Sapphire (1997). The use of AAVE in character development metonymically foregrounds and affirms African Americans' lived experiences in a racialized society. The same point can be made when it comes to the use of Chinese writing to represent local speech. For instance, headlines in Hong Kong news media are commonly written in a local script based on Cantonese. The script appeals to readers more than does the national one because it has well captured their everyday speech. Newspapers in Shanghai are making similar attempts, using Shanghai dialects to better capture local residents' experiences and feelings. These local scripts use Chinese characters as phonetic symbols to represent certain words in the local dialects, often abandoning the traditional meanings assigned to these characters. As a speaker of Hakka and Standard Chinese, I often fail to grasp these dialectal writings. The writings can pose a threat to the state because they mark local rather than national identities. While the state can tolerate the flavors of local culture these writings capture, it abhors the separatist vehicle they can also serve as. Even a small state can have great diversity in population, socioeconomic culture, and language—hence writers' desire to capture these diversities faithfully. The state promotes monolingualism to maintain national coherence and unity amid these diversities.

The monolingual perspective, sponsored by the state, has long shaped the literacy classroom. In the United States, historical accounts of such abound (Dayton 2005; NeCamp 2014; Spack 2002; Wan 2014; Webster 2010). For instance, after studying the public discourse and beliefs about literacy during the Progressive Era (1890–1920), Amy E. Dayton (2005) unveiled the conflicts between the monolingual, nationalist pedagogy sponsored by the Americanization programs and the community-based pedagogy sponsored by the labor union programs. In Americanization program classes, immigrants were taught literacy in its most narrow, utilitarian form. The authors of a widely used text-book that Dayton examined, for instance, presented writing only as an exercise in penmanship and correctness. They suggested teaching penmanship and letter formation, then copying and dictation, very gradually advancing to more original assignments such as responding to newspaper ads or sending telegrams. Writing was presented as a skill with narrowly defined monolingual rules, best learned by repeti-tion. In contrast, the union educators encouraged students to use their multilingual literacy to meet their diverse, community-based needs and goals. They emphasized small-group learning and student discussion instead of drills, memorization, or lectures. Their pedagogy focused on student leadership, preparation for real-world work, activism, and cultural plurality. Dayton's description calls our attention to two distinct pedagogical approaches, one inspired by nationalism and the other by class consciousness, in improving immigrant workers' literacy levels.

Reviewing the historical tensions between translingual writing and a monolingual state helps generate several insights. First, the rise of the state has led to boundary building both physically and culturally. To bring its people together, the state tends to foreground their sameness and downplay their difference. It makes conscious efforts to create a script system based on a particular dialect and to promote it through the state apparatus, including schools, official scribes, and printing presses. Second, because of the sedimentation of language as well as cross-cultural contact, writing always involves drawing expressions, structures, and meanings from different languages and cultures. Thus writing is always a translingual practice. Third, this translinguality matters tremen-dously to writers and their communities, particularly those historically marginalized, such as foreigners and ethnic minorities. Highlighting translinguality as a key feature in communication in a monolingual state calls people's attention to these groups' marginalization and demands an ethical response.

ETHICS IN THE TEACHING OF WRITING

This historical overview of translingual writing and a monolingual state helps raise a series of ethical and political questions for writing teachers. Specifically, how do we position ourselves and our students in relation to the dominant society? Who will benefit from our teaching? Should we teach writing assuming it as a monolingual or a transling-ual practice? Answers to these questions are somewhat divided along disciplinary lines.

In the field of second-language writing, a field that intersects with applied linguistics and writing studies, much of its scholarship and pedagogy has centered on the traditional notion of English as a second language (ESL) writers in the United States, including international students, immigrants, and native-born bilinguals. In terms of ethics in the teaching of writing, Tony Silva (1997) proposed a code of conduct for treating ESL writers based on respect. He suggests that ESL writers "need to be (a) understood, (b) placed in suitable learning contexts, (c) provided with appropriate instruction, and (d) evaluated fairly" (Silva 1997, 359). Silva positions the writers as outsiders of the nation-state who want to learn the language of its citizens. These writers have been understood based on fixed national and cultural identities, on the features of their texts and composing behaviors measured against native speaker norms: "These writers may be very different from their native English-speaking (NES) peers in important ways . . . The results of the relevant research suggest that, in general, ESL writing is distinct from and often simpler and less effective (in the eyes of NES judges) than that of their NES peers. ESL writers' composing processes seem constrained in some salient ways" (Silva 1997, 359). Although the field of second-language writing has focused on ESL writers with multilingual backgrounds, it traditionally views writing as monolingual. That is, aligned with the nation-state, it focuses on helping ESL students master the skills required to produce monolingual texts rather than on challenging the monolingual ideology.

In a recent "update" on the ethical treatment of English as an additional language (EAL) writers, Christine Tardy and Erin Whittig (2017) advocated for a multilingual framework for teaching second-language writing and adopted a social justice perspective to ethics. They first underscore that the world is both more globalized and "simultaneously more fractured, conflict-ridden, and inequitable" (Tardy and Whittig 2017, 920) than it was two decades ago. In terms of instruction, they recommend that it be conducted based on the recognition that "multilingual writers write multilingually" (924). Teachers need to negotiate between valuing this practice and supporting students to learn to function successfully in contexts that value monolingualism. They embrace a social justice perspective for ethics, suggesting that "many EAL writers are members of marginalized groups" (927) and therefore that teachers and writing programs should advocate for these writers by providing them with resources to support them emotionally and legally, speaking for them when making decisions that would affect them, and recognizing and challenging material and discursive structures that disadvantage these writers. In contrast, writing studies in the United States has positioned students as members of the nation-state. But like the field of second-language writing, it has long viewed writing as a monolingual practice, aligning itself with the monolingual ideologies propagated by the state (Horner and Trimbur 2002). It assumes that students in the United States need to learn how to write in English, the de facto official language, rather than in other languages. Further, the written script needs to conform to Standard English, through which one may communicate with other members of the state or an academic audience. When it attends to language and cultural differences, it focuses on explicit ones, as reflected in student texts as measured against Standard Written English. As the textual deviations are often explained through social factors, such as ethnicity and class, writing studies takes as its ethical responsibility making sure that ethnic minority and working-class students are able to produce texts conforming to Standard English.

The rationale for attending to cultural and language difference in US writing studies has primarily been social injustice. Certain ethnic minorities, such as African Americans, were historically oppressed and exploited by the white majority. Responding to their wretched situations, African Americans developed strategies for survival and solidarity, including their distinct AAVE. Likewise, other ethnic groups, such as Chicano, Hispanic, Chinese, and Korean Americans, may want to maintain their own languages for survival and communal solidarity. The importance of minority languages and dialects for minority students was first affirmed in the historic document "Students' Right to Their Own Language" published by the Conference on College Composition and Communication in 1974 (Committee 1974). Speaking their heritage languages or dialects at home, students may struggle with the acquisition of Standard English. The ethnicity factor is further compounded by a class factor. Students from lower working-class families tend to lack material resources to support their schoolwork, including the acquisition of literacy skills in Standard English. However, as the social justice argument goes, without Standard English, students would be deprived of the opportunity to succeed in mainstream society and would remain second-class citizens.

Another argument for attending to language and cultural difference arose more recently from the demands of the post-Fordist workplace and globalization, which have propelled writing studies to examine its language ideologies and embrace a multilingual or translingual perspective. In literacy education, the New London Group argues that traditional literacy pedagogy is inadequate in the post-Fordism era in which communication channels and media have multiplied and cultural and linguistic diversity have increased. They advocate for a pedagogy of multiliteracies, which assumes that "language and other modes of meaning are dynamic representational resources, constantly being remade by their users as they work to achieve their various cultural purposes" (Cope and Kalantzis 1999, 5). In globalization, the increasing mobility of people and social and economic super-diversity requires a similar mobility of language resources. The new fluid and dynamic environment demands that we cultivate new forms of competence among our students. As Hina Ashraf (2018, 1) notes, "Current research in multilingual countries supports local languages and recognizes plurilingual practices as proficiency." These are the linguistic, discursive, and, in more diffuse ways, cultural values the more fluid and dynamic global context calls out (Donahue 2018). In writing studies, Bruce Horner and his colleagues (2011) proposed a translingual approach to teaching writing, acknowledging language differences as both rights (supporting a social justice argument) and resources (supporting a globalization argument). They suggest that we should honor "the power of all language users to shape language to specific ends" and recognize "the linguistic heterogeneity of all users of language both within the United States and globally" (Horner, Lu, Royster, and Trimbur 2011, 305).

Advocating a dynamic, fluid, and mobile perspective to language and literacy practice, this plurilingual, translingual, or multilingual perspective has been criticized by some for having unwittingly aligned itself with neo-liberal multiculturalism "that celebrates individual cosmopolitanism and plurilingualism for socioeconomic mobility" (Kubota 2016, 475). The critics are concerned that the perspective has not seriously considered how racial and other power relations might affect the ways people use, learn, and teach language. They are worried that the perspective does not improve the lives of those who are linguistically, racially, and economically marginalized by globalization. Responding to the neo-liberalism charge, Suresh Canagarajah (2015) suggested that while neo-liberals use translingualism as a product and a commodified branding mechanism, proponents of the translingual perspective view it as a practice that is politically savvy and socially conscious, as well as sensitive to power, social norms, and audience.

Indeed, as some critics charge, while combining a social justice and a resources argument, the translingual approach may still risk losing ethical ground (Gilyard 2016). This concern may be illustrated using an example from the classroom, initially introduced by Steven Fraiberg and colleagues (2017). I taught a public speaking class in an

English-medium summer program a few years ago for Chinese international students who studied in the United States and returned to China for the summer. In class, students needed to deliver a few scripted speeches. One of them is a practice speech called "Inspire Me," in which a student needs to follow several rhetorical moves commonly found in an inspirational speech. Students were divided into speakers and judges. The speakers chose whichever topic could inspire the audience. One of the students was Michael. His scripted speech put a judge or the teacher in an ethically challenged position when evaluating it. He chose to speak about homosexuality:

> Four scores ago, when our country was still young and wild, we made lots of mistakes. We raise the flag of freedom and ring the bell of liberty from the high of the Rocky to the low of the Ocean Pacific. Meanwhile, we cast intolerable looks on homosexuality. Then, I asked myself, and my country asked itself: Where is the freedom we believe in? We need freedom, from religion to love, from politics to relationship, everything! Yes, everything, because we all do not want to forget what this country is found[ed] on. Yes, Philadelphia, freedom, 1776. I have a dream. One day from now on, our despicable look will be found nowhere across the Appalachian mountain, sweep the Mississippi. I have a dream. One day boys and girls, boys and boys, girls and girls, are able to lay in the same bed of pure love passionately, purely, and freely. And I have a dream. One day, black, yellow, white are all able to choose whatever partners they want to choose no matter what gender they are all over the universe. And yes, I have a dream. From today, from now on, nobody, me, she, you, and I, none of us will be afraid to pick up soul dropped on the floor accidently [sic] or not accidently [sic]. Let homosexuality ring, let liberty ring, for world freedom. God bless you all. (Fraiberg, Wang, and You 2017, 216)

Michael's mixing of discourses and styles evidences his translingual practice. He adopted the language styles of two renowned speeches in American history. The opening of his speech echoes that of the Gettysburg Address delivered by Abraham Lincoln on November 19, 1863. Lincoln declared, "Four score and seven years ago our fathers brought forth on this continent a new nation, conceived in Liberty and dedicated to the proposition that all men are created equal." The Gettysburg Address was Michael's favorite, as he once mentioned in class. In the rest of the speech, he imitates Martin Luther King Jr.'s "I Have a Dream" speech. In addition to his repetitive use of the phrase "I have a dream," Michael borrowed sentence structures from King. For example, King says, "I have a dream that . . . one day right here in Alabama little black boys and black girls will be able to join hands with little white boys and white girls as sisters and brothers." Michael says, "I have a dream. One day boys and girls, boys and boys, girls and girls, are able to lay in the same bed of pure love passionately, purely, and freely." Like King, Michael capitalized on the power of repetition, parallelism, and rhyming.

While adroit in stitching these references together, however, Michael showcased the negative side of being an uncritical writer. On the surface, he staged sympathy to homosexuality as a social practice in the United States. He seemed to understand that gays and lesbians and, by extension, the LGBTQ community had been prejudiced against for years. He criticized social inequality and oppression in the United States. While critical on the surface, deep down, Michael's speech was rather facetious and carnivalesque. He called on everyone to practice homosexuality: "I have a dream. One day boys and girls, boys and boys, girls and girls, are able to lay in the same bed of pure love passionately, purely, and freely." He did not seem to be a member of the LGBTQ community and thus was limited in his understanding of the community's experiences and feelings. He oddly integrated Lincoln's speech with Martin Luther King's, showing insensitivity to their socio-historical contexts. Michael's cross-border practice remained at a superficial level. What the audience gained was entertainment rather than a heightened, critical awareness of the topic. Behind the playfulness, one could also read the speech as homophobic. While Michael seemed sympathetic to gays and lesbians, his carnivalesque description reinforced a negative image of homosexuality.

Michael's speech helps raise questions about the ethics of translingual practice, questions barely addressed by Horner and colleagues (2011). Taking the translingual approach they proposed, we can only go so far as identifying the various translingual strategies Michael has deployed in his speech—as I have done in the above analysis—and offering appreciative readings. While honoring language users' linguistic heterogeneity and power, shouldn't we demand that they learn to communicate critically and responsibly? What could writing teachers do in cases like this?

Perhaps an ethical argument couched in cosmopolitanism can be made for the translingual approach. Of its various formulations across time and geographic space, cosmopolitanism carries a fundamental meaning: though sometimes defined by kindred relations, ethnicity, nation, race, or class, all people are first and foremost members of the human race and as such are morally obligated to those outside their categories; further, they have the agency to develop and sustain new allegiances across cultures, communities, and languages. To communicate successfully and responsibly in the age of globalization requires that one respect another as an equal human being. One must strive to transcend national, racial, ethnic, gender, and class divides when interacting with the other. The translingual approach to writing pedagogy and program administration should underscore this universal, humanist outlook alongside the social justice argument. This cosmopolitan frame will allow students to more easily perceive the multiplicity and fluidity of their identity that naturally comes with their learning and use of an additional language, allow them to see the need for negotiating the use of the language in each context, and allow them to see the constraints of nationalism and monolingualism in their everyday communication (You 2016, 2018).

A cosmopolitan pedagogy proposed by Miriam Sobré-Denton and Nilanjana Bardhan (2013), You (2016), and Fraiberg and colleagues (2017), for instance, centers ethical issues in communication education. This pedagogy would teach Michael the value of valuing humanity and social justice at local and global levels through multiple learning styles, such as experiential learning, dialogue, and reflection. While the pedagogy honors Michael's alternative voice, it would also emphasize engagement with the cultural other (the Americans, the homosexual community) as well as critical self-reflexivity. It would encourage Michael to sample multiple perspectives to inculcate the value of empathy, focusing on the interconnectedness of the local and global, and it would encourage him to use imagination to link the two. Further, it would encourage Michael to shoulder an ethical obligation to the other both at home and at a global level.

A review of the discussions of ethics in the teaching of writing generates the following insights. First, ethics has been discussed and handled largely within disciplinary boundaries. While writing studies focuses on domestic students, treating them as subjects of the nation-state, second-language writing has focused on international, immigrant, and heritage students—students inhabiting the margins or outside the state. However, both fields have traditionally viewed writing as a monolingual practice and taught students using this ideology. Second, ethical arguments for attending to language and cultural difference have evolved to embrace both social justice and resources arguments, pushing both fields to embrace a multilingual or translingual perspective. Third, while the translingual approach has focused centrally on language difference, it has fallen short in addressing ethical issues in teaching writing in a transnational context. It can be complemented by a cosmopolitan argument that emphasizes students' moral responsibility within and beyond the national, ethnic, and racial boundary.

CONCLUSION

Language and cultural difference has figured prominently in rhetorical studies since ancient times. In their works, Eastern and Western thinkers drew on resources, such as stories, metaphors, and expressions, from different languages and cultures in developing their rhetorical thinking; and they positioned themselves differently from the dominant society. However, because of the imposing power of the state, rhetoricians have not factored into their thinking the fact that speaking and writing is a translingual practice. As globalization intensifies in our everyday life, rhetoricians have increasingly recognized the mobility of people, products, and language resources. They came to perceive that in reality, conventions of language and writing are always heterogeneous, fluid, contested, and negotiable. They proposed a multilingual or a translingual approach to affirm students' agency in constructing and conveying meanings by drawing on their multiliterate resources. This approach can be complemented by a cosmopolitan perspective so that it will not only focus on the pragmatic side of translingual practice but also attend to ethical questions—questions that ask how we position ourselves in relation to the other and whether we have taught our students how to communicate critically and responsibly in an era of globalization.

REFERENCES

Anderson, Benedict. 1991. *Imagined Communities: Reflections on the Origin and Spread of Nationalism.* Revised ed. New York: Verso.

Aristotle. 2006. *On Rhetoric: A Theory of Civic Discourse.* 2nd ed. Trans. George A. Kennedy. New York: Oxford University Press.

Ashraf, Hina. 2018. "Translingual Practices and Monoglot Policy Aspirations: A Case Study of Pakistan's Plurilingual Classrooms." *Current Issues in Language Planning* 19 (1): 1–20.

Canagarajah, Suresh. 2015. "Suresh Canagarajah on Translingualism: A Four Part Interview, Part 1." Transnational Writing, a blog. https://transnationalwriting.wordpress.com/2015/08/04/suresh-canagarajah-on-translingualisma-four-part-interview-part-i/.

Committee on CCCC Language Statement. 1974. "Students' Right to Their Own Language." *College Composition and Communication* 25 (3): 1–18.

Cope, Bill, and Mary Kalantzis, eds. 1999. *Multiliteracies: Literacy Learning and the Design of Social Futures.* New York: Routledge.

Dao Jing: Making This Life Significant. 2003. Trans. Roger T. Ames and David L. Hall. New York: Ballantine.

Dayton, Amy E. 2005. "Representations of Literacy: The Teaching of English and the Immigrant Experience in Early Twentieth-Century America." PhD dissertation, University of Arizona, Tucson.

Dicker, Susan J. 2003. *Languages in America: A Pluralist View.* 2nd ed. London: Multilingual Matters.

Donahue, Christiane. 2018. "Rhetorical and Linguistic Flexibility: Valuing Heterogeneity in Academic Writing Education." In *Transnational Writing Education: Theory, History, and Practice,* ed. Xiaoye You, 21–40. New York: Routledge.

Fraiberg, Steven, Xiqiao Wang, and Xiaoye You. 2017. *Inventing the World Grant University: Chinese International Students' Mobilities, Literacies, and Identities.* Logan: Utah State University Press.

Gilyard, Keith. 2016. "The Rhetoric of Translingualism." *College English* 78 (3): 284–89.

Horner, Bruce, Min-Zhan Lu, Jacqueline Jones Royster, and John Trimbur. 2011. "Language Difference in Writing: Toward a Translingual Approach." *College English* 73 (3): 303–21.

Horner, Bruce, and John Trimbur. 2002. "English Only and US College Composition." *College Composition and Communication* 53: 594–630.

Kachru, Braj. 1990. *The Alchemy of English: The Spread, Functions, and Models of Non-Native Englishes.* Urbana: University of Illinois Press.

Kaplan, Robert B. 1966. "Cultural Thought Patterns in Intercultural Education." *Language Learning* 16 (1): 1–20.

Kubota, Ryuko. 2016. "The Multi/Plural Turn, Postcolonial Theory, and Neoliberal Multiculturalism: Complicities and Implications for Applied Linguistics." *Applied Linguistics* 37 (4): 474–94.

Laertius, D. 1972. *The Lives of Eminent Philosophers,* Book 6. Cambridge, MA: Harvard University Press. Online text in English at the Perseus Project. http://www.perseus.tufts.edu/hopper/text?doc=Perseus:text:1999.01.0258.

Martin, W.A.P. 1896. *A Cycle of Cathay; or, China, South and North, with Personal Reminiscences.* New York: Fleming H. Revell.

Morrison, Toni. 2004. *Song of Solomon.* New York: Vantage.

NeCamp, Samantha. 2014. *Adult Literacy and American Identity: The Moonlight Schools and Americanization Programs.* Carbondale: Southern Illinois University Press.

Plato. 2003. *Phaedrus.* Trans. Robin Waterfield. New York: Oxford University Press.

Sapphire. 1997. *Push.* New York: Vintage.

Seeley, Christopher. 1991. *A History of Writing in Japan.* Leiden, the Netherlands: E. J. Brill.

Silva, Tony. 1997. "On the Ethical Treatment of ESL Writers." *TESOL Quarterly* 31 (2): 359–63.

Smitherman, Geneva. 1985. *Talkin and Testifyin: The Language of Black America.* Detroit, MI: Wayne State University Press.

Smitherman, Geneva. 1999. *Talkin That Talk: Language, Culture, and Education in African America.* New York: Routledge.

Smitherman, Geneva. 2000. *Black Talk: Words and Phrases from the Hood to the Amen Corner.* New York: Mariner Books.

Sobré-Denton, Miriam, and Nilanjana Bardhan. 2013. *Cultivating Cosmopolitanism for Intercultural Communication: Communicating as Global Citizens.* New York: Routledge.

Spack, Ruth. 2002. *America's Second Tongue: American Indian Education and the Ownership of English, 1860–1900.* Lincoln: University of Nebraska Press.

Tardy, Christine, and Erin Whittig. "On the Ethical Treatment of EAL Writers: An Update." *TESOL Quarterly* 51 (4): 920–30.

Walker, Alice. 1982. *The Color Purple.* New York: Washington Square Press.

Wan, Amy. J. 2014. *Producing Good Citizens: Literacy Training in Anxious Times.* Pittsburgh, PA: University of Pittsburgh Press.

Webster, Anthony K. 2010. "'Still, She Didn't See What I Was Trying to Say': Toward a History of Framing Navajo English in Navajo Written Poetry." *World Englishes* 29 (1): 75–96.

Yang, Tiancai, and Shanwen Zhang. 2011. *Zhou Yi* [The Book of Change]. Beijing: Zhonghua shuju [Zhonghua Book Company].

You, Xiaoye. 2016. *Cosmopolitan English and Transliteracy.* Carbondale: Southern Illinois University Press.

You, Xiaoye. ed. 2018. *Transnational Writing Education: Theory, History, and Practice.* New York: Routledge.

7

ETHICS AND ACTION
Feminist Perspectives on Facing the
Grand Challenges of Our Times

Jacqueline Jones Royster
Gesa E. Kirsch

AN EVOLVING CONCEPTUAL VIEW

Over recent decades, feminist scholarship has been a lever for change in many arenas for contemporary action. One area of focus has been ethical values and practices that had been frequently neglected in prior scholarship in both theory and practice. With the surge of feminist studies, however, several scholars have devoted specific attention to concepts such as care, compassion, empathy, social responsibility, collaboration, and rhetorical listening. Consider, for example, American philosopher Martha C. Nussbaum, who has spurred our thinking about ethics, education, and viable approaches to problem solving. Nussbaum (1998, 84) states:

> It is up to us, as educators, to show our students the beauty and interest of a life that is open to the whole world, to show them that there is after all more joy in the kind of citizenship that questions than in the kind that simply applauds, more fascination in the study of human beings in all their real variety and complexity than in the zealous pursuit of superficial stereotypes, more genuine love and friendship in the life of questioning and self-government than in submission to authority.

We could not imagine more important goals for higher education than teaching students about discovering beauty and joy in citizenship, about engaging in meaningful work, about fostering curiosity and wonder in life, and about the genuine friendship and love that emerges from a commitment to community and to a good that is greater than ourselves. Such goals are optimistic, bold, and courageous. They inspire hope and optimism that our work in higher education can and does matter deeply.

At the same time, we acknowledge that we live in dark times. As Kirsch (2018) writes elsewhere:

DOI: 10.7330/9781607329978.c007

In 2018 many pieces of civil rights legislation are under attack. The #MeToo hashtag is drawing attention to continued sexual harassment and flagrant abuses of power. The Southern Poverty Law Center is tracking and mapping the dramatic increase of hate speech and hate crimes across the country. Growing xenophobia and anti-immigrant sentiments are shaping immigration policies and threatening a generation of Dreamers who now live in fear of deportation to countries they have never known. Gun violence and school shootings haunt every city and state in the nation.

Drawing on *new materialism*, many scholars in cultural studies, philosophy, and literary theory are beginning to address these dark times. In this work, the emphasis shifts more explicitly to the physical, material world, to the ways we are dependent, interdependent, and connected with all the physical elements that make up the fabric of the world that touches and envelops us, as demonstrated most recently by the COVID-19 pandemic. New materialist scholars draw our attention to the ways we are embodied—configured by the air we breathe, food we digest, microbes that inhabit our guts, places in which we live, and the animate and inanimate objects that surround us and shape our lives. In "Posthumanist Performativity:" (2003), often-cited feminist scholar Karen Barad set the stage for a feminist take on new materialism, while Stacy Alaimo and Susan Hekman (2008) further solidified feminist concerns about the interconnected, material, ecological nature of the world in their edited volume *Material Feminisms*.

Recent work in rhetorical, writing, and literacy studies (RWL) has taken up new materialism by exploring how our work can *matter*, both inside and beyond the academy. Laura Micciche (2014, 489), for instance, defines new materialism as "a transdisciplinary effort to reshape materialist critiques in order to acknowledge and reckon with a much-expanded notion of agency, one that includes humans, nonhumans, and the environmental surround." Furthermore, Micciche (2014, 490) notes, "on the whole, new materialists seek critical frameworks that honor daily life experiences in coexistence with ordinary and complex matter, from the life-supporting activity of worms to the web-like structure of geopolitical conflicts." It is this emphasis on interconnectedness and on material realities that informs our thinking in this chapter.

We find that critically important to the enriched view of the interconnectivity of new materialism is a de-centering of actors that matter in the world. In other words, a brighter light is cast on de-centering humans as the end-all, be-all actors in the world with absolute agency and authority; as the only beings with perspectives that should be included in considerations for planning, design, and consequence; as the only beneficiaries or victims of choices and decisions. Instead, new materialists challenge us to reframe our perspectives more holistically to include all sentient beings—human and non-human, all natural objects, and all elements that are part of the environment, part of our earth—in search of a deeper, more multidimensional understanding of interdependency as a grand global challenge. As Micciche (2014, 490) notes, "For new materialists, human exceptionalism is a dangerous fiction that distorts reality, identity, culture, and politics by giving little due to energies or actors that coexist with humans." In like manner, David M. Grant (2017, 62) positions a dialogic relationship between the work of new materialist scholars and indigenous scholars like himself as he articulates this focus: "What remains is a loose coalition of thinkers and scholars who are working to shift us away from assuming the primacy of human subjectivity by pushing the human actor off center stage while still retaining a role for it to play."

Worthy of note is that in RWL we have two instructive examples of conferences in 2018 that focused on such challenges. The Thomas R. Watson conference theme was Making Future Matters. Conference organizers invited participants to reflect on at least two meanings of the word *matter*:

> We use the concept of matter and mattering in two ways, both addressing how we might direct our work toward material futures. First, we use matter colloquially to ask, what work do we find valuable and how do we make that work consequential with, to, and for others? Second, we use matter methodologically, to ask how we assemble, analyze, and share our work so that it materializes (in) the world. Emerging from both lines of inquiry is detailed attention to the questions we ask, the partners we engage, and the theories/methodologies we draw upon to pursue our work of mattering. (Watson 2018, 5)

We find this call for proposals (CFP) compelling because it asks us to imagine bold futures, futures worth living, fighting, and working for; futures that begin to address grand challenges while training our rhetorical ear and eye toward the consequences and impact of words and actions, both as we engage with the world at large and as we reflect on our contributions in a local context, from our classrooms to the communities in which we live. For the provocative essays that resulted from this CFP, see Rick Wysocki and Mary P. Sheridan (2018).

A Reflection

We feature this CFP because we were impressed by the conference organizers' deliberate efforts to highlight work that matters in and beyond the academy, their aims to contribute to social justice, and their desire to include diverse voices and perspectives. We were impressed as well by their deliberate effort to feature diverse scholars, generations, and subfields of RWL studies, all in an effort to create a rich and generative platform for discussion, engagement, and deliberation. At the conference, scholars were engaged in important but challenging conversations, one of which led to a controversy that has circulated across various social media platforms and deserves attention in our discussion, not to further the controversy that arose but to underscore the complexities of taking ethics and action seriously.

As readers may know, the controversy centered on one of the keynote speaker's remarks. The speaker narrated her experience of growing up in Alabama and hearing racist language as a child. However, rather than narrating those experiences in descriptive terms, the speaker chose to repeat the actual slurs she remembered hearing. Audience members were taken aback—angry, hurt, and insulted—but during the moment of the conference itself, no one challenged the speaker on her language use. Silences enveloped the moment. Kirsch, who served as conference moderator, is implicated in these silences since she did not object to the speaker's use of hurtful language. Anger surfaced after the conference, mostly on social media, and occasioned several responses. One of them was an open letter published by the Black, Latinx, American Indian, Queer, and Asian/Asian American Caucuses of the National Council of Teachers of English and the Conference on College Composition and Communication (NCTE/CCCC), condemning the speaker's choice of language and the conference organizers' lack of immediate intervention. The letter calls for sustained anti-racist education in our discipline. The speaker and conference organizers posted letters of apology online, but a shadow has inevitably been cast on the whole conference.

The point to be emphasized is that engaging in difficult conversations related to ethics and action amplifies the need for all of us, especially those of us in RWL, to be more consciously, deliberately, and consistently attentive at such moments to the ways we use language and story as both speakers and listeners. Moreover, we cannot escape a basic observation. At the core of our own profession, despite our inclinations to think of ourselves as "good actors," we continue to face the quite basic challenge not simply of talking about a more inclusive and welcoming environment within which scholars of diverse backgrounds, conditions, and ideological perspectives can function but also of actually exhibiting and normalizing how such an environment can function and be managed and maintained as a respectful, reflective, and reflexive space. In this regard, we appreciate Mary P. Sheridan's (2018) call for "all sorts of thoughtful, generous and generative engagement that both challenges and supports people to *do* better, moves which are so lacking in our nation's public discourse that it seems easy to forget their importance." Equally important, we appreciate and support the NCTE/CCCC joint caucuses' call for sustained education and systemic anti-racist work that goes beyond simple apologies. We consider both calls for action to be responsive to the ever-present challenge in RWL to address conundrums: How do we acknowledge issues and conditions without being outrageously offensive to others? How can we be honest and truthful without being hurtful? How do we speak our truths and respond to truths spoken by others without silencing or being silenced? The path to *doing better* is necessary, important but not simple. We need to work on this goal consciously, deliberately, persistently, with an eye toward care, compassion, empathy, and respect.

Second, consider the CFP for the 2018 Western States Rhetoric and Literacy Conference, Matter and Mattering. Conference organizers asked participants to reflect not only on new materialist perspectives but also on non-Western[1] ways of knowing and the contributions of indigenous scholars. They write:

> In recent years, resonating with many indigenous and nonwestern discourses, rhetorical and literacy studies have taken up the question of mattering more literally. Scholars draw on diverse sources and methods to explore how material realities unfold not only through human words and ideas, but also through affect, emotion, sensation, bodies, performance, animality, environments, land, things, and more. This intimate embrace of matter and mattering has surely deepened our understanding of rhetoric and rhetorical mechanisms of change. But what can those intimacies do? What, for instance, do they indicate about how rhetoric and literacy connect to justice and power; oppression and discrimination; ethics and care? How can close attention to material life reveal rhetorical options and participate in making better rhetorical futures? What insight can it offer on what matters? (Western States 2018)

These CFPs draw attention to the increasing impact of new materialism on scholarship related to ethos formation and operational practices in RWL. They draw attention also to the need for research and scholarship to take more fully into account a broader spectrum of scholarly perspectives. The second CFP indicates explicitly that we need to recognize and, by extension, incorporate and naturalize indigenous and non-Western research and scholarship in our work.

Amid the vibrancy of these discourses, we surmise that recognizing humans as only one of many diverse beings that matter with regard to the future of life sets in motion the recognition of the habitual constraints of our perspectives even within the category *human*. What becomes more legible are the ways by which we envision, process, interpret, and respond to what we see. Given long-standing values in RWL, enhancing legibility strikes us as a necessary and positive move, despite the likelihood that such enhancements may feel like a threat for those who have historically dominated legibility. The obvious example is Western viewpoints, where the history of practice has been unbridled agency, the suppression and de-valuing of other cultural values and perspectives, and the presumption of superiority—often with military might as the most compelling tool for conformity.

Rasha Diab (this volume) pursues this line of thinking when she complicates the term *transnationalism*, challenging readers to take a hard look at the ethics, impact, and consequences of the Western gaze. She sets out to "ward off a romanticized version of transnationalism" and instead reminds readers that the concept can make invisible, or in her words, "crop out global capitalist forces; histories and legacies of colonialism, racism, nationalism, and other-isms; and the immobility and precarity facing many around the world." Diab draws our attention to the fact that we often fail to recognize the humanity of others—such as refugees, immigrants, victims of war violence, and many others—until we learn about tragedy or death. Using the case of a photo that went viral in 2015 (a photo of Aylan Kurdi, a five-year old Syrian boy whose body was found on a beach in Turkey along with those of several of his family members), Diab calls on us to recognize the humanity of all people, independent of their national, transnational, or refugee status. She asks, "How do we recognize the other *before* and not just *after* the calamity? How do we relate with others across nations and borders?"

The question is whether those who hold Western perspectives as superior and who have held dominant power and authority historically can adjust to the need to de-center and broaden the operational space for the presence and possibility of others. While this question is indeed an open one, new materialists are moving forward with frameworks that offer a different way of thinking and acting. Focusing on matter and mattering, these scholars are influencing the design of conceptual, analytical, interpretive, and thereby problem-solving and policymaking paradigms that transform the very enterprise of what it means to be human in the world. In this chapter, therefore, we draw attention to what strikes us as the growing capacity of feminist rhetorical perspectives on ethics and action to address deeply challenging presumptions not only about legacies but also about the future of life in terms that suggest more broadly, richly rendered, and thoughtful insights about identity, agency, power, and authority and about creating frames that hold greater promise for actions that accrue a wider range of positive and sustainable effects for all.

In declaring this focus, we are mindful that (1) new materialist lenses enhance the scope of vision in examining and teaching ethics and action in contemporary contexts; (2) it remains important to connect rhetoric and literacy to our understanding of justice and power, oppression and discrimination, compassion, empathy, and care in interrogations of important ethical challenges; (3) one imperative is to help students understand (to paraphrase Nussbaum) the joy, beauty, friendship, and love that can emerge when we wrestle with difficult, global challenges; (4) another imperative is to help them understand that through these efforts we all have an obligation to cultivate consciously and deliberately an ever-evolving sense of what it means to be human in the context of a shared world, filled with miraculous coexistences.

BROADENING SCHOLARLY INCLUSION FOR RWL FRAMEWORKS

We begin an articulation of this mandate, as the CFP from the 2018 Western States Rhetoric and Literacy Conference suggests, with the inclusion of *indigenous American perspectives* and ontologies. Particularly pertinent to our thinking in this case have been indigenous scholars such as Viola F. Cordova, David M. Grant, Angela M. Haas, Sarah Klotz, Malea Powell, and Zoe Todd. These scholars challenge us to rethink radically our understanding of the material world and Western philosophy and ontology. Todd in particular has been outspoken, as the title of her blog and published article reveals, "An Indigenous Feminist's Take on the Ontological Turn: 'Ontology' Is Just Another Word for Colonialism." She takes to task famed European- or American-trained theorists, philosophers, and anthropologists who exhibit great ignorance of indigenous cultures, law, and scholarship when they credit new materialist theories with novel insights into ecological principles and the interconnectedness of the material world. With a clear sense of exasperation, Todd (2016, 7, original emphasis) asks:

When *will* I hear someone reference Indigenous thinkers in a direct, contemporary, and meaningful way in European lecture halls? Without filtering ideas through white intermediaries . . . but by citing and quoting Indigenous thinkers directly, unambiguously and generously. As thinkers in their own right, not just disembodied representatives of an amorphous Indigeneity that serves European intellectual or political purposes, and not just as research subjects or vaguely defined "collaborators." As dynamic Philosophers and Intellectuals, full stop. Rather than bequeathing climate activism to the Al Gores of the world, when will Euro-American scholarship take the intellectual labour and activist work of Inuit women like Rosemarie Kuptana and Sheila Watt-Cloutier seriously?

If we are to address with deeper, more positive, and more sustainable consequence the grand challenges of our times, we need to heed Todd's advice to learn about and engage more fully with indigenous and other non-Western scholarship. The challenge is to de-center not only the positioning of humans as the prime anchor in problem solving and policy making but also purposefully and deliberately to de-center as well the familiarity of our Western-derived theoretical and ethical frameworks. As Todd (2016, 19) reminds us, "Reciprocity of thinking requires us to pay attention to who else is speaking alongside us" or to listen to those who may actually have spoken quite insightfully before us.

Grant (2017) interrogates the relationship of new materialism and indigenous studies even further. He writes that "in order to put indigenous philosophies and new materialisms in dialogue, divisions such as mind-body, religious-mundane, and human-animal must be troubled, and to honor rhetorical sovereignty, we must understand those divisions and the troubles caused by their undoing as grounded in a Eurocentric worldview. It is not arriving at objective truth that matters, but arriving at a place to begin equitable dialogue" (Grant 2017, 65). There are signs that this kind of dialogue, this "paying attention to who else is speaking alongside us" (Todd 2016, 19), is beginning to happen in RWL, as evidenced by the 2018 conferences as well as by articles published in 2017 in both *College English* (*CE*) and *College Composition and Communication* (*CCC*). This set of journal issues brought into our scholarly discourses a steady flow of diverse voices, topics, and theoretical perspectives. The very presence of such publications confirms that in RWL, prestigious tone-setting venues are beginning to acknowledge the value and importance of inviting not only insights that have not been previously included but also the innovations to our thinking that inevitably can be accrued. More narrowly defined scholarly frameworks are being disrupted, and we are setting aside with increasing frequency presumptions that have historically constrained the breadth and depth of knowledge-making enterprises.

The December 2017 issue of *CCC*, for example, features articles on "Romantic Correspondence as Queer Extracurriculum: The Self-Education for Racial Uplift of Addie Brown and Rebecca Primus" by Pamela VanHaitsma; "Impossible Rhetorics of Survivance at the Carlisle School, 1879–1883" by Sarah Klotz; "Talkin' bout Good and Bad Pedagogies: Code Switching vs. Comparative Rhetorical Approaches" by Bonnie J. Williams-Farrier; and "Cripping Time in the College Composition Classroom" by Tara Wood. Here, then, we find scholarship, informed by queer, African American, indigenous, and disability studies perspectives, that unsettles business as usual in RWL and successfully so, we would add. The September 2017 *CE* issue is equally rich in perspectives; it offers "A Pedagogy of Rhetorical Looking: Atrocity Images at the Intersection of Vision and Violence" by Kristie Fleckenstein, Scott Gage, and Katherine Bridgman; an exploration of "Literacy Instruction in Jim Crow America" by Sue Mendelsohn; and "Freshman Composition as a Precariat Enterprise" by James Rushing Daniel. These articles are informed by theoretical frameworks that tangle with class-based, racial, and visual rhetorics and acknowledge the embodied, lived, and material realities of voices we do not always hear in our discipline. In other words, we are observing that recently, RWL journals have begun to feature, highlight, and embrace theoretical, analytical, and interpretive frames that recast scholarly work across a richer spectrum of perspectives. We can see thereby a slow shift in our rhetorical lenses, a shift that gives us reason for optimism—that scholars are focused more critically than ever before on ethics and action, on points of view, impact, and consequence. These evolving frames constitute the foundation on which this chapter stands. In the sections that follow, we offer our own contributions to these recalibrating processes.

DESIGNING AN INTEGRATED ETHICAL OPERATIONAL SYSTEM

As indicated by the discussion above, in feminist rhetorical scholarship, we are expanding conceptual, analytical, and interpretive frameworks that are useful for addressing grand challenges. This process requires that we articulate both how we are expanding these frameworks and how we are demonstrating best practices in using them. In addition, we are also called upon to articulate what we mean by *grand challenges*. Often the term *grand challenges* refers to problems we now recognize as having global consequence, such as clean energy and green environments; healthy foods and clean water; economics as a global enterprise; global peace, human rights, civil rights; issues of healthcare and the impact of devastating disease; climate change; and on and on—all compelling and of tremendous concern. However, as indicated by the discussion above, we are suggesting that, in effect, we have an *uber* challenge before we can even get to these specific problem spaces. We posit that to address the materiality of our grand global challenges as articulated in various contemporary discourses, we need simultaneously to address the ethical framing not only of the challenges but the solutions we might propose. The quintessential opportunity is to garner our evolving insights in feminist rhetorical studies about ethics and action to create strategies and practices for:

- Sharpening rhetorical listening and responding skills
- Enhancing our abilities to interact with others across social, political, and cultural identities, conditions, contexts, and stakeholders
- Enhancing our capacities to engage in meaningful, respectful, sustainable dialogues capable of giving rise to the sorts of collaborations that are necessary to address complex material challenges
- Figuring out what it means amid all of the complexities that surround us to foment and sustain peace—locally and globally—knowing that the future of life on Earth and the future of the Earth itself depend on it.

This *uber* challenge is a core and critical one. In making this rhetorical shift in strategic planning and design, we find that the questions we need to explore cannot be contained or adequately interrogated by feminist ethical framing alone, again as suggested by the explanation above. Rather, in this chapter we suggest that we need frames informed by an intersection of systems that are constantly interrogated with a deliberate de-centering of the primacy of human beings and the primacy of Western ontologies, theories, and practices. *Here there be dragons.* Here be also the potential to forge pathways toward an ethics of care, compassion, empathy, courage, commitment, collaboration—value constructs we have long proclaimed in RWL as necessary for active engagement in research, education, and community interactions that are innovative and impactful while simultaneously ethical and honorable (see Agnew, this volume, for further discussion of how these values can be enacted by recovering an ethics of style).

Cathy N. Davidson (2017, 15, original emphasis) states:

> The goal of higher education is greater than workforce readiness. It's *world* readiness. No road map shows what lies ahead in the time after college, when there are no more grades and requirements, theses and

dissertations, professors and advisers. *Here be dragons.* The new education prepares students for a journey where anything might happen, the journey that is about to begin.

Focused on a reframing of the educational enterprise, this quotation draws attention to the realities of the work of higher education occurring in a world in flux, amid contested value systems, shifts in points of view, terms of engagement, and decision-making paradigms; and it casts a bright light on the need to acknowledge that within such a dynamic context, nothing seems stable, absolute, or certain. From our perspective, such uncertainty for educational enterprises generally, as well as for research and community engagement, suggests the need for a compass, a path-finding system for negotiating the terrain. We suggest that this path-finding system is keyed by an ethics model that integrates and operationalizes both inner-facing and outer-facing analytical and interpretive frameworks for action.

The need to think of ethics and action as an integrated operational system is illuminated quite provocatively when various social hierarchies and cultural differences in our contemporary world step in to complicate what we have considered to be basic concepts, such as:

- *Ethos formation* (the assumption of a standpoint for vision and action). By what means, mechanisms, and models do we form ethos in an uncertain world?
- The development of operational *principles and frameworks* based on this standpoint. Demonstrating an awareness of standpoint, how do we articulate and interrogate our choices using a *standpoint* and then hold ourselves accountable for these choices in an interdependent world?
- The establishing of *protocols and processes* for decision-making, action, and the creation of impact and consequence. How do we design solutions and pathways for action in an interdependent world—that is, with the awareness that actions create swirls of impact and consequences and with an understanding that because of our interconnectedness, these swirls really need to be thoughtful, well-balanced, and justifiable in terms of creating forces that rebound to ourselves, whether for good or evil?

To be noted, *ethics* as a rhetorical concept emerged in earlier eras in more contained spaces, conceptually and geographically—where viewpoints, principles, processes, and practices were not so directly, deliberately, and deeply interrogated (as materialist, feminist, indigenous, and other non-Western scholars have described so poignantly) as functioning within hierarchies of social, cultural, linguistic, and ethnocentric constructions of power. In the twenty-first century, however, we have come to understand far more clearly the multidimensionality of the grand array of hierarchies of difference in human value systems and practices we have created across time, place, communities, and cultures and about which we must now be deliberately aware and accountable (see Agnew; Diab; Wang, this volume). We no longer enjoy the comfort of simple presumptions—even in academic arenas. We have come to understand that a convergence of knowledge offers leverage for action, with our suggestion for facing this *dragon*—the *uber* grand challenge—being to design a better *compass*, a dynamic integrated ethical operational system.

STARTING WITH EXPERIENCE

With this design challenge before us, we suggest that one place to focus on innovative opportunity is with our own work environments. Royster's workplace is a technological university, a place where engineering, technology, and science have normalized and naturalized their status of operational power and privilege. Colleagues take great pride in being master problem solvers who are innovative, entrepreneurial, and quick. Even so, in recent decades there has been a growing understanding that their ecosystem is not set by technology and scientific enterprises alone but by these enterprises in the company of other values, systems, and practices. In the face of the complex problems they want to solve, they are developing a habit of partnering and collaborating with others of us in the humanities, the social sciences, and the arts to prepare students who will be local and global leaders and to engage in research that in like manner has local and global impact. Kirsch's workplace is a business university. Similarly, with a focus on *globalization* and *engagement*, colleagues at her institution know that successful business leaders need to understand how, when, and why social, political, cultural, gendered, and environmental factors will shape business outcomes. At her institution, as with other schools of business, they have begun to recognize that their success depends on educating students, as Davidson indicates, not only for "workforce readiness" but for "world readiness." In fact, Bentley University's mission is "to create new knowledge within and across business and the arts and sciences and to educate creative, ethical and socially responsible organizational leaders" (Bentley University Mission Statement 2019–2020). These local views are not unusual among academic institutions across the nation, as indicated by the many articles, conferences, and symposia that have been focused, for example, on the need to take advantage of intersections between STEM education and the liberal arts or to make clearer that the humanities and the arts add value to our world and serve useful and meaningful functions in modern societies—especially amid the many uncertainties and unknowns we face. What is striking, however, about addressing such concerns in technological or business universities instead of more traditional universities is that liberal arts areas, including RWL, have been called upon to de-center. We recognize that historically the liberal arts, rather than more applied areas (such as business and engineering), have proclaimed ourselves to be the center of the academic universe. In specialized institutions like our own, however, we are not. We have had to think beyond our presumptions of centrality and consider very seriously viewpoints, ontologies, and practices that have emerged from other communities of knowledge making and practice. Such de-centering has been good for us in rejuvenating our thinking and in enriching the frames we use to pose problems, collect and analyze data, interpret findings, make use of the thinking and operational tools of others, and create solutions in time and place. In the context of a broader spectrum of values and interests, we have been pushed constantly to be explicit about:

- **Vision and Mission:** As scholars and teachers who are not the center of the academic enterprise, we have learned to thrive in the company of others. With this adjustment to our disciplinary and interdisciplinary agency and identities, we have the opportunity to remind ourselves that even in our de-centered state, we are neither new to these environments nor peripheral. Our areas have been present in one form or another throughout our institutional histories. We have just needed to share—in not thinking of ourselves as the only ones with agency and authority. We are not. Moreover, we recognize that not having the luxury of being the primary or ultimate lens of engagement is not intimidating. A more modest identity has not affected our capacity to be amazingly good at what we do in these specialized spaces. In fact, one might easily assert that de-centering has enabled us to develop and evolve in interconnected ways, understanding the full force of our strengths, our capacity to understand past, present, and future knowledge more holistically, to help students and colleagues utilize their knowledge, skills, and expertise powerfully from varying perspectives, and to help them to see and understand the impacts and consequences of their actions and inactions—locally and globally.

We have garnered benefits in our work in knowing firsthand the importance of articulating this vision of ourselves in the company of colleagues who are noticeably different, as well as within a context where we might be easily classified not as *native* but as *cultural (im)migrants.* Of note is that both of our institutions declare that their missions are to educate innovative, entrepreneurial, ethical, and socially responsible leaders by creating and disseminating cutting-edge knowledge within and across various boundaries. What we know in RWL is that we have, and should have, a place at these tables as important partners in the narratives of academic success. On a more personal level—as we look more directly at our own scholarly interests in ethics and action and at the professional adjustments we ourselves have needed to make, learn from, and incorporate into our own operational systems in our institutional contexts—we posit from this experiential learning that *de-centering* is a key factor in designing a dynamic ethical operational system. It shifts the vision, which in turn creates opportunities for paradigmatic shifts capable of enabling and enhancing the ethical compasses by which we negotiate our professional lives.

- **Place and Purpose:** Indisputably, we have discovered that de-centering while simultaneously claiming space at the table shifts the task. In universities where enterprises are typically more outer-facing (such as a business university and a technological university) than the liberal arts have been historically, the task is to show what we know and know how to do—not just narrate, analyze, and interpret it. We are consistently called upon to show how our expertise and experience matter and how they do work in the world. In other words, we have to declare and substantiate the materiality of our frameworks and practices from the perspective of a larger academic arena and typically on a larger landscape for action. We have to document not just our insights and credibility but our potential for impact and consequence in making a meaningful difference. Every day we must take as a given that the ability to survive and thrive is not our academic primacy but very much our interdependence. We excel based on our ability to be extraordinarily clear about who we are and what we do, to bring these strengths boldly to a cross-disciplinary table, not only as we make our own stories in this enriched arena but as we partner and collaborate also dynamically with others to create larger stories than just our own. In working from this de-centered perspective, we demonstrate in robust fashion the consequence, impact, and the values added that we bring to the larger institutional enterprises that surround us and as they bring these business, technological, and scientific enterprises to the global marketplace. Our experiences convince us, then, that these recalibrated frameworks are instructive for designing a better ethical operational compass as we commit ourselves to facing ever-present complex global challenges.

More broadly stated, our experiences suggest that scholars and teachers in feminist rhetorical studies partake in research, education, and community engagement as part of legacies in the humanities more broadly, as evidenced by RWL's long and deep commitment to excellence in these areas. However, we have also come to understand that in our contemporary world we benefit, as our narratives above suggest, from continual reflection, reflexivity, recalibration, and the opportunities for reinvigoration these processes offer in helping us to be more consciously and deliberately aware of context, purpose, and interconnectedness. With our long-standing operational principles and practices, emanating from the fifth century BCE in Western cultures (and longer than that in other geopolitical spaces around the globe), we certainly appreciate the remarkable base of knowledge and experience in RWL from which our presumptions have been drawn (see Wang, this volume, for an exploration of Confucius's contributions to contemporary rhetorical theory and ethical considerations). We rightly treasure these values and the strengths that constitute that part of ourselves. However, over the millennia of cross-cultural contacts, the diversity of experiences we have garnered, and a sparkling array of distinctive accomplishments as scholars and teachers in the humanities, we have learned to broaden our geopolitical scope as critical and creative thinkers and astute communicators and problem solvers. At this point, we confirm that our historical strengths are worthy, including, for example, an understanding of human history, current circumstances, and future prospects; critical frameworks for interrogating and assessing human behavior and action; tools and models for creating and using knowledge; the ability to articulate and communicate ideas, perspectives, and implications through multimedia and multimodal forms; the ability to analyze and predict impacts and consequences; and so on.

At the same time, in the twenty-first century, fairly or unfairly, we are pushed to recognize the need to translate our work, interpret it in various contexts, apply and connect what we know and do to the work of others, and actually show evidence of impact, not just presume and proclaim it. We are literally surrounded by this imperative as we face the constant barrage of questions about the value of higher education and in our case the viability of the humanities and the systems that support our work as a public good (with regard, e.g., to defending the necessity of the National Endowment for the Humanities or the importance of sustaining our standards of practice for classroom excellence, such as small classes, face-to-face encounters and not just online relationships, libraries with books and not just technologies of various kinds, graduate student fellowships that are not supported by external funding, and so on). We face constant scrutiny, and we are constantly at risk of increasingly severe under-funding, de-funding, financial starvation, and, indeed, elimination. What we face, thereby, is an evolving ecology for leadership and learning that keeps many of us on edge with the feeling that we are indeed surrounded by *dragons*.

The question, then, is not whether such realities exist. Of course they do. The question is whether we are up to the challenge of facing these imperatives righteously and well. Well, we are—if we resist spending all of our time and energy quaking in our boots in fear and trepidation about being de-centered and no longer being *loved, respected, and understood* as disciplines that were once centralized by default but are no longer so. Instead, we have the opportunity to devote our time to preparing ourselves, not just our students, to gather the resources that enhance our capacity to rise to contemporary challenges. We are suggesting that one resource—for ourselves and others—results from the refining of our frameworks for ethics and action as a dynamic compass capable of functioning at the crossroads (an integrated ethical operational system) and our developing as well action paradigms that embody and enable practices that matter.

A SEARCH FOR RESPECTFUL AND INCLUSIVE ENGAGEMENT

In proposing the idea of offering the world a better compass with an integrated ethical operational system, how might such an instrumentation work? To illustrate the opportunity, consider the example of recent advances in face recognition capabilities enabled by Artificial Intelligence (AI). Face recognition technologies are increasingly used for security purposes by banking systems, law enforcement, and border patrol agencies, among others. Disturbingly, we are now learning that a lot of this technology is biased: it is better at recognizing the faces of men, in particular white men, than it is at recognizing the faces of women. It performs worst at recognizing the faces of women of color

(Schwab 2018). So, who needs to be involved in design, development, and testing to preempt or minimize bias and to embed inclusion? How do operational protocols need to be normalized to enhance the capacity to be both accurate and respectful in the engagement of a broad diversity of expected end users? In hindsight, with face recognition development processes, one of the reasons for the bias that has become evident is that the benchmarking data for training and testing the technology contain a very high proportion of white male faces, with an instructive interconnection being that the majority of AI developers are white men. White male faces are centralized as the default, dominant, and definitional examples. Is it surprising that the technology is better at recognizing white male faces? A more critical question in terms of ethical operational practices is, how might the developers have de-centered white maleness and balanced more inclusive data as a normalized part of their protocols?

The need to de-center with this innovation did not become strategic until a smart woman of color, a researcher at MIT, Joy Buolamwini (2018; Buolamwini and Gebru 2018), decided to test the systems produced by Microsoft, IBM, and Face++ and discovered bias in facial recognition software. As Katherine Schwab (2018) notes, such bias can have "dire consequences, determining who gets a job, who gets a loan, and even who goes to prison." The data spoke and made national and international news, illustrating the critical need to provide richly cast operational frameworks to interrogate concept, design, development, and analytics. This example opens up critical dialogue. It illustrates the importance of diversifying the workforce to enhance viability and credibility of the work, as well as the ethical implications of the processes and practices. In addition, it brings to bolder relief the opportunity we now have to shift operational paradigms and create better models of engagement. The *uber* challenge, especially given the ever-present flow of technological innovations that affect all of our lives, is to acknowledge the increasingly pressing need to create a dynamic convergence for ethics and action—and we dare say for ethics *before* action. The abiding question is this: What as scholars and teachers do we know now—in the twenty-first century—about how and where we are functionally as human beings in the company of many others? What as scholars and teachers do we need to account for in research, education, and community engagement in our own professional responsibilities to meet the needs of the human enterprise? At this point in research and scholarship, we understand, as indigenous scholars remind us, that human actors in all of our variety are intricately connected to each other, to all other beings, and to

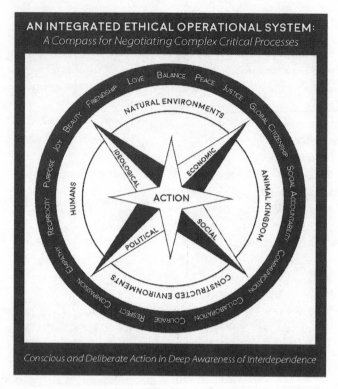

Figure 7.1. An integrated operational system: A compass for negotiating complex critical processes

the planet. We understand that the materiality of the interdependence
of the broad range of beings that live on the earth means that humanity
has no prima facie case for always occupying center stage—which sets
in motion the need to acknowledge that these triangular relationships
constitute an ethical stance.

Such value propositions are compelling. The question, though, is,
how do we bring the complexities of the operational task into scope
in an integrative, coherent, and manageable way? In the visualization
shown in figure 7.1,[2] we use a compass to represent the multidimensionality and fluidity that constitute these decision-making processes
and to suggest that the interdependencies of perspectives and various
intersections between ethics and action form a deliberative operational
ecosystem. Imagine, for example, that the design is dynamic rather
than static. Consider the notion that (1) all of the rings can move independently, with the outer ring offering a fluid stream of virtues, values,
and practices that inspire insights and beliefs; (2) the second circle

represents a fluidity of points of focus intended to suggest interactions among varieties of living beings and the habitats in which they live without a presumed primacy of humans dominating the center; (3) the two stars are, in effect, ethics (the larger star) and action (smaller star), and together they represent the complex convergences of our decision-making processes.

In practice, this schema raises basic implications for RWL in our work on ethics and action that center on two fundamental queries.

QUERY ONE: CONTEMPORARY CHALLENGES

The idea of an integrated ethical operational system underscores obligations and accountabilities for RWL, beginning with the question: How can/should we think about the goals of rhetorical education in addressing contemporary challenges? Is it reasonable to think about writing, reading, speaking, listening, thinking as isolatable skill sets rather than interdependent skill sets? Is it reasonable to think about rhetorical decision-making as isolatable practice rather than practice that enhances legibility, interconnectedness, impact, and consequence? In thinking about such educational challenges, we suggest that setting goals—whether for research, education, or community engagement—benefits from a clustering of intentions so that we might grab hold of our patterns of action. Energy and effort can be directed toward:

- **Personal development:** People need to develop their talents, skills, and abilities in learning about what various collectives of humanity have come to know in and about our world; how to interrogate ourselves, reflectively and reflexively, as human beings in triangular relationships; how to hone and sharpen their sensibilities about what is going on around them that might help them see what swirls of impact they themselves might wish to engender; how to use critical and technological resources to connect their knowledge vibrantly and meaningfully in efforts, large and small, to make the world a better place. This long-standing imperative for RWL remains.

- **Workforce development:** People also need good and meaningful work. The ideal would be, of course, that more people might get paid to do things they would be inclined to do for free because they are inspired and excited and find joy in doing the work and wanting to do it well. Realistically, however, many of us don't actually have this luxury within the complicated societies in which we live. Short of meeting this ideal goal, then, at minimum, people need to do work that permits them to feel that it's purposeful, that allows them to support and care for themselves and their families, that enables them to contribute to the prosperity of their communities. In RWL, our academic enterprises are called upon to engage more explicitly with this imperative as we offer qualitative opportunities that help students and employers to function ethically as they create value, impact, and consequence through the work they do.

- **Global citizenship development:** People need to understand themselves in the context of others who may be like and unlike themselves. Our planet is just too small and too fragile to do otherwise. In accepting the truth of human similarity, in accepting the truth of our triangular relationships, the question is: How much imagination do we need to stop blustering and beating our national chests, to begin valuing the goal of fomenting peace with each other instead of war, to have the courage and commitment to take seriously our collective obligations as caretakers of the future of life on earth? RWL has ethical operational frameworks, particularly as enriched by new materialism, capable of providing leverage in meeting this challenge well.

- **Human inspiration:** This cluster is perhaps the most challenging of all. Over the centuries, those of us in RWL and the humanities more generally have been affirmed in our understanding that human beings need to be *inspired* as a whole body experience—by way of the head (logos), backbone (ethos), heart and stomach (pathos). They need to figure out how to sustain a sense of joy and purpose in their lives, whether their learning opportunities move them toward a career pursuit or not; to find ways to think of themselves as a positive factor on the globe rather than a negative one or, perhaps most damaging, rather than a neutral one. With the ever-present opportunities we have for devastation, destruction, death, and inhumanity in the context of ubiquitous technologies, none of us can really afford to be neutral. This challenging innerscape is a terrain that RWL and the humanities more generally have been negotiating for centuries as we have committed ourselves through our disciplinary and interdisciplinary lenses to helping ourselves and others think critically and creatively with senses and sensibilities sharply attuned and in focus.

QUERY TWO: GLOBALIZED THINKING AND ETHICAL ACTIONS

This dynamic integrated ethical operational system is defined by its embracing of complexity and its understanding of the necessity of flexible, multi-layered, multidimensional strategic solutions. How do we resist our own inclinations toward hubris and our territorial desires to work collaboratively with multiple stakeholders to create balances amid complexity? The imperative is to create heuristics that help us to think in interconnected ways, perhaps in defiance of habits and comfort zones. The challenge is to resist simple solutions and focus instead on keeping the horizons of our operational paradigms dynamic and open. The basic goal would be to help students develop a fuller range of motion as they prepare themselves to lead productive professional lives in a highly innovative scientific and technological world that is simultaneously a thorny and complex ecological system in which social, cultural, political, economic, and environmental factors converge.

In setting forth the idea of a dynamic integrated ethical operational system, an ethics-action compass, as it were, globalization quickly rises as the koine of our academic realm. The cautionary tale, however, is to consider the idea of globalization not as a state of being or a condition but instead as an ongoing process of engagement with a deliberately cast global scope. More than that, consider it a process that requires critical thinking. The working definition of *critical thinking* that we have found to be useful is one that emerged from the community of practice that developed during Royster's early days of leading Writing Across the Curriculum workshops. It is *the ability to see what is there and not there, to* ✓ *stand back reflectively and reflexively, to be able to imagine what could be there instead while taking deliberately into account the impacts and consequences of social hierarchies, the need for information drawn from multiple perspectives and experiences, the need to understand human and non-human beings in context, the imperative of caring for the earth as a fragile ecosystem that supports the future of life.* Added to this working definition are obligations that require us to connect these globalized critical thinking processes to ethical actions, actions that are respectful and inclusive, that normalize compassion, empathy, partnership, and collaboration.

CODA

As we acknowledged at the outset of this chapter, we live in deeply troubling times, with toxic discourses on the rise—xenophobia, misogyny, racism, bigotry, white supremacy, extreme nationalism, and more. As scholars and teachers in RWL who aim for respectful and peace-generating public discourses that participate in the negotiation of a collective sense of public good, the exigencies for mitigating these toxicities are urgent. Royster (2016, 7) writes elsewhere:

> Given our long experience in [and our deep commitment in rhetorical studies to] educating both leaders and citizenry, we have a deep sense of mission. We understand that in order to create top tier academic experiences [rhetorical and otherwise]; to make it possible for top tier leaders to emerge from these experiences; and to secure peace and prosperity as a global reality, we need to keep in focus, not simply . . . the development of knowledge and skills, but the nurturing of the whole human being with regard to head, heart, stomach, backbone, and most provocatively perhaps imagination—in the sense of helping our fellow human beings to exercise and sustain an operational sense of compassion, empathy, courage, and commitment.

This perspective of ethics and action, informed by histories of research and practice in the liberal arts, by feminist rhetorical scholarship, by new materialism, and by indigenous studies, creates a generative space for intersectionality; for deliberately taking into account multidimensional knowledge, expertise, and experiences; for utilizing multimedia, multimodal means of expression; for understanding the interconnectedness of science, technology, business, humanities, social sciences, arts at the same time that we are deliberately attuned to the complexities of social hierarchies and the dynamics of power and privilege that surround them. All of us—students, academics, leaders, citizens—must negotiate and traverse these precarious terrains. We must be both *work ready* and *world ready*.

In RWL, our conceptual, analytical, and interpretive frameworks suggest that we are equipped to have a place at the table in enterprises that are designing *work readiness*. We also need to secure a place at the table in enterprises that are designing *world readiness*. We have, in fact, the potential to create an amazingly elegant set of tools and assets. Our *uber* challenge is to partner with others to transform them, given our twenty-first-century context, into a dynamically rendered ecosystem within which we enhance our capacities to negotiate the intersections between ethics and action and face our grand challenges well.

NOTES

1.   We were persuaded by current practices of indigenous scholars not to capitalize Western in non-Western but thought also of not capitalizing "western" at all—which is not common practice in standardized spelling. This issue of habit, consistency, and equity underscored for us the fact that despite what seem to be

better instincts, in the end often we de-center only the other, not the dominant structure. We considered, then, that not capitalizing non-Western is too simple a solution and that a better choice would be to encourage dialogue about these habitual practices, raising specifically the issue of who is called upon to adjust at moments of change and who has the privilege of not adjusting even when the goal is equity and inclusion.

2. We thank Lillian H. Steele, co-lab intern, School of Literature, Media, and Communication, Ivan Allen College of Liberal Arts, Georgia Institute of Technology, for designing this elegant compass figure. Currently, we are working with Michael Vogel and other staff in Georgia Tech's Digital Integrative Liberal Arts Center to create a web-based interactive version intended for use as a pedagogical tool.

REFERENCES

Alaimo, Stacy, and Susan Hekman, eds. 2008. *Material Feminisms*. Bloomington: Indiana University Press.

Barad, Karen. 2003. "Posthumanist Performativity: Toward an Understanding of How Matter Comes to Matter." *Signs: Journal of Women in Culture and Society* 28 (3): 801–31.

Bentley University Mission Statement. 2019–2020. Course Catalogue. https://catalog .bentley.edu/graduate/mission/.

Black, Latinx, American Indian, Queer Caucus, Asian/Asian American Caucuses of NCTE/CCCC. 2018. "Open Letter to the Watson Conference Organizers." Posted on Facebook and Google Docs, December 4. https://docs.google.com/document/d/ 1fsD-D5Y-KyQ007lLiMDmuIv7QV2TJ07qMUxJqQZIzHk/edit.

Buolamwini, Joy. 2018. "How I'm Fighting Bias in Algorithms." TED Talk, November 12.

Buolamwini, Joy, and Timnit Gebru. 2018. "Gender Shades: Intersectional Accuracy Disparities in Commercial Gender Classification." *Proceedings of Machine Learning Research* 81: 1–15.

Davidson, Cathy N. 2017. *The New Education: How to Revolutionize the University to Prepare Students for a World in Flux*. New York: Basic Books.

Grant, David, M. 2017. "Writing *Wakan*: The Lakota Pipe as Rhetorical Object." *College Composition and Communication* 69 (1): 61–86.

Kirsch, Gesa E. 2018. "The Challenge of Making Our Work Matter in Dark Times: Afterword." In *Making Futures Matter*, ed. Rick Wysocki and Mary P. Sheridan. Logan: Computers and Composition Digital Press/Utah State University Press. https://ccdigital press.org/book/makingfuturematters/kirsch.html.

Micciche, Laura. 2014. "Writing Material." *College English* 76 (6): 488–505.

Nussbaum, Martha C. 1998. *Cultivating Humanity: A Classic Defense of Reform in Liberal Education*. Cambridge, MA: Harvard University Press.

Royster, Jacqueline Jones. 2016. "Bold Futures: Integrative Liberal Arts as Leverage for Evolutionary Change." Middlebury College, Middlebury, VT. http://envisioning.middle bury.edu/our-process/speaker-series/.

Schwab, Katherine. 2018. "Facial Recognition Systems Are Even More Biased Than We Thought." *Co-Design Newsletter*. https://www.fastcodesign.com/90160327/facial-recog nition-systems-are-way-more-biased-that-we-thought.

Sheridan, Mary P., director. 2018 Thomas R. Watson Conference "Open Letter to Conference Participants." Distributed to conference participants via email. December 10.

Southern Poverty Law Center. Hate Map. https://www.splcenter.org/hate-map.

Todd, Zoe. 2014. "An Indigenous Feminist's Take on the Ontological Turn: 'Ontology' Is Just Another Word for Colonialism." Blog post, *Urbane Adventurer: Thoughts of a Metis Urban Scholar*. October 24. https://zoestodd.com/2014/10/24/an-indigenous -feminists-take-on-the-ontological-turn-ontology-is-just-another-word-for-colonialism/.

Todd, Zoe. 2016. "An Indigenous Feminist's Take on the Ontological Turn: 'Ontology' Is Just Another Word for Colonialism." Revised and expanded blog post from October 24, 2014. *Journal of Historical Sociology* 29 (1): 4–22.

Watson, Thomas R. Conference on Rhetoric and Composition. 2018. Call to the Conference for the Twelfth Biennial Conference "Making Future Matters." Louisville, KY, October 25–27. Call to the Conference is included in the Conference Program, p. 5. https://louisville.edu/conference/watson/files/watson-2018-program.

Western States Rhetoric and Literacy Conference. 2018. Call for Proposals. Theme: Matter and Mattering. http://www.public.asu.edu/~petergo/wsrl/2018cfp.html.

Wysocki, Rick, and Mary P. Sheridan, eds. 2018. *Making Futures Matter*. Logan: Computers and Composition Digital Press/Utah State University Press. https://ccdigitalpress.org/book/makingfuturematters/kirsch.html.

SECTION TWO

Disciplinary and Pedagogical Perspectives

8

ETHICS, PSYCHOMETRICS, AND WRITING ASSESSMENT
A Conceptual Model

Robert J. Mislevy
Norbert Elliot

Providing a coherent conceptual model for relationships among ethics, psychometrics, and writing assessment is a complex undertaking. Challenges are apparent at a moment's thought: the landscape is vast, sources of evidence are field-dependent, and the points of entry are contested. A possible way forward is to propose a broad definition of ethics and then to narrow that definition as its elements apply to writing assessment. Psychometrics may then be added to the model as a sociocognitive framework in which language is understood as situated and constitutive. In this way, we may then proceed to the details of a conceptual model for writing assessment informed by the fields of ethics and psychometrics.

Let's begin with a basic definition of ethical philosophy proposed by James Rachaels (1986, 11)—his minimum conception of morality:

> Morality is, at the very least, the effort to guide one's conduct by reason—that is, to do what there are the best reasons for doing—while giving equal weight to the interests of each individual who will be affected by one's conduct.

Rachaels (1986, 11) extends the definition by linking it to the capabilities needed to be a conscious moral agent:

> Someone who is concerned impartially with the interests of everyone affected by what he or she does; who carefully sifts facts and examines their implications; who accepts principles of conduct only after scrutinizing them to make sure they are sound; who is willing to "listen to reason" even when it means that his or her earlier convictions may have to be revised; and who, finally, is willing to act on the results of this deliberation.

This definition has distinct advantages as the general philosophical background for our conceptual model of writing assessment. Published in

DOI: 10.7330/9781607329978.c008

1986, the definition benefits from three philosophical traditions—the categorical imperative of Immanuel Kant (2012 [1785], 31): "Act only in accordance with that maxim through which you can at the same time will that it become a universal law"; the greatest happiness principle of John Stuart Mill (1879 [1861], 17): "The ultimate end, with reference to and for the sake of which all other things are desirable (whether we are considering our own good or that of other people), is an existence exempt as far as possible from pain, and as rich as possible in enjoyments, both in point of quantity and quality"; and the social justice theory of John Rawls (1999 [1971], 96): "We are not to gain from the cooperative labor of others without doing our fair share." Informed by philosophical perspectives of conscience, capability, and community, it seems wise to adopt a complementarity model yielding overlapping consensus an endorsement of principles, as philosopher Martha C. Nussbaum (2011) observes, for a given purpose and not as a guide to life. Put straightforwardly, we advance complementarity in our conceptual model as an overarching way to establish new directions for research leading to the advancement of individual capability.

Extending this ethical framework—a sense of reason tempered by consequence understood as particularized, convictions revisited by reflection, and fairness enacted in communities—we now offer a definition of ethics in writing assessment:

> Fairness in writing assessment is defined as the identification of opportunity structures created through maximum construct representation. Constraint of the writing construct is to be tolerated only to the extent to which benefits are realized for the least advantaged. (Elliot 2016, §3.1)

In advancing a minimum concept of morality that informs the actions of a conscious moral agent, this definition provides needed focus. First, it yields an overarching frame in which the advancement of opportunity is understood as the aim of writing assessment. Here we recall James Paul Gee (2008) and his identification of the rights of students in terms of opportunity to learn: universal affordances for action, participation, and learning; attention to experiential ranges of students; equal access to relevant technologies; accountability for the communities of practice who manage that information; and emphasis on identity, value, content, and characteristic activities associated with language across academic areas. Thus the definition's emphasis on opportunity to learn plays a unique role. Second, the definition aims to lessen the social inequality resulting from writing assessment while emphasizing the benefits to be gained by assessment. Third, the definition bridges the philosophical and the psychometric with its emphasis on fairness in relationship to validity and reliability. Here the definition leverages the 2014 edition of the *Standards for Educational and Psychological Testing* (American Educational Research Association, American Psychological Association, and National Council on Measurement in Education 2014) in which fairness in testing has been considered as its own category of evidence alongside foundational concepts of validity and reliability. Fourth, the definition advances construct-based assessments—those assessments that have at their core a well-defined, evidence-based conceptualization of the writing construct—and links those assessments to fairness. Thus the definition implicitly advances recent efforts by the Institute of Education Science to bring forward recommendations of writing instruction based on empirical evidence meeting exacting research demands (Graham et al. 2012, 2016). Since the definition takes as the aim of writing assessment advancement of opportunity to learn, teaching and assessing writing are taken as inextricably interrelated under defined construct models. Fifth, the focus of the definition on opportunity structures aligns the Western philosophical tradition with non-Western traditions. As Nussbaum reminds us, emphasis on human rights and capabilities exists in both Indian and Chinese traditions. Thus the philosophers we reference, although Western, need not lead us to value imperialism. As Bo Wang argues in this volume, Confucian perspectives provide alternatives to the values of autonomy and individualism. Our definition of ethics in writing assessment is therefore open to all philosophical traditions that value the pursuit of human capabilities. With Rawls and Nussbaum, we affirm those philosophical traditions in which diverse perspectives, formed through collaboration, are used to advance justice and capability.

The standpoint we are proposing in this chapter is therefore a confluence of three lines of work: the growing understanding of fairness, validity, and reliability as both categories of evidence and ethical frameworks (Kelly-Riley and Whithaus 2016); an ecological view of human cognition as applied to writing (White, Elliot, and Peckham 2015); and a sociocognitive view of assessment as an expression of contextualized, purposive arguments (Mislevy 2018). Significantly, our model thus resonates with that of David Slomp's (2016) framework for using consequential validity evidence in evaluating each step in writing assessment design. These lines of work inform the structure of our chapter and the model proposed in it.

We first turn to an integrative perspective in which a defined view of psychometrics (identified as sociocognitive) is used to design a construct-driven approach to writing (identified as nomothetic). We then combine the desire to use situative perspectives with efforts to describe the span of the writing construct. We conclude with a summary of four ethical principles that are implicit in our model that, taken together, call for enhanced attention to construct validity and the integrative framework that is provided by evidence of fairness. In emphasizing this integrative approach, we believe researchers can structurally design assessments that, in context and use, are ethical in nature. With the reservation that conceptual models are limited in terms of their applications—as are all human endeavors intending to structure opportunities—we hold that ours bakes a certain kind of ethical perspective (identified with fairness) into the assessment itself.

Our proposed model comes with a warning label for our readers. Our work is based on two fields of research—psychometrics and writing assessment—in which empirical techniques are used to gather evidence of fairness, reliability, and validity. Our chapter is therefore complex at times in its use of terminology. As well, our discussion is based on current empirical knowledge of educational measurement in general and writing assessment in particular. Ellen Schendel and Peggy O'Neill (1999) were among the first assessment scholars to remind us that quantitative research is an ethical obligation to our students, and we extend their belief here—with eyes wide open to the costs and effectiveness when mathematical models are used to make inferences about human behavior. The decisions we make when we prepare our writing assessment programs nevertheless raise questions that can only be answered empirically: Are there performance differences among sub-groups that are related to the writing assessment task? Does the assessment task operationalize an explicit model of the writing construct that all groups may access equally? Is there inter-topic reliability among those tasks for all student groups? Required, therefore, is a willingness to engage current programs of research in fields that are uncommonly intricate.

Our model also comes with an admission. The chapter seeks to extend an existing theory of ethics for writing assessment by emphasizing the benefits to be gained from psychometrics—key concepts and methods, that is, as opposed to rote applications of long-standing practices. We therefore seek a restorative vision in which quantitative methods are seen as one important way of understanding students as they make language visible on notebook pages and computer screens. Many of our colleagues continue to depict assessment as a uniform activity of oppression, and their work is important if we are to understand the consequences of our actions. Our vision, however, carries nothing of the tacit conservatism inaccurately attributed to anyone who uses traditional and advanced empirical techniques in educational research. As such, we invite our readers to understand our work as driven by a liberal imagination.

PSYCHOMETRIC MODELING: A SOCIOCOGNITIVE PERSPECTIVE ON ASSESSMENT

Paul Holland, a former president of the Psychometric Society, described the history of psychometrics in educational and psychological assessment, or test theory, in terms of four generations (Holland 2008). Neil J. Dorans (2011, 259) summarized the first three like this:

> The first generation, which was influenced by concepts such as error of measurement and correlation that were developed in other fields, focused on test scores and saw developments in the areas of reliability, classical test theory, generalizability theory, and validity. This generation began in the early twentieth century and continues today, but most of its major developments were achieved by 1970. The second generation, which focused on models for item level data, began in the 1940s and peaked in the 1970s but continues into the present as well. The third generation started in the 1970s and continues into today. It is characterized by the application of statistical ideas and sophisticated computational methods to item level models, as well as models of sets of items.

Most large-scale assessments in writing and other disciplines remain grounded in first-generation concepts and methods even while drawing on second- and third-generation machinery to improve quality and efficiency to the same ostensive end: to measure a trait that is qualitatively the same for all the test takers, who can be assessed with samples of the same tasks, have their performances evaluated in the same way, and have their results reported as locations on the same proficiency scale. In the second generation, the mid-century emergence of Item Response Theory (IRT) under psychometricians such as Frederic M. Lord (1952) allowed for the more flexible designs in the National Assessment for Educational Progress. Generalizability theory, developed by Lee J. Cronbach and his colleagues (1972), enabled illuminating analyses of ratings of multiple aspects of students' performances and the consistency of evaluations of multiple raters. Third-generation efforts draw on elements from IRT and generalizability and other techniques such as latent class analysis, hierarchical modeling, diagnostic classification, and mixture models to build models tailored to assessment designs, response formats, aspects of performance, and student-population structures (see, for example,

De Boeck and Wilson 2004). Third-generation psychometrics assimilated emerging technologies, with computer-based testing and automated scoring of essays to produce scores to match humans' ratings.

Not much of this history of test theory matches our narratives of interactions among writing teachers and their students. Measurement error seems to have little bearing on, for example, the ways teachers help student prepare initial drafts for an assignment. These interactions address no single writing proficiency. Rather, the interactions encompass unique aspects of writing as drawn down in the writing task at hand. Classroom and online discussions focus on the particulars of genre, purpose, audience, context, and the language evoked by the task. Ever situative, students have different backgrounds, goals, and writing experiences to build on as they engage the task. Teachers do not merely take into account such contexts; rather, using process-based approaches, teachers build on the situatedness of each student in ways that foster individual learning. Teaching writing comes down to finding the sweet spot between informed pedagogy for the class and the fit of that pedagogy to the individual student.

One frontier in psychometrics looks in just these directions. Dorans (2011, 259) continues:

> The current fourth generation [of test theory] attempts to bridge the gap between the statistician/psychometrician role and the role of other components of the testing enterprise. It recognizes that testing occurs within a larger complex system and that measurement needs to occur within this larger context.

Here is where writing pedagogy intersects with the measurement theory. We find in the fourth generation growing attention to the sociocognitive foundations for peoples' capabilities, how they develop, and how they are used in a social and cultural milieu—and just how ideas and methods from test theory might be reconceived, extended, and brought to bear in ways that are consistent with what we are learning about learning (Chalhoub-Deville 2003; Mislevy 2018; Zumbo 2007). Figure 8.1, which we will parse shortly, reflects this view of psychometric modeling. In the field of psychometrics, figure 8.1 is a big leap.

Quietly, at the edges of practice, the ground is shifting. The idea is to give attention to modeling patterns in the dynamic interplay of individuals and the social structures—but with models that reflect patterns as we can now view them through a sociocognitive perspective. Valuing the impact of flux, a sociocognitive view sees human activity as a complex adaptive system involving interactions among and within individuals (Gee 1992; Sperber 1996). Although every social situation is unique,

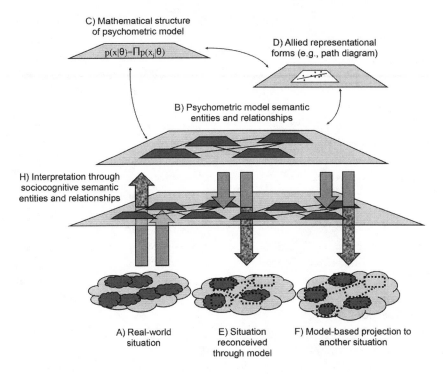

C) Mathematical structure
of psychometric model

$p(x|\theta)=\Pi p(x_j|\theta)$

D) Allied representational
forms (e.g., path diagram)

B) Psychometric model semantic
entities and relationships

H) Interpretation through
sociocognitive semantic
entities and relationships

A) Real-world
situation

E) Situation
reconceived
through model

F) Model-based projection to
another situation

Figure 8.1. Model-based reasoning from a psychometric perspective (Mislevy 2018, reprinted with permission)

regularities emerge in interactions among persons, which collectively might be called linguistic, cultural, and substantive patterns (LCS patterns). It is LCS patterns that make interactions among individuals possible and to which individuals become attuned through experiencing situations constructed around them. Linguistic patterns, for example, span lexicon and syntax; there are typical uses of given words and structures, but every situated meaning depends on context, users' intentions and hearers' expectations, and the interpersonal functions they serve. Genres are examples of cultural patterns—encompassing typical ways people structure writing but intertwined with kinds of purposes and uses people have in recurring kinds of social situations. Substantive patterns address knowledge structures and activity structures in the social and physical world, from repairing toasters to greeting friends to writing research proposals. In every situation, we perceive, act, and interact by assembling resources attuned to LCS patterns of many kinds and at different levels and blending them with the situation at hand (and, in the process, further developing our resources for future experiences).

Figure 8.1 illustrates core properties of model-based reasoning in psychometrics, reconceived through a sociocognitive perspective. It represents aspects of a particular quantitative model as applied in a particular assessment application. At the top left of the figure, representational form C is the mathematical expression of the model, a set of statements in the symbol system of mathematical reasoning and probabilistic expression. Let's take the example of IRT—second-generation models known for their ability to characterize individual item difficulties and test-taker abilities separately but on the same scale, a feature not possible with first-generation models (Lord 1952). IRT contains conditional probability distributions for some variables Xj given another variable θ—which by themselves say nothing about people or performances. Here is the world of mathematical modeling, elegant equations that, if we are fortunate, allow us to learn something about how we are with each other. Representational form D suggests one of perhaps several aspects of the model, such as visualizations, geometric expression of relationships, or computer code for carrying out calculations (as examples, displays of relationships between scores as scatterplots, algorithms for computing Pearson correlation coefficients, and interpreting correlations as cosines between score vectors).

The plane labeled B in the center of the figure, holding a place for psychometric model entities and relationships, is the semantic connection between the equations and the world; it lies in the realm of "as if" thinking (as does all our use of language). There we begin to give semantic expression to concepts involved in the construct at issue, which will take situated meanings in the application. Returning to representational form C, we can now better understand the Xj variables associated with aspects of performance in tasks indexed by j and by θ as an aspect of a person's capability. While these expressions surely do not capture the entirety of the term at hand, the process of establishing a relationship among a concept, the word used to define that concept, and a quantitative expression of some aspects of a real-world situation provides a practical tool for working through certain kinds of complex problems. As a process of enactment, plane B is a gateway to further reasoning.

In real-world situation A at the lower left, the cloud represents the candidates (in our case, the students) sitting for the assessment and their performances. It is here that the concepts used to model entities and relationships come into force. In reconceived situation E, the cloud represents the way we approximate aspects of how that student experiences the assessment within the identified setting in terms of the entities and relationships of the model space represented in plane B.

In the bottom right of the figure, the final cloud, shown in F, represents this assessment as it is envisioned and then extended to another environment—with special attention to the things the student might do in an unknown situation (expressed by that empty box).

Put in motion, figure 8.1 represents a series of considerations and reconsiderations as we move through the model: mathematical reasoning and probabilistic expressions are either expanded or narrowed as they are considered in terms of the model entities and relationships—as are the ways these expressions are visualized (and thus manifested for assessment stakeholders). The real-world situation, in turn, allows reconceptualization of the entities and relationships that are, in turn, further modified as the assessment situation is reconceived and what is learned there is projected (with caveats and qualifiers) to other assessments, instructional activities, or real-world situations.

What is new is the plane labeled H, a reconception of all the variables in the model, all the patterns among aspects of peoples' performances approximated in the model, and all the decisions and inferences supported by the model through a sociocognitive perspective. Importantly, the patterns emerge from their personal histories and the sociocultural context and could be quite different for other test takers and in other sociocultural contexts; careful checking of inferences through the model requires investigation when certain individuals or groups understand tasks or perform qualitatively differently than other students. Reasoning through a model can strengthen inference about individuals by leveraging broader patterns, but it can in these cases distort inferences for certain individuals. The statistical machinery comes with tools to highlight such instances, and a score user has an ethical imperative to use them.

The idea is not to give the same writing tasks over and over and watch some students succeed and others fail. The idea is to advance opportunities to learn for all students by recognizing and making use of the information in the variation. Advances in computer technology and accompanying assessment platforms have enabled modelers to make more nuanced distinctions among student responses to varied tasks. These advancements are not the same, of course, as a perceptive teacher, but even with their limitations, the fine-grained information provided by technology is far more helpful as feedback at a larger scale than an overall measure can be: providing more refined, variegated automated feedback on genre-tuned aspects of a writing sample, for example, or supporting dialogue among peers critiquing each other's work in an internet community, or providing analyses of patterns of performance across teachers who share assignments and use an online tool to facilitate their evaluations. As a result, students can learn in real time what they know and what they need to know. While, for example, a student may have strong skills in knowledge of conventions, that same student may have difficulty in achieving cohesion in varied writing genres. With this knowledge, instructors can plan in greater detail how to help individual students. The takeaway is straightforward: figure 8.1 is ideally suited to support formative assessment and is, in fact, readily adaptable for settings in which sociocognitive modeling in local settings is desired.

The match between the situation and the model is never perfect, nor do we claim it to be so. Nevertheless, our understanding of the situation—and our ability to make inferences beyond the situation—are now both enhanced by a framework the situation does not in itself possess. We now re-understand (and incompletely understand and sometimes misunderstand) the situation in terms of the patterns the model can provide, built around both the regularities and the variations of students, tasks, and performances.

This may sound good in the abstract, but how do we actually go about building models that are suited to contexts and purposes? We draw on what we know globally from sociocognitive research and studies of the domain at issue and what we know locally about the students, purposes, contexts, and constraints at play for the job at hand. We turn now to an example that uses a representation of the writing construct to help an assessment developer think through the design process.

WRITING ASSESSMENT: A CONSTRUCT
REPRESENTATION PERSPECTIVE

As is the case with psychometrics, quietly, at the edges of practice, the ground is also shifting for writing assessment. Research at the present time emphasizes the need for greater construct validity in our research practices (Sparks, Song, Brantley, and Lou 2014) and the turn to social justice as a stance framing the validity and the reliability/precision of our theory building and empirical research (Poe, Inoue, and Elliot 2018). Informed by recent developments such as these, a new view of the writing construct has emerged that is congruent with a more sociocognitive view of psychometric model-based reasoning. Figure 8.2 is a visualization of that construct.

The top row spans the three environments in which students communicate: digital, print, and blurred. The second row captures a language arts framework for writing, including writing, reading, speaking,

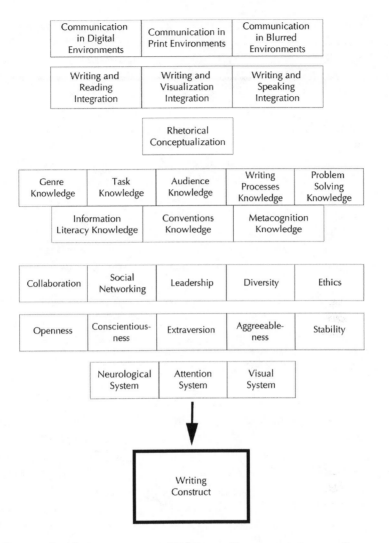

Figure 8.2. Construct representation from a writing assessment perspective (White, Elliot, and Peckham 2015, reprinted with permission)

and listening. The third row identifies rhetorical conceptualization in its attention to language and its sources of knowledge. The fourth and fifth rows identify the cognitive domain of writing. The sixth row identifies the interpersonal domain of writing. The seventh row identifies the intrapersonal domain of writing. The eighth row, often neglected in construct mapping, attends to the neurological, attention, and vision capacities necessary to perform language arts tasks.

As noted above, this view of the writing construct is described as nomothetic—a taxonomy of the span of written communication that is understood to be both constant and general and therefore a way to generate ideographic representations that are detailed and specific. In other words, the rows in figure 8.1 are meant to represent all possible facets of writing as a part of language arts (writing, reading, speaking, and listening). Under this broad taxonomy, specific representations may be created, such as those consensus frameworks used in the *Framework for Success in Postsecondary Writing* (Council of Writing Program Administrators, National Council of Teachers of English, and National Writing Project 2011) and the empirical models derived by John Hayes (2012). The more research we have, the more we can refine the general taxonomy and the better we can create specific models for specific episodes of instruction and assessment. In the field of writing assessment, figure 8.2 is a big leap.

Both figures 8.1 and 8.2 are high-level abstractions. Let's see how they inform and particularize each other when we design a writing assessment in a particular context, for particular students, for a particular purpose. To position the writing construct, imagine sliding figure 8.2 into plane B in the center of figure 8.1 so we can begin the "as if" thinking process. It is here that we begin to enact the semantic expressions by which we give precision to particular communication environments, language arts frameworks, rhetorical conceptualizations, and the cognitive, interpersonal, intrapersonal, and neurological domains of writing that are at issue in the application at hand. While we acknowledge that any definition we give these entities and their relationships is limited, we now have a conceptual gateway to work through our assessment. In figure 8.1, we illustrate how elements of the writing construct interact when they are specified in a given situation—the relationships among the four domains, what we know about the students, what we (and they) need to find out, and what genres and environments are in play. This kind of consideration tells us the kinds of narratives we need to build to support claims about students in the semantic space of the model (B).

In terms of representational form A in figure 8.1, we now begin to consider and select the forms of mathematical reasoning and probabilistic expression—classical test theory, IRT, multidimensional scaling, or something else—that will be of use to situate the writing construct and the psychometric model jointly. That is, we now specify what variables and relationships we need to express in the particularized semantic needed to suit the assessment aim and context. As they are useful to various stakeholders, we also begin to consider the visualizations of these models in representational form B—as well as interpretation (H), contextualization (A), reconceptualization (E), and generalization (F) based on the construct model. As we turn to the real-world situation, we imagine the individual student and those students of similar and dissimilar backgrounds who will be involved. As we project our thought experiment to other settings, we begin to understand the complexities of the particularized model in terms of interactions within the broader construct model itself as determined by contexts. The model is simplified, but if we have done our work well, it is simplified in a way that is useful for the job at hand. In other work complementary to that which we are presenting in this chapter, we have demonstrated that such particularization may prove useful in supporting the success of diverse student groups in international higher education contexts by improving connections between assessments and instruction for admitted students (Oliveri, Mislevy, and Elliot 2020).

As an example of just one of the many considerations involved in this process, we will do well to reflect on the significance of *genre* in this kind of construct modeling. Carolyn R. Miller (1984, 151) noted that traditionally, "rhetorical genres have been defined by similarities in strategies or forms in the discourses, by similarities in audience, by similarities in modes of thinking, and by similarities in rhetorical situations." She was after something entirely different:

> The classification [of genre] I am advocating is, in effect, ethnomethodological: it seeks to explicate the knowledge that practice creates. This approach insists that the "de facto" genres, the types we have names for in everyday language, tell us something theoretically important about discourse. To consider as potential genres such homely discourse as the letter of recommendation, the user manual, the progress report, the ransom note, the lecture, and the white paper, as well as the eulogy, the apologia, the inaugural, the public proceeding, and the sermon, is not to trivialize the study of genres; it is to take seriously the rhetoric in which we are immersed and the situations in which we find ourselves. (Miller 1984, 155)

In other words, genre is not simply about forms of writing, reading, or speaking but about those forms as ways of using language in recurring situations. Speakers and writers know the kinds of things that are meant to happen and structures their hearers and readers expect to help them produce and to make sense of new information. Becoming proficient means not simply knowing structures but understanding their role in practice, using them to create and to apprehend information in the ways people communicate in those practices. Yes, genre "embraces both form and content . . . [but also] the use of genres simultaneously constitutes and reproduces social structures; and . . . genre conventions signal a discourse community's norms, epistemology, ideology, and social ontology" (Berkenkotter and Huckin 1993, 475). Writing a research proposal or completing a tax form are genre uses that serve to structure individuals' thinking and acting in a complex network of coordinated activity.

To become proficient in a genre, then, is not simply knowing how to write decontextualized text in a certain form but to write in forms and ways that connect intimately to what people know, what people expect, and what people do in some activity. As John Duffy demonstrates in this volume, alertness to genre theory itself promotes virtue by allowing the formation of bridges (our term is crosswalks) that allow students to understand writing as an achievable task—a form of conceptualization that is important to assessment as we seek to see students at their best. It does no good to simply throw one five-paragraph essay topic after another and watch a student succeed or fail when the goal is to help her improve her skill in crafting résumés or assembling engineering proposals. If we want our students to learn to write in a network of coordinated activities, our curricula cannot be one essay after another. If our aim is to advance opportunity to learn through fairness, then genre selection becomes an ethical matter.

Remaining alert to the power of genre goes a long way in helping us understand topics such as transfer, so important to education in general (National Research Council 2012) and writing research in particular (Yancey, Robertson, and Taczak 2014). A moment's reflection on how genre shifts the writing process makes us realize again the contingent nature of assessment. In their examination of how a professional communication designer constructs a proposal, Mariëlle Leijten and colleagues (2014) acknowledge that the recorded activities—the construction of visual content and the accompanying attention and motivation management—are not apparent in current models of writing. With a genre shift from academy writing (the source-based essay) to professional writing (the proposal), the landscape shifts radically. Without recognizing the impact of such shifts at the lexical and grammatical level, tracking writing transfer becomes impossible.

In the design process, then, we must examine the role of a particular genre in a given assessment, what the students know (and do not know) about the social milieu in which it takes meaning, and what types of feedback will be needed. The genre we highlight in a writing assessment for engineering students, the practices it draws on, and the qualities in performance we attend to will be quite different from those we must address when helping job-seeking adults prepare their résumés—yet both are derived from the same broad writing construct and the same broad sociocognitive conception of assessment. These considerations shape our decisions about task types, substantive content, evaluation procedures, and the nature and grain size of reports. Together, such contextualizations, articulations, and design choices give the variables and relationships in our models a meaning that is situated and hence useful in the situation.

More generally, educational experiences in school, work, and recreation are meant to help people develop resources associated with targeted LCS patterns and practices that draw on them. Educational assessments are meant to evoke aspects of peoples' diverse capabilities so construed, for a variety of purposes and in a variety of contexts that concern past, present, or potential development. The challenge for assessment and measurement is reconceiving its very foundations accordingly (Mislevy 2018). Models and concepts developed throughout the previous generations can continue to be useful, although with interpretations and uses reconsidered. Others will need to be extended, such as models that characterize the more qualitative aspects of writing performances that are the basis of individual feedback or models that examine patterns of variation and regularity across distributed networks of students and teachers as they critique and support each others' development. Still others will be developed anew, such as incorporating natural language processing tools to supplement learning locally and developing ways to evaluate distributed performances both economically and authentically.

In terms of the offered psychometric perspective and writing construct, their validity is not just the correspondence between the model and the system being modeled. Viewing models as tools people use for reasoning, we recognize that validity depends on the aptness of the relationship among the situation, the model, a user, and a purpose (Suárez 2004). Becoming proficient in the use of models therefore means more than becoming fluent with their mechanics. Becoming proficient means being able to build models to suit real-world situations, evaluating where they fit and when they need to be revised or abandoned, and continually evaluating the quality of reasoning about the real world through the lens of the model. It means understanding which inferences derived through a model are warranted and which are not—as well as which are robust and sensitive to various ways the real-world situation might differ from the model. Psychometric models and assessments are constructive to the extent that they are at once faithful to the construct as we understand it, support sound inferences for their intended purposes, and suit the contexts and constraints of the application at hand.

ETHICAL UNDERSTANDING THROUGH CONCEPTUAL MODELING

Far from a monolith, writing assessment exists along a continuum. At one end, we find standard assessments designed to be distributed across contexts; on the other, we find local assessments intended to provide information tuned to particular students, contexts, purposes, and surrounding information. Along this continuum, the conceptual model we offer, in which model-based reasoning from a psychometric perspective enriches our understanding of the LCS span of the writing construct, will be of varied use. Yet wherever one is located on this continuum, the kind of model-based thought experiment offered in this chapter will be of use in understanding the complexity of the assessment task at hand.

It is within this very complexity that we find the need for ethical understanding. Designing writing assessments and using psychometric models is not a matter of objectively constructing a scientific measure of some unitary capability. It is rather the fashioning of a means to gather, represent, and use information about the resources students can bring in some space of writing activities, for some purpose, in some context, under some constraints. This we can do well or poorly. Issues of evidence and inference arise, and psychometrics can help with those. But equally important are issues of fairness, of opportunity, and of consequences, in various ways to various stakeholders. These are not simply measurement issues but ethical issues, which statistical reasoning may help us clarify but cannot by itself resolve. While we do not have the space here to devote to all the implications of our model, we can conclude with a summary of ethical principles implicit in our approach.

- *There exists an inextricable bond between the technical and the ethical.* This Stoic belief that nothing is good or bad but by its use does not pass the smirk test. With Langdon Winner (1980), we all learned in the twentieth century to realize that artifacts have politics. Harder to recognize, however, is that our technical artifacts are deeply related to our ethical perceptions. The formulas in figure 8.1, representational form A, are based on premises that, in turn, reflect worldviews. Because equations have politics, ethical stance exists at the level of the equation. Without an understanding of the four generations of psychometric research defined above—accompanied by the ability to work with specialists to ensure that attendant measures are used in principled ways—there is as much chance that the writing assessment specialist will throw darkness as cast light. To those who would dismiss empirical knowledge outright, this is a very hard message, but its truth will not go away. If a researcher is involved in the assessment of writing abilities across time and space—and over many students and many instructors—little can be done to help students without an understanding of quantitative methods. Because we need commonalities between the technical and the ethical, we can do no better than remind ourselves, as does James E. Porter in this volume, that when combined with *techne, praxis* means making something beautiful, positive, and communal. Just as equations have politics, they may also be elegant in their creation of change and their ability to disrupt traditional thinking.

- *There is value in infusing contingency into language-based conceptual systems.* In the interplay between figure 8.1 and figure 8.2, stakeholders participate in a principled system of planning before the assessment episode is begun. In this kind of anticipatory thought, the assessment design runs along an iterative path so that the standpoints of those involved in the assessment community are understood from the beginning. In placing the conceptual system in the referential frame of the test taker, specific attention is oriented to the candidate and others like and unlike that candidate. Here we find useful William Duffy's interpretation of *phronesis* in this volume as a stance requiring balance between what is good and what is expedient, thus encouraging us to rise to the demands of exigencies even as we refuse to foreclose the possibility of future exchange. While seemingly at odds, acknowledgement of contingency and the desire for practical action need not forestall each other. There is an important connection between practical action and anticipatory thought that begins with acknowledgment of contingency.

- *The complexity of a language-based conceptual system should reflect both the intracity of human capability and the humility required to engage that capability.* As one becomes alert to contingency, one is limited in the claims made and inferences drawn from a given assessment. This expanding sense of humility thus serves as an obligation to those who design assessments and interpret their results to qualify findings even as knowledge about writing studies is expanded. With Gesa Kirsch and Jacqueline Jones Royster, we are committed to the pursuit of human capability as imagined by Nussbaum. Focus on virtues related to humility—compassion, empathy, courage, and commitment—is integral to the new materialist view these virtues adopt in which exceptionalism is abandoned and replaced with affiliation. Seen in this way, figures 8.1 and 8.2 support what Kirsch and Royster reference in their chapter as the deliberate and conscious cultivation of what it means to be human.

- *To continue to advance knowledge, a multidisciplinary perspective is needed to build language-based conceptual systems.* As we hope we have demonstrated in this chapter, our collaboration has resulted in a conceptual model that is beyond that of any single disciplinary perspective. No psychometric scholar will understand the writing construct from the perspective of a teacher of writing, and no writing studies researcher will understand the intricacies of psychometric perspectives. Together, however, one field forces the other to make clear the assumptions and premises behind their models and thus, to the benefit of students, new systems are developed. These perspectives will require what Patrick W. Berry terms an ethics of listening in his chapter—interrogating deeply held beliefs and listening to the perspectives of others. As John Duffy (2014, 2019) proposed, needed are ethical dispositions in which confirmed beliefs are revisited and expression is considered generously; perhaps an ethics of listening and ethical dispositions are the two most important preconditions for multidisciplinarity, foundations without which harmony between figure 8.1 and figure 8.2 cannot exist. Significantly, we also wish to make explicit that multidisciplinary perspectives allow us to move beyond the lone philosophical voice that establishes a singular ethics agenda. Used wisely, collaborative thinking advances justice and capability. Multidisciplinarity is not only good practice; it is also philosophically justified and morally virtuous.

While much more work remains to be done, these four principles support calls for greater construct validity in our research practices and desires for fairness as an integrative framework for validity and reliability. Perhaps of most significance, these principles support a view of writing assessment as a formative, generative process that can be understood in terms of contextualized, purposive arguments designed, at the end of the day, to advance opportunity.

REFERENCES

American Educational Research Association, American Psychological Association, and National Council on Measurement in Education. 2014. *Standards for Educational and Psychological Testing.* Washington, DC: American Educational Research Association.

Berkenkotter, Carol, and Thomas N. Huckin. 1993. "Rethinking Genre from a Sociocognitive Perspective." *Written Communication* 10 (4): 475–509.

Chalhoub-Deville, Micheline. 2003. "Second Language Interaction: Current Perspectives and Future Trends." *Language Testing* 20 (4): 369–83. http://dx.doi.org/ 10.1191/0265 532203lt264oa.

Council of Writing Program Administrators, National Council of Teachers of English, and National Writing Project. 2011. *Framework for Success in Postsecondary Writing.* http:// wpacouncil.org/aws/CWPA/asset_manager/get_file/350201?ver=1624.

Cronbach, Lee J., Goldine C. Gleser, Harinder Nanda, and Nageswari Rajaratnam. 1972. *The Dependability of Behavioral Measurements: Theory of Generalizability for Scores and Profiles.* New York: Wiley.

De Boeck, Paul, and Mark Wilson. 2004. *Explanatory Item Response Models.* New York: Springer.

Dorans, Neil J. 2011. "Holland's Advice for the Fourth Generation of Test Theory: Blood Tests Can Be Contests." In *Looking Back: Proceedings of a Conference in Honor of Paul W. Holland,* ed. Neil J. Dorans and Sandip Sinharay, 259–72. New York: Springer.

Duffy, John. 2014. "Ethical Dispositions: A Discourse for Rhetoric and Composition." *JAC: A Journal of Composition Theory* 34 (1): 209–37.

Duffy, John. 2019. *Provocations of Virtue: Rhetoric, Ethics, and the Teaching of Writing.* Logan: Utah State University Press.

Elliot, Norbert. 2016. "A Theory of Ethics for Writing Assessment." *Journal of Writing Assessment* 9 (1). http://journalofwritingassessment.org/article.php?article=98.

Gee, James Paul. 1992. *The Social Mind: Language, Ideology, and Social Practice.* New York: Bergin and Garvey.

Gee, James Paul. 2008. "A Sociocultural Perspective on Opportunity to Learn." In *Assessment, Equity, and Opportunity to Learn,* ed. Pamela A. Moss, Diana C. Pullin, James P. Gee, Edward H. Haertel, and Lauren J. Young, 76–108. Cambridge: Cambridge University Press.

Graham, Steve, Alisha Bollinger, Carol Booth Olson, Catherine D'Aoust, Charles MacArthur, Deborah McCutchen, and Natalie Olinghouse. 2012. *Teaching Elementary School Students to Be Effective Writers: A Practice Guide* (NCEE 2012-4058). Washington, DC: National Center for Education Evaluation and Regional Assistance, Institute of Education Sciences, US Department of Education. https://ies.ed.gov/ncee/wwc/Docs/practiceguide/writing_pg_062612.pdf.

Graham, Steve, Julie Bruch, Jill Fitzgerald, Linda D. Friedrich, Joshua Furgeson, Katie Greene, James S. Kim, Julia Lyskawa, Carol Booth Olson, and Claire Smith Wulsin. 2016. *Teaching Secondary Students to Write Effectively* (NCEE 2017-4002). Washington, DC: National Center for Education Evaluation and Regional Assistance, Institute of Education Sciences, US Department of Education. https://ies.ed.gov/ncee/wwc/Docs/PracticeGuide/wwc_secondary_writing_110116.pdf.

Hayes, John R. 2012. "Modeling and Remodeling Writing." *Written Communication* 29 (3): 369–88. http://dx.doi.org/10.1177/0741088312451260.

Holland, Paul W. 2008. "The First Four Generations of Test Theory." Paper presented at the Association of Test Publishers on Innovations in Testing. Dallas, TX, March.

Kant, Immanuel. 2012 [1785]. *Groundwork of the Metaphysics of Morals.* Rev. ed. Trans. and ed. Mary Gregor and Jens Timmerman. Cambridge, UK: Cambridge University Press.

Kelly-Riley, Diane, and Carl Whithaus. 2016. A Theory of Ethics for Writing Assessment. Special issue of *Journal of Writing Assessment* 9 (1). http://journalofwritingassessment .org/archives.php?issue=19.

Leijten, Mariëlle, Luuk Van Waes, Karen Schriver, and John R. Hayes. 2014. "Writing in the Workplace: Constructing Documents using Multiple Digital Sources." *Journal of Writing Research* 5 (3): 285–337. http://dx.doi.org/10.1111/j.1745-3984.1976.tb00178.x.

Lord, Frederic M. 1952. "A Theory of Test Scores." *Psychometric Monograph no. 7.* Princeton, NJ: Educational Testing Service. https://www.psychometricsociety.org/sites/default /files/pdf/MN07.pdf.

Mill, John Stuart. 1879 [1861]. *Utilitarianism.* 7th ed. London: Longmans, Green.

Miller, Carolyn R. 1984. "Genre as Social Action." *Quarterly Journal of Speech* 70 (2): 151–67.

Mislevy, Robert J. 2018. *Sociocognitive Foundations of Educational Measurement.* New York: Routledge.

National Research Council. 2012. *Education for Life and Work: Developing Transferable Knowledge and Skills in the 21st Century.* Washington, DC: National Academies Press.

Nussbaum, Martha C. 2011. *Creating Capabilities: The Human Development Approach.* Cambridge, MA: Harvard University Press.

Oliveri, Maria Elena, Robert M. Mislevy, and Norbert Elliot. 2020. "After Admissions: What Comes Next in Higher Education?" In *Higher Education Admissions Practices: An International Perspective,* ed. Maria Elena Oliveri and Cathy Wendler, 347–75. Cambridge, UK: Cambridge University Press. https://doi:10.1017/9781108559607.019.

Poe, Mya, Asao B. Inoue, and Norbert Elliot, eds. 2018. *Writing Assessment, Social Justice, and the Advancement of Opportunity.* Fort Collins and Boulder: WAC Clearinghouse and University Press of Colorado.

Rachaels, James. 1986. *The Elements of Moral Philosophy.* Philadelphia: Temple University Press.

Rawls, John. 1999 [1971]. *A Theory of Justice.* 2nd ed. Cambridge, MA: Harvard University Press.

Schendel, Ellen, and Peggy O'Neill. 1999. "Exploring the Theories of Consequence of Self-Assessment through Ethical Inquiry." *Assessing Writing* 6 (2): 199–227. https://doi.org/10.1016/S1075-2935(00)00008-8.

Slomp, David. 2016. "An Integrated Design and Appraisal Framework for Ethical Writing Assessment." *Journal of Writing Assessment* 9 (2): 1–14. http://journalofwritingassessment.org/article.php?article=91.

Sparks, Jesse R., Yi Song, Wyman Brantley, and Ou Lydia Lou. 2014. *Assessing Written Communication in Higher Education: Review and Recommendations for Next-Generation Assessment.* ETS Research Report no. RR-14–37. Princeton, NJ: Educational Testing Service. http://dx.doi.org/10.1002/ets2.12035.

Sperber, Daniel. 1996. *Explaining Culture: A Naturalistic Approach.* Oxford, UK: Blackwell.

Suárez, Mauricio. 2004. "An Inferential Conception of Scientific Representation." *Philosophy of Science* 71 (5): 767–79. http://dx.doi.org/10.1086/421415.

White, Edward M., Norbert Elliot, and Irvin Peckham. 2015. *Very Like a Whale: The Assessment of Writing Programs.* Logan: Utah State University Press.

Winner, Langdon. 1980. "Do Artifacts Have Politics?" *Daedalus* 109 (1): 121–36.

Yancey, Kathleen Blake, Linda Robertson, and Kara Taczak. 2014. *Writing across Contexts: Transfer, Composition, and Sites of Writing.* Logan: Utah State University Press.

Zumbo, Bruno D. 2007. "Three Generations of Differential Item Functioning (DIF) Analyses: Considering Where It Has Been, Where It Is Now, and Where It Is Going." *Language Assessment Quarterly* 2: 223–33. http://dx.doi.org/10.1080/15434300701375832.

9

WRITING CENTER ETHICS AND THE PROBLEM OF "THE GOOD"

Michael A. Pemberton

Education is the art of making man ethical.

—Georg Hegel

Consider the following situation. The writing center at Big State U, a four-year state university, is staffed with five graduate student tutors and twelve undergraduate tutors from a variety of majors, though most of the tutors come from humanistic disciplines such as English and speech communication. The writing center is open only about six hours a day, five days a week, and students generally place a tremendous demand for tutorial assistance during those hours. Though most students can be accommodated sometime on the same day they contact the center for an appointment, during busy times of the semester they sometimes have to sign up for conferences two days in advance to be assured of getting a time slot. The center's budget is stretched thin, there are no more funds to hire additional tutors, and the writing center director must struggle with campus administrators annually to justify continued funding at the same level. The director is a non-tenured, though tenure-track, assistant professor in the English department, and the administrative duties of running a writing center have detracted somewhat from her ability to establish a strong publication record on a par with her peers in the department.

Into this writing center and this context comes a student with a paper. The student is twenty-five years old and working on his master's degree in civil engineering, and English is not his native language. The text he brings in is a draft of his master's thesis, a fifty-page document on "The Tensile Dynamics of T-Rod Supports in Suspension Bridges: A Computer Model," and nearly every page contains complex formulas and detailed charts. The paper is filled with handwritten notes, circles, and arrows,

DOI: 10.7330/9781607329978.c009

most of them suggestions and comments from the student's graduate adviser; on the last page is a note from the adviser berating the student for his poor grammar skills and demanding that he take the paper to the writing center for "repair." The student resents having to come to the center, saying it makes him feel "stupid," and he demands that the tutor proofread the paper and fix it for him. The conference is scheduled to last one hour.

What should the tutor do in a situation like this? What is the appropriate response? Should the tutor be accommodating? Should she be confrontational? Should she be manipulative? Should she cite writing center policy? Should she explain writing center goals?

Though these questions, on one level, address the immediate exigencies of tutorial work in a writing center—quick assessments of texts, of needs, of personalities and stress levels, of the appropriate tutorial pedagogy—they are also intrinsically *ethical* questions that require tutors to make complex and cognitively challenging judgments about what constitutes the most responsible course of action in a specific situation; further, they demand that tutors weigh in the balance a diverse assortment of overlapping contexts, desires, and institutional demands. As Ian McGreal (1970, 1) states, "Ethics is the attempt to abstract, clarify, and examine the ideas of good and evil, right and wrong, duty and obligation"; and tutoring decisions that call upon our senses of "good" outcomes, "right" behaviors, and professional "obligations" are all, in some sense, *de facto* ethical decisions.

If we use the hypothetical case above as an example, we can see how ethically convoluted even the most seemingly straightforward decisions can be in tutorial conferences. To begin with, the student's agenda for the conference—that the tutor must do the proofreading—must be addressed, and the response to this agenda will be inflected in part by any explicit *policies* for or against proofreading in the writing center. If there are formal guidelines that prevent tutors from proofreading student papers in conferences, then it may be the tutor's responsibility to ignore or finesse the student's stated wishes. Similarly, if the *instructional mission* of the writing center emphasizes the higher-order problems of discourse (e.g., organization, development, tone) over the lower-order matters (e.g., grammar, spelling, punctuation), then the tutor may feel an even greater sense of obligation to direct the conference away from the text-based, surface-level agenda the student came in with. On the other hand, if the paper's most significant problems seem to be at the level of surface features—problems with idioms, definite articles, or other English as a second language (ESL) markers—then the tutor might feel that some type of proofreading in the conference session would actually be the most helpful to the student, in spite of general dicta to the contrary.

The *instructor's comments* also make it fairly clear that grammatical issues are the teacher's primary concern for the next revision, so the tutor may feel compelled to help the student make the kinds of changes that might lead to a higher grade on the paper and give faculty the sense that the writing center is responding to their needs. Belinda Wood Droll (1993, 3) sees such instructor expectations as "a powerful third force in tutoring sessions" and makes the case that overlooking or ignoring the instructor's rhetorical emphases in a conference may actually hurt both the student and the writing center in the long run. Tutors must therefore weigh the consequences of subverting the explicit agendas put forth by instructor and student and determine whether the outcome of doing so will lead, on balance, to a preferable and therefore (according to some frameworks) a more ethical result. If the *director's status* in the university is tenuous and uncertain, she might be more willing to have her tutors remain flexible about proofreading policies in the interest of generating goodwill among faculty who might have some influence on future funding or tenure decisions. Each of the stakeholders in this interaction, then—instructor, student, tutor, and director—makes judgments about how the writing conference should best proceed, and they do so in ways that likely align with both their personal and professional ethics.

It seems evident, even from this brief example, that ethics—particularly ethics in the writing center—is an extraordinarily complex matter, and the few issues I've listed here represent only a portion of the many contexts and considerations that might influence a director's or a tutor's ethical decision-making process.

My purpose in this chapter is not simply to argue that ethical decision-making in writing centers is complicated but to reflect critically on what we *mean* when we talk about writing center ethics: How do we define ethical tutoring, and what are its features? What ethical philosophies undergird our understanding of "ethics"? What values do we embrace? What belief systems do we adopt? What goals do we pursue? What outcomes do we prize? And how might we make decisions if some of these values, beliefs, goals, and outcomes conflict? Further, if we are to understand what it means to conduct ourselves in an ethical manner while working with *students* on *texts* for *teachers* in *institutions*, then we must be fully aware of the ways in which all of these contexts and stakeholders (and their associated ethical perspectives) intersect and impact the work we do and the decisions we make.

This is no simple task, particularly when the complex web of social, institutional, and pedagogical interactions that affect a writing center's ethical positioning seems to argue against a universal or "one-size-fits-all" set of standards. In truth, few ethical principles exist that can be applied unilaterally to all writing centers (except for obvious and trivial ones, of course, like "tutors should not verbally abuse students or belittle student writing in conferences"), but this probably says more about the diverse nature of writing centers than it does about the constitution or validity of their ethics. To paraphrase a statement once made about Writing Across the Curriculum (WAC) programs, "there are as many different *kinds* of writing centers as there are writing centers," so it should come as no real surprise that writing center ethics is likely to reflect this diversity as well.

But given these innate complexities, how might tutors and directors think productively about ethics in the writing center? Writing center scholars have certainly written about a variety of ethical issues over the last forty years, sometimes focusing on how to resolve specific, particularly vexing ethical problems (Pemberton 1993–99) and sometimes grappling with accusations that writing centers are by their very nature unethical because the collaborative pedagogies they employ will likely lead to inappropriate levels of help, plagiarism, and academic dishonesty (Behm 1989; Clark 1988; Clark and Healy 1996). Other researchers have considered the ethical dimensions of working with nontraditional students (Gardner 2002), the ethics of social justice advocacy in the writing center (Greenfield and Rowan 2011; Grimm 1999; Pemberton 2006), the degree to which our natural empathy for students might compromise our professional ethics (Hoskins 2007), and the ethics of working with multilingual writers (Olson 2013). Still, relatively few of these pieces have considered writing center ethics from the perspective of ethical philosophy (notable exceptions being Trachsel 1995 and Duffy 2012), so it seems useful, then, to consider how these philosophies have defined and discussed the term *ethics* and how those definitions might inform our understanding of ethics in a writing center context. In the following sections, I will briefly discuss some tenets of ethical philosophy related to the problem of identifying the most ethical course of action in specific situations and then consider how we might apply some of these ethical principles to writing centers.

DEFINING "ETHICS"

In the Western canon, the study of ethics might be said to begin with Plato's dialogues *Gorgias* and *Philebus* and Aristotle's *Nicomachean Ethics*

(1934). Plato's primary interest in *Gorgias* and *Philebus* was a characterization of "the good" and a determination of its principal features. In both dialogues, Plato explores whether "good" is synonymous with "pleasure" (as Socrates's interlocutors claim), whether it is more closely related to "wisdom," or whether it is some other abstract quality connected to both. Aristotle investigates "the good" as well, though his approach—perhaps unsurprisingly—evidences a distinctly different style, tone, and analysis of the problem than Plato's. In the *Nicomachean Ethics*, Aristotle does admit that there may indeed be some ideal quality of goodness (the "Supreme Good") that may be equivalent to "happiness" or "the virtuous life," but he nevertheless realizes that "goodness" is not a concept that is easily defined or realized:

> We may now return to the Good . . . and try to find out what exactly it can be. For good appears to be one thing in one pursuit or art and another in another: it is different in medicine from what it is in strategy, and so on with the rest of the arts. What definition of the Good then will hold true in all the arts? (1934, ch. 7, sec. 1)

The shared themes in the works of both Plato and Aristotle—good, bad, right, wrong, duty, responsibility, moral behavior, and immoral conduct—comprise the core topics, the tropes of ethics and ethical philosophy. William Lillie (1961) notes that ethics is a distinctly social phenomenon as well. "Ethics," he says, "has been defined as the normative science of conduct, and conduct is a collective name for voluntary actions" (Lillie 1961, 3). Societal norms determine what constitutes "good conduct," and these norms are constructed "voluntarily" (that is, as an expression of free will and free choice among a variety of options) rather than involuntarily as the result of an authoritative mandate. "Right" and "wrong" may be abstract qualities, but they have concrete social consequences in their effects on collective behavior and individual actions. Some behaviors are held up for approbation, others are not, and people are generally expected to conform to the consensual norms. The act of murder, for example, is generally considered to be a "wrong," a violation of the socially enacted moral principles that allow people to live together in relative harmony; and criminal penalties—themselves constructed with reference to socially determined hierarchies of transgressive behavior—exist to punish those who violate these principles. In the more specialized context of the writing center, the forces of social approbation and scorn operate in like fashion to codify the "norms" of tutoring. Some behaviors, such as writing students' papers for them or ridiculing student texts in conferences, are disapproved of, while other behaviors, such as active listening and using non-directive questioning strategies, are strongly encouraged.

But neither of these principles or sets of behavior can be claimed as absolutes, independent of contextual considerations. Under some circumstances—such as in the case of war or self-defense—killing can be excused by society at large in the name of some "higher" moral principle, and in some situations tutors may find good reasons to generate some of the original writing in student texts or be more directive in conferences with some students than they would normally be with others.

But if ethics—in most cases, if not all—is relative and situational, if it depends on an accurate and measured analysis of all possible contexts, strategies, and outcomes, then what becomes of "the good"? How is it to be determined? What is the relationship between relative degrees of "goodness" and context, and how can this relationship be employed to construct an ethics for a writing center? The task of answering these questions may seem insurmountable at first. As Ian McGreal (1970, 15) puts it, "No area within ethics is more likely to challenge the critical thinker than that problem area we have entitled 'The Problem of the Good.'"

ETHICAL THEORIES AND "THE GOOD"

One way to understand ethical systems that might be applicable to writing centers, though, is to categorize them in terms of the ethical standard they uphold, the overarching ethical principle in a given philosophy of moral conduct that can be used to adjudicate relative degrees of "goodness" across contexts and argue for an appropriate set of behaviors. Though it is certainly true that no ethical philosophy (or philosopher) can be adequately described in terms of a single standard or core principle, a number of ethicists such as William Lillie (1961), John Stuart Mackenzie (1901), and others have found this method of categorization useful as a rich starting point to see some of the ways ethical philosophies clash, contrast, and overlap. Lillie's (1961) discussion of ethical standards is particularly useful for this purpose, and it is also useful as a framework for discussing important aspects of ethical decision-making in a writing center context. Lillie's schema collapses the moral/ethical standards embraced by dozens of philosophers into five core categories, and though this number may at first seem surprisingly small, other ethicists (e.g., Mackenzie) have employed a similar set of categories when discussing ethical standards. In brief, the standards Lillie identifies are: Intuition, Law, Pleasure, Evolution/Perfection, and Value.

Lillie (1961) attributes the standard of "intuition" to the philosophies of Shaftesbury, Hutcheson, and Butler; and it is in essence an argument for moral innateness. Human beings are, according to this perspective, born with a fundamental, intuitive understanding of right and wrong, and they can appeal to this inborn sense to determine the proper solutions to ethical problems. This perspective is closely related to "virtue ethics," though virtue ethics recognizes that community values and social norms also contribute to our innate sense of what constitutes virtuous behavior (Duffy 2012).

The standard of intuition stands in notable contrast to the standard of "law," however, which maintains that there are certain indisputable, law-like principles—not innate in the human psyche but discernible by objective observers—that can be used to assess the ethical value of a given behavior. Some philosophers, like Samuel Clarke (*Discourse of Natural Religion*), look to "natural law" (viewing nature and natural phenomena as exemplars of God's will) as the basis for moral standards, while others like Kant (*The Metaphysics of Morals*) turn to the laws of reason and logic as the ultimate arbiters of morality.

The standard of "pleasure," like law, has been interpreted in a variety of ways, from a kind of unrestrained individualism (egoistic hedonism) to a view that people should always try to achieve "the greatest good for the greatest number" (utilitarianism). The central question for many philosophers is, of course, 'What is pleasure,' and the answers they propose range from pleasurable physical sensations to intellectual satisfaction to the fulfillment of an abstract goal.

The standard of "evolution" or "perfection" advances the general principle that human beings should work toward their own ethical self-realization. Herbert Spencer (*The Principles of Ethics*) maintained that life consists of a protracted series of adjustments based on consequences. We are faced with ethical problems, we try out solutions, we judge the results of our solutions, and we adjust our ethics depending on whether or not we feel the outcomes were beneficial. In this way, our ethical systems evolve over time, gradually becoming better and better.

The final standard in this taxonomic system, the standard of "value," is in some ways as abstract and amorphous as the concept "good" and is subject to the same diversity of interpretation. What exactly is "value," and how does one measure it? According to Lillie (1961), philosophers have assessed value on the basis of either *intrinsic* worth (innate qualities) or *extrinsic* worth (that is, its usefulness, consequences, or teleology). In his *Principia Ethica*, for example, George Edward Moore (1903) makes a case for the intrinsic goodness of some things like "beautiful objects" or "the pleasure of human intercourse," while an example of extrinsic value might be "helping others in time of need [resulting in] these people's needs being satisfied, or their experiencing pleasure, to which helping them is related in some causal way" (Zimmerman 2014).

ETHICAL STANDARDS AND WRITING CENTERS

So what implications, then, do these ethical frameworks hold for writing centers? How might these standards apply to tutors or directors or conferences, and how might they inform the construction of a writing center ethics? We can certainly see how the ethical standards referred to in each of the above theories might explain—or at least provide one explanation for—certain aspects of writing center practice. Tutors in a writing center, for example, will be guided by their intuitions and motivated by their consciences in conferences, however we might choose to construct either of those terms. Their intuitional impulses, whether the result of a biological imperative or a socially constructed behavioral schema, cannot help but shape their activities when working with students. Tutors, for the most part, tutor in the spirit of benevolence, out of a sincere desire to help students improve their writing; and they conduct themselves in a kind, civil, and sympathetic manner as well. In this regard, they enact the principles of mindfulness advocated by Paula Mathieu (this volume) and relational ethics, which Rasha Diab (this volume) argues is a critical component of ethical interaction.

Yet we can also see that the standard of law pervades much of what goes on in the writing center and in tutorials. Writing center theory and research—derived in principle from the empirical foundations of "natural law" and the studied observation of activities in tutoring conferences and their effects—has a tremendous impact on pedagogy and policy. Writing scholarship informs practice and helps tutors understand what works and what doesn't in tutorials. Interactions between tutors and students are studied in multiple ways using a variety of research strategies, and reasoned conclusions about those interactions are drawn from the resulting data. These conclusions, in turn, are used to shape tutor training and to suggest particular teaching strategies for particular situations. If a given tutorial practice has been shown by research to be ineffective, then it would be unethical to continue using that practice (unless a tutor believes the research is flawed or that the practice she chooses to pursue will lead to a "good" that she prizes more highly). In the same fashion, we can see that a different kind of law—composed of the rules, regulations, traditions, and mandates attached to a specific institution—also affects writing center ethics. Some policies such as hiring regulations and reporting requirements may be imposed upon writing centers and tutors by agencies outside the center itself. These policies certainly have the force of law, and they can impact a writing center's ethics in significant ways.

"Pleasure" touches both the affective and the cognitive ethics of a writing center. We want students to feel good about their writing, and much of what we do in conferences is point out student strengths and indicate what we like about what they've written. By doing so, we help the student feel good, and this makes us feel good as well. But we also recognize that the value of this "good feeling" can extend beyond the immediate pleasure of the moment. It has useful, practical value as well. By helping students believe in themselves and their writing abilities, we can help them overcome their fear, their tentativeness, and their writing blocks; and we also enhance their sense of self-efficacy, which has proven, beneficial effects on their writing and learning. These seem to be reasonable goals for a writing center, and most people would probably agree that achieving them would qualify as an ethical "good." On a purely utilitarian level as well, much of writing center practice and virtually all of its day-to-day operating policies (e.g., length of conferences, frequency of visits) are guided by the spirit of pragmatism and a controlling desire to provide "the greatest service to the greatest number" (within the restrictions of its operating budget). Ethical decisions about the optimum conference time/student ratio will ultimately be based in assessments of relative utility and how to garner the greatest amount of total "happiness."

"Evolution" and "perfection" are in some ways at the heart of a writing center's instructional mission. Writing centers exist in part to intervene in and support student writing processes. We work with students and texts as they develop over time. Tutors want to teach students how to become better writers, and one of the ethical criteria we can use to measure what we do is our effectiveness in helping students realize this end. Are the students evolving as writers—becoming better and more capable as a result of our tutorial conferences? And are texts moving toward "perfection"? Admittedly, it makes no sense to talk about a text ever becoming literally "perfect," nor should the achievement of that unrealistic goal be considered the only true measure of success in a conference. Yet tutors (and students) cannot help but construct an abstracted image of the "ideal paper" or the "ideal writer" in their minds, for whatever paper they happen to be working on in whatever genre, and they often use this as a goal to work toward in conferences and to guide the operation of their writing processes. Similarly, tutors' growth as tutors, whether through the acquisition of knowledge and skills relevant to writing (see Porter's discussion of *techne*, this volume) or the development of context-specific strategies for ethical decision-making (see Duffy's discussion of *phronesis*, this volume), must also be considered an ethical good in an evolutionary framework.

Perceptions of "value," as indicated earlier, can also influence a writing center's ethics, though perhaps in a less obvious or significant way than some of the other standards. I think most writing center personnel, for example, have a sense that writing centers are innately ethical, that a writing center's value is embodied in the very activities that go on there, independent of any externally imposed standard or criterion or set of consequences. If we accept G. E. Moore's example of "the pleasure of human intercourse" as an instance of innate goodness and if we tie it to other pleasing "organic wholes," such as the emergent discourse in a student text, the teaching and learning relationship enacted in a tutorial conference, and the reciprocal cognitive benefits of working collaboratively to solve a perplexing textual problem, then the standard of value can also help us to see and understand the ethical worth of what we do.

Each of the ethical theories described here—or, more accurately, each of the ethical standards that underlie the ethical theories described here—can be brought to bear on writing centers, then, and used to explore (or justify) some of the practices that take place within them. Yet opting to embrace any single set of ethical principles in this list seems insufficient to a full elaboration or understanding of a writing center ethics. For one thing, each of these theories taken individually says little about either the particular ethical problems that face writing centers or the multiple contexts and conflicting ethical agendas writing centers (and tutors) often have to face. In idealized circumstances, it might be possible to say that the standard of natural law should reign supreme in writing center ethics, that rational thought, logical deduction, and empirical research should determine how to act ethically in tutorial conferences. But tutorial conferences are rarely so easily constructed or described that empirical approaches alone can point to adequate solutions. When a student like the one described in the opening example comes into the writing center—a student with his own individual set of language difficulties, emotional responses, and cultural and educational contexts—existing research is likely to offer only limited help, and logical deduction will find itself hard-pressed to account for the innumerable social and personal factors that make this student and this conference unique.

RESPONSIBILITY, CONTEXT, AND SITUATIONAL ETHICS

If writing center tutors accept the notion that it is their responsibility to act ethically in tutorial conferences, then they will have to decide on a regular basis what ethical conduct is. Though, as discussed above, some ethical theories provide general principles and standards for determining ethical behavior, in real-life situations, those standards are often not so easily applied. A tutor's perceptions of "value" may not be shared by others, what "pleases" a student or a tutor in the short term may not be beneficial to that student's long-term development as a writer, and a tutor's predictions about the consequences of her tutorial approach can never be 100 percent certain. But even though ethical decision-making is a fraught endeavor even in the best of circumstances, as Moore (1903, §91) asserts, "there still remains a humbler task which may be possible for Practical Ethics. Although we cannot hope to discover which, in a given situation, is the best of all possible alternative actions, there may be some possibility of shewing which among the alternatives, likely to occur to any one, will produce the greatest sum of good."

We can, in other words, make educated guesses about how best to proceed, even if those guesses might sometimes lead to unforeseen or undesirable consequences. By doing so, we will fulfill our duty—to the extent humanly possible—to behave in an ethical manner, and this is probably the best we can ever hope for. Even so, if we accept Moore's assessment at face value, writing centers are still left with the troubling questions of how to distinguish the features of the "given situation" he refers to and how to determine what might comprise the "greatest sum of good," especially when that good must be negotiated among the multiple ethical frameworks that often intersect in writing center tutorials.

Writing center tutors face these dilemmas on a daily basis. What is the most urgent textual problem to address in a conference? What would be most useful for the student? What would be the most useful for the paper? What can be covered satisfactorily in the time available? How should tutors proceed if their perception of the "best" plan for the conference violates general writing center or administrative guidelines? Is it even possible to talk about being "ethical" in a writing center conference when tutors are faced with so many competing "ethical" agendas?

According to John Dewey, it is indeed possible to be ethical in such circumstances; in fact, Dewey believes ethical conflicts such as these are the norm rather than the exception:

> Conduct as moral may thus be defined as *activity called forth and directed by ideas of value or worth, where the values concerned are so mutually incompatible*

as to require consideration and selection before an overt action is entered upon.
(Dewey and Tufts 1913, 209, original emphasis)

The science of applying ethical principles and theories to particular circumstances is called *casuistry,* and it is one of the central methodologies of situational ethics. Charles Eugene Conover's (1967, 48–49, 51) reflections on situational ethics define the philosophy's basic principles concisely, and in doing so, he also describes, unintentionally yet quite poignantly, the real-life experience of tutoring in a writing center:

> In situational ethics, the persons involved are expected to take a social point of view in the search for solutions to their problems. This interpretation of morality finds its focus in the give-and-take of human life. Our problems, our temptations, our opportunities to add to the good and evil that mark our common life arise in the changing situations within which we must choose and act . . .
>
> Human experience is "interactional"; the individual experiences the qualities of changing contexts of objects and events. Situations are of many kinds—threatening, embarrassing, joyful, satisfying. Reflection and decision are called for when the situation is "problematic," the outcome uncertain, and the solution not obvious . . . Ethical problems arise in the changing contexts of persons and events within which we live. We make our choices and act—for better or worse—in situations.

Threatening, embarrassing, joyful, and satisfying situations; the interactional experience of human life; solutions that are not often obvious; the special characteristics and distinctive needs of the students we see . . . These are certainly features that are common to many kinds of teaching, but they seem especially evocative of the close, personal, dynamic, and collaborative teaching that takes place in writing centers. Writing conferences are deeply immersed in the full range of "changing contexts of persons and events" that can be brought to any teaching situation, and ethical responses to problematic situations in the writing center must demonstrate an awareness of those contexts, events, and influences. Though different writing centers and different individuals may construct their ethics in different ways, it is important as a matter of critical self-reflection that they understand the principles that undergird their ethical decisions and the relative value they place on the possible outcomes of their actions.

FINDING ETHICAL PATHWAYS IN THE WRITING CENTER

So let me return to the example described at the beginning of this chapter, a somewhat annoyed student coming into a busy writing center with a long paper whose subject matter is unfamiliar to the tutor. Depending on the ethical principles most valued (or the needs most quickly identified) by the tutor, the course of the conference could follow very different tracks—each equally ethical in the sense that it relies on the application of ethical principles to determine what will accomplish the most "good"—but resulting in distinctly different outcomes for the conference, the paper, and the student. Lillie's framework can be particularly useful here as a means of identifying the varying (and multiple) ethical standards that can affect a tutor's ethical decision-making process.

For example, the tutor might establish a social and interactive context for the conference by beginning with introductions and a bit of small talk, gathering information about the assignment and the class. This establishes the tutor's benevolence and willingness to help (intuition) and also enacts a tutorial strategy that tries to equalize power differentials in the conference, an approach that is sanctioned by the community of writing center professionals and supported by empirical research (law). Because the paper is fifty pages in length and the conference time is short, she asks the student to summarize the document briefly and also asks what section of the paper the student would like to work on. The student resists this approach, in part because he is uncomfortable about his level of English fluency (speaking will lead to embarrassment and a decrease in pleasure) and in part because he wants to address his instructor's grammar concerns first (law/pleasure/perfection). The tutor ultimately decides that it is important and ethical to respect the student's agenda, especially given the level of discomfort and anxiety he displays, and to ensure his satisfaction with the conference overall (intuition/pleasure). Though in some respects this approach violates the dominant pedagogical model for writing conferences (law), the tutor believes several other beneficial outcomes will be achieved, leading to a greater overall good: the student will continue to see the tutor as someone who respects him and his goals (intuition), he will likely be satisfied with the conference (pleasure), he will learn more about English grammar and syntax (evolution), and he will be more willing to return to the writing center for help with other projects (evolution).

In another conference, the tutor might decide to take an entirely different approach with this student but still marshal a core set of ethical principles in support of her course of action. After beginning with small talk and focused questions about the topic and rhetorical situation, the tutor determines that despite the student's preference, the session should be focused largely, if not entirely, on rhetorical and organizational concerns; it will be more beneficial and ultimately more ethical to insist that most of the conference be spent focusing on those matters in a single troublesome section of the text the student identifies. This may require an explanation from the tutor about the center's policies against proofreading (law) as well as some friendly advice about how important it is to have strong arguments, good evidence, and a well-organized paper (law/evolution). The tutor also makes clear that this approach will make the student a better writer overall (evolution) and that she thinks this would be the best way to make his entire paper stronger (intuition/value) and his professor happier (pleasure). Though the student may remain skeptical and have some concerns about not responding to all the professor's comments in the conference, the tutor is certain that the student will be satisfied with the outcome (pleasure) and be motivated to make future writing center appointments in which other parts of the paper can be discussed (evolution).

Two tutors, two decisions about what constitutes an appropriate, ethical structure for the conference. Is one approach superior to the other? That depends, as I've argued here, on how one chooses to define "the good," but ultimately I would argue that the question of superiority is, if not largely inconsequential, certainly less important than the process of ethical decision-making itself. By encouraging tutors to be self-aware and reflective, helping them analyze and articulate their own ethics of tutoring, and emphasizing how the "best" or the most ethical approach to take in a conference session will almost always be inflected by context and circumstance, then we fulfill some of the most important goals of writing center ethics overall: critical awareness, thoughtful and supportive tutoring, goodwill toward others, and a commitment to learning and personal growth. If writing center ethics could be said to have any universal principles, I suspect these would be among them.

REFERENCES

Aristotle. 1934. *Nicomachean Ethics.* Aristotle in 23 volumes, vol. 19. Trans. Harris Rackham. Cambridge, MA: Harvard University Press. www.perseus.tufts.edu/hopper/text?doc= Perseus:text:1999.01.0054.

Behm, Richard. 1989. "Ethical Issues in Peer Tutoring: A Defense of Collaborative Learning." *Writing Center Journal* 10 (1): 3–12.

Clark, Irene Lurkis. 1988. "Collaboration and Ethics in Writing Center Pedagogy." *Writing Center Journal* 9 (1): 3–12.

Clark, Irene L., and Dave Healy. 1996. "Are Writing Centers Ethical?" *WPA: Writing Program Administration* 20 (1–2): 32–48.

Clarke, Samuel. 1969. "A Discourse of Natural Religion." In *British Moralists: 1650-1800,* vol. 1, ed. David D. Raphael, 191–225. Oxford: Clarendon.

Conover, Charles Eugene. 1967. *Personal Ethics in an Impersonal World.* Philadelphia: Westminster.

Dewey, John, and James H. Tufts. 1913. *Ethics.* New York: Henry Holt.

Droll, Belinda Wood. 1993. "Teacher Expectations: A Powerful Third Force in Tutoring Sessions." *Writing Lab Newsletter* 17 (9): 1–5.

Duffy, John. 2012. "Virtues of Conversation: Ethics in the Writing Center." *Another Word: From the Writing Center at the University of Wisconsin-Madison.* writing.wisc.edu/blog/virtues of-conversation-ethics-in-the-writing-center/.

Greenfield, Laura, and Karen Rowan, eds. 2011. *Writing Centers and the New Racism: A Call for Sustainable Dialogue and Change.* Boulder: University Press of Colorado.

Grimm, Nancy Maloney. 1999. *Good Intentions: Writing Center Work for Postmodern Times.* Portsmouth, NH: Boynton/Cook.

Hoskins, Betty. 2007. "Ethics and Empathy in the Writing Center." *College English Association Forum* 36 (1). files.eric.ed.gov/fulltext/EJ1097334.pdf.

Kant, Emmanuel. 1996. *The Metaphysics of Morals.* Trans. Mary J. Gregor. Cambridge, UK: Cambridge University Press.

Lillie, William. 1961. *An Introduction to Ethics.* London: Methuen.

Mackenzie, John Stuart. 1901. *A Manual of Ethics.* New York: Hinds and Noble.

McGreal, Ian. 1970. *Problems of Ethics.* San Francisco: Chandler.

Moore, George Edward. 1903. *Principia Ethica.* Cambridge, UK: Cambridge University Press. http://fair-use.org/g-e-moore/principia-ethica/.

Olson, Bobbi. 2013. "Rethinking Our Work with Multilingual Writers: The Ethics and Responsibility of Language Teaching in the Writing Center." *Praxis: A Writing Center Journal* 10 (2). www.praxisuwc.com/olson-102.

Pemberton, Michael A. 1993–99. "Writing Center Ethics." *Writing Lab Newsletter* 17 (5)–24 (1) (columns).

Pemberton, Michael A. 2006. "Critique or Conformity? Ethics and Advocacy in the Writing Center." In *The Writing Center Director's Resource Book,* ed. Christina Murphy and Byron Stay, 261–69. New York: Routledge.

Plato. 1987. *Gorgias.* Trans. Donald J. Zeyl. Indianapolis: Hackett.

Plato. 2019. *Philebus.* Trans. James L. Wood. Peterborough, ON: Broadview.

Spencer, Herbert. 2012. *The Principles of Ethics.* Auburn, AL: Ludwig von Mises Institute.

Trachsel, Mary. 1995. "Nurturant Ethics and Academic Ideals: Convergence in the Writing Center." *Writing Center Journal* 16 (1): 24–45.

Zimmerman, Michael J. 2014. "Intrinsic vs. Extrinsic Value." *Stanford Encyclopedia of Philosophy.* plato.stanford.edu/entries/value-intrinsic-extrinsic/.

10

WHERE ETHICS DWELLS
Ethical Writing in the Disciplines

Vicki Tolar Burton

Michael Hyde (2004) notes a meaning of ethos that pre-dates its meaning as "moral character" and "ethics." Rather, he says, "the *ethos* of rhetoric" refers to "the way discourse is used to transform space and time into 'dwelling places' (*ethos*; pl. *ethea*) where people can deliberate about and 'know together' (*con-scientia*) some matter of interest. Such dwelling places define the grounds, the abodes or habitats, where a person's ethics and moral character take form and develop" (Hyde 2004, xiii).

Expanding on this rooting of ethics and ethos in the notion of dwelling place, this chapter examines the concept of disciplinary discourse as a dwelling place of disciplinary ethics: a location where members of a discipline dwell together to work out the understandings and knowledge of the field, a habitat where students' ethics and moral character as members of the field develop. The academic disciplines are literally the places where our students go when they leave our composition classes, the places where their professional character (ethos) and knowledge develop and where they learn to write as ethical citizens of their field. It is true that college writers briefly abide in first-year composition (now frequently located in the high school classroom) and lightly touch down in general education classrooms, but for most college writers, their first true dwelling place is the major, the suite of courses that build, expand, and define their academic identities as undergraduates.

How students can learn the rhetorical ethics of writing in their major is the focus of this chapter. After situating ethics and Writing in the Disciplines within a scholarly and historical context, I turn to Michael Carter's (2007) theory of the disciplines as constituted by their distinctive ways of knowing, doing, and writing. Extending Carter's idea of metagenres, I argue that one way to understand the rhetorical ethics of a discipline is through the ethics implicit in that discipline's written genres. As James E. Porter (1998, original emphasis) maintains, "Ethics

DOI: 10.7330/9781607329978.c010

pertains to a *process of inquiry* by which we determine what is right, just, or desirable in any given case." Further, "Ethics pertains to the *subjectivities of writers and readers*" as they enact their character, their ethos, "through the process of writing and reading" (Porter 1998, 29, original emphasis). For writers in the disciplines, rhetorical ethics develops through disciplinary discourse.

LOCATING RHETORICAL ETHICS IN THE WAC/WID MOVEMENT

One route to understanding disciplinary discourse is through the curricular reform movement known as Writing Across the Curriculum (WAC), of which Writing in the Disciplines (WID) is a part. According to Chris Thaiss and Tara Porter, WAC has impacted the teaching of writing at 55 percent to 65 percent of higher education campuses in the United States. While 42 percent of programs are more than ten years old, indicating program stability, nearly two-thirds of programs that were operating in 1987 no longer exist. (Thaiss and Porter 2010, 541–42). The fact that WAC programs commonly come and go, start and stop and start again, often has locally idiosyncratic contexts, but it also may signal resistance from faculty in the disciplines who do not want—or do not feel qualified—to teach writing, as well as the reluctance of institutions to fund WAC programs in preference to the next shiny educational thing. WAC has also suffered "friendly fire" from colleagues in English and writing studies, some of whom have implied that WAC/WID pedagogy is less ethical than pedagogy in their own specializations.

For example, Kurt Spellmeyer (1989) famously argued against a WAC model for first-year writing. Targeting by name such notable scholars as Charles Bazerman, Patricia Bizzell, and Elaine Maimon, Spellmeyer argued for the value of the personal essay in first-year writing. His primary supporting evidence consisted of excerpts from two student essays: one a dry student summary of a sociology article on suicide among young people, the other a graceful freshman essay placing an analysis of Sartre in the context of the illness of the writer's pet rat. Heartened by the ethical implications of the Sartre essay, Spellmeyer (1989, 270) offered a dark vision of student writing in a WAC context, saying he "suspect[s]" that "the prevailing tradition of discipline-specific writing instruction encourages both conformity and submission" by presenting a monologic discourse model, with no sense of Bakhtinian "heteroglossia" and little sense that writing occurs in context. Not only do those with a WAC approach teach "submission" to a single way of writing, he claimed, but by "reifying the prevailing configuration of knowledge, by accepting this configuration as a fait accompli and supporting the narrow vocationalism which has created it, proponents of discipline-specific writing may . . . discourage these same science majors from thinking that might culminate in necessary social change" (Spellmeyer 1989, 269). He further charged, without evidence, that those who teach Writing in the Disciplines fail to teach the values of those disciplines (Spellmeyer 1989, 269).

Spellmeyer's narrow view that students learning writing in their discipline have no sense of the context of their writing within and beyond their discipline seems mistaken, for, as Bazerman and others suggest, Writing in the Disciplines is largely focused on understanding the rhetorical foundation of contexts and audiences for one's writing—key for ethical writing. However, Spellmeyer's point about the need for students to be *taught* the values of the discipline as well as the content is valid. More specifically, there is a need to teach the rhetorical ethics implied by the discourse forms and practices of the discipline the student is entering, just as there is a need to teach the broad concept of rhetorical ethics of writing in a general first-year composition classroom.

Attention given to ethics in the teaching of writing has a long history in the field of composition/writing studies and in the history of rhetoric and has recently been re-theorized by scholars such as John Duffy and James Porter. Duffy (2017) has argued persuasively for using an Aristotelian model of *virtue ethics* in the composition classroom as a way of teaching students to make ethical rhetorical choices. Duffy distinguishes virtue ethics from an ethics of rules (deontology), an ethics of consequences (Kantian), and a postmodern ethics that emphasizes finding the right thing to do in the context of a specific moment. A pedagogy of virtue ethics encourages taking a stand for justice and flourishes with the use of exemplars (Duffy 2017, 240–46). However, while virtue ethics may be a good fit for first-year writing, it might be a harder sell to WID faculty—folks who are looking for practical wisdom (*phronesis*), something they can implement with ease within their already content-heavy curriculum and, frankly, something that does not sound like theory from another (Aristotelian) world.

Beyond the realm of first-year writing, James E. Porter (1998, 50) explores the possibility of a postmodern rhetorical ethics, "grounded in fluctuating criteria, in difference, or in community or local practices." Porter frames a postmodern theory of ethical praxis for inter-networked communication based on three principles: (1) respecting audiences/respecting differences, (2) exercising care for audience/care for the concrete (i.e., specific) other, and (3) not oppressing/doing no harm.

These principles are enacted through procedural strategies that include consulting with diverse sources, attending to the local as one situates and contextualizes an ethical decision, and acknowledging ethical complexities and ambiguities (Porter 1998, 143–62). Porter is especially interested in how postmodern rhetorical ethics applies to and affects networked writing.

Duffy's virtue ethics and Porter's postmodern ethics for the online environment have helped place the subject of rhetorical ethics on composition studies' scholarly table, but neither seems quite to align with the challenges of teaching rhetorical ethics in the disciplines. Looking further afield, I find hints of alignment with the early Sophists, especially as interpreted by Susan Jarratt (1991). Jarratt seeks to reclaim the Sophists from centuries of criticism based on Plato's and Aristotle's negative views of them. Drawing from Eric Havelock, Jarratt points us to the Sophist Protagoras, who "explains how group values evolve out of custom or habit as 'pragmatic solutions to temporal and historical needs'" (Havelock 1957, quoted in Jarratt 1991, 10). This reference to "group values" is echoed eons later in the formation of academic disciplines.

In fact, Jarratt (1991, 96) argues, Sophistic ethics flow from their epistemology, "their insistence on the relativity of meaning and, consequently, value . . . questions of value must be referred to subjective perception and the historical and geographical specificity of local custom." Jarratt (1991, 96) notes that "the formation of ethical norms within communities" takes the Sophists beyond the accused relativism "to a discourse about enlightened self-interest based in the notion of 'self' as constituted by the community," such as a disciplinary community college students are joining in their major. Jarratt (1991, 97) notes that the Sophists, much like sociologists of knowledge, "anticipate writing-across-the-curriculum programs, which have the potential to provide critical perspectives from outside disciplinary frames of reference."

WAC/WID programs have provided outside perspectives by introducing teachers in the disciplines to such important elements of composing as process writing with its emphasis on invention and revision, rhetorical considerations of audience and purpose, and authentic writing assessment, among others. The ethics of Writing in the Disciplines, however, has not been a routine topic for WAC/WID faculty development, nor has it received much attention in WAC/WID scholarship. How do we initiate this important conversation?

As a possible method for understanding where disciplinary ethics dwells and opening the rhetorical ethics conversation with disciplinary faculty, I suggest extending the frame Michael Carter (2007) constructs in his Braddock Award–winning essay, "Ways of Knowing, Doing, and Writing in the Disciplines." Using evidence gathered from faculty at his own land-grant university, Carter argues, along with Charles Bazerman and James Paradis (1991) and others, that academic disciplines are socially constructed; that ways of knowing, doing, and writing in a discipline are linked; and that disciplinary faculty can come to understand and articulate this to students. Carter (2007, 394–403) suggests a system of four metagenres under which most disciplinary ways of knowing, doing, and writing will reside: academic situations that call for empirical inquiry, situations that call for problem solving, situations that call for research from sources, and situations that call for performance. I will explore the possibility that the ethics of a field dwells in doing, knowing, and writing in the discipline through these metagenres and that for college students these disciplinary dwelling places are "the abodes or habitats where a person's ethics and moral character take form and develop" (Hyde 2004, xii).

EMPIRICAL INQUIRY AND ETHICAL WRITING

I begin this pursuit of rhetorical ethics with the metagenre Carter (2007, 396–97) calls "Responses to Academic Situations That Call for Empirical Inquiry," which includes the sciences and the laboratory experience (a way of doing), through which students learn the tasks of forming research questions, forming a hypothesis, gathering data, using a particular method with which to test the hypothesis, analyzing results, and drawing conclusions about the research questions and hypothesis based on the results. Empirical inquiry pertains to many disciplines in STEM fields, as well as to some social sciences, for example, to political scientists who gather survey data and report and interpret results.

Science students learn the ways of doing in science in part through laboratory experiences and through written genres like the laboratory report, as well as an earlier genre through which social actions and the accountability of science occur even before the lab report: the lab notebook. Through the lab notebook, students learn not only the conventions but also the ethics of recording and tracking empirical results.

A comparison of the lab notebook instructions from three universities reveals that institutions may emphasize different values through assignment design for the notebook. The lab notebook instructions for experimental biosciences at Rice University (n.d.) begin with the observation that few students and even few researchers record enough information in the lab notebook. Not only are students urged to record everything, but the protocol for the notebook itself is prescribed in detail. Genre ethics requires writers to follow certain conventions/rules of the genre. Every page must be numbered in a certain spot, dated, and covered completely with data. Any blank sections of the page should be marked out with a diagonal line. Students must use ink, and mistakes can be noted by drawing a single line through the error, but nothing can be erased or blanked out with correction fluid. An honest account of the complete laboratory experience along with all procedures and observations must be recorded. If any change in protocol occurs, that must also be recorded. It is unethical to go back into the lab notebook and make changes later. The process and findings must be recorded clearly and honestly in real time. After a description of the notebook that seems centered on student learning, the Rice (n.d.) document justification for all the strict guidelines for the lab notebook is that "it is a legally valid record that preserves your rights or those of an employer or academic investigator to your discoveries. A comprehensive notebook permits one to reproduce any part of a methodology completely and accurately." So at Rice University, the ethics of the notebook relates to reproducible results and intellectual property.

Similarly, the lab notebook guidelines for students in mechanical engineering at Massachusetts Institute of Technology (Hunter and Hughey 2007) opens with a brief rationale for the notebook based on student learning ("establish good habits that will serve you throughout your career"), but the rationale is then dominated by a discussion of the engineer's notebook being key legal evidence of owning intellectual property when applying for or defending a patent. The lab notebook is quickly linked to other genres like the disclosure report (the first step in applying for a patent). The specific requirements for the notebook are presented in a colorful checklist that includes the admonition that after each lab, "you must have your lab notebook signed by Dr. Hughey or your lab professor before you leave lab each day. Any pages not signed on the day the experiment was performed will adversely affect your lab notebook grade" (Hunter and Hughey 2007). These mechanical engineers appear to be joining a regimented discipline in which they will be expected daily to meet high legal standards, an ethics based on strict rules and enforcement.

The lab notebook instructions from these two universities convey different values. The Rice University instructions seem learning-centered and clearly try to prepare students to join the disciplines of experimental biosciences. The audience to whom students are ethically responsible is other scientists, with legal audiences mentioned only briefly. By contrast, the MIT instructions are more centered on the role of the lab notebook in protecting intellectual property, including the university's property, and in obtaining and defending patents. Rice students are required to follow certain ethical notebook procedures in order to join the community of biological scientists, whereas MIT mechanical engineering students are scared straight into correct notebook keeping because the notebook may become legal evidence and protect a patent. Focusing research ethics on protecting patents is problematic, say Wayne C. Booth and colleagues (2003, 67, original emphasis), because at times, "profits from patents not only determine the choice of research problems, but also color their solutions: *Tell us what to look for, and we'll provide it.*"

A third science writing guide, the *Microbiology Writing Guide for Oregon State University* (n.d.), seems atypical in that it contains a page specifically titled "Ethics." As might be expected, the guide offers advice on ethical quotation and paraphrase of borrowed information, using examples from the discipline. But the "Ethics" page begins with a statement related to both conducting the lab experiment and writing about it in a lab notebook or lab report, explicitly pointing out that because one's results may influence others, the researcher must report accurate results. The guide notes the advice on ethics of Henry Bauer of Virginia Polytechnic Institute:

> But what if an experiment doesn't give the result you expected? What if it gives a result that you just *know* is wrong in some way? Isn't there the temptation to fudge a bit? Since you know what the right answer *ought* to be, why not just round the numbers off a bit? (*Microbiology Writing Guide for Oregon State University* n.d., original emphasis)

The ethical guidance calls the temptation to fudge data "a huge ethical dilemma" in science, concluding with this advice:

> Obviously, the falsification of any data is unacceptable. If the "rounding of numbers" significantly changes the outcome of the experiment, it is unacceptable as well. It is important that scientific researchers remain as ethical as possible in reporting their data, since that is the only way that real discoveries in science will be made. (*Microbiology Writing Guide for Oregon State University* n.d.)

The ethical stakes of the lab notebook, indeed all aspects of research, are even higher when human subjects are involved in research. In addition to providing its well-known training for ethical research using human subjects, the National Institutes of Health (2008) offers instruction in ways of doing and ways of writing a lab notebook when human subjects are involved. Although formal institutional human subjects review and approval may not be required for undergraduate research performed as inquiry for a course and limited in publication and distribution to that course, nevertheless, instructors in appropriate methods courses typically offer explicit guidance in the ethical challenges of working with human subjects and especially with vulnerable populations; they also cover the conventions of ethical recordkeeping when working with human subjects.

This is not to imply that being proficient in the academic expectations of a genre like the lab notebook is inherently ethical. Other ethical implications of laboratory experiments must be discussed with students, whose labs and outcomes are typically designed by instructors. Students might be forming ethical habits, but for what ends? Ethical pedagogy gives students a sense of how their research acts in the world, how it might be part of larger studies, larger goals. And then students can practice critical thinking by writing informally—individually or in groups—about the value or harm to the community and the public of these larger goals, for example, the experiment's impact on the environment. Students grow as ethical writers by examining multiple perspectives and perhaps identifying places where their personal values conflict with the goals of laboratory research they have been asked to do. They might begin to discern the larger ethical issues around the social actions of their discipline and articulate and discuss choices they might have to make as graduate researchers and in the workplace.

Although I have focused on the ethical keeping of a lab notebook in various disciplines and locations, ethics also obviously abides in other genres of empirical research. Some courses move students beyond the lab genres to practicing the genre of the scientific article. The structure of the scientific article is fairly standard across disciplines: abstract, introduction/literature review, methods, results, discussion, conclusion, with figures integrated or attached in an appendix. Many readers read only the abstract of an article, so the writer's ethical responsibility to those readers includes clearly and accurately representing the findings of the article in the abstract. The methods must be described in sufficiently accurate detail that they could be replicated, with any alterations in methods noted and explained. In addition, in many studies there may be more results than can be reported in a single article. Here the writer proceeds ethically by including key relevant findings, being sure selections and omissions do not distort the overall results or their relationship to the original hypothesis/research questions. In the discussion section, the writer should attempt to interpret the results without bias. The ethical depiction of results in figures is a huge learning challenge whose discussion is beyond the scope of this chapter. My experience teaching a course for advanced dissertation and thesis writers across the disciplines suggests that even graduate students receive little explicit instruction in the disciplinary ethics of writing the methodology, results, discussion, and figures. If ethical questions arise, students are expected by their advisers to figure them out themselves from reading published articles. I see this pedagogy of osmosis across the curriculum as highly problematic and unfair to students because it leaves them ethically untrained.

PROBLEM SOLVING AND ETHICAL WRITING

In disciplines that focus on problem solving, Carter's (2007) second megagenre, students are given tasks that offer them the opportunity to identify and investigate problems and then to design solutions. Disciplines whose ways of doing involve problem solving include business, agricultural economics and research, public health, food science, and capstone engineering courses, among many others. Genres typical for these disciplines include "business plans, feasibility reports, management plans, marketing plans, reports to management, project reports, project proposals, technical memoranda, [and] technical reports" (Carter 2007, 396). These genres ask students to write for an audience, imagined or real, to whom they have an ethical responsibility for honesty. As implied in the explicit ethics advice to microbiology students not to fudge the lab results, the rhetorical and ethical decision to be honest and report in good faith in the end depends on the character of the student to make choices that reflect their responsibility to behave ethically toward their audience. Faculty in fields whose students may enter the for-profit sector need to prepare writers for understanding and responding to the complexity of situations where the ethical choice may be in conflict with the employer's profit motive.

In certain problem-solving disciplines, students may be aware of their ethical responsibility not only to a human audience but also to the environment. A sustainability course at Oregon State University asks students to "analyze controversial agricultural and environmental issues, synthesize information from diverse sources, and apply scientific knowledge to recommend specific courses of action to solve real world problems" (Lloyd 2018). Students submit five case study reports, each in a different "form of writing" (genre)—including two genres, a letter to the editor and an Extension publication—that communicate with the public (Lloyd 2018). Students in this course commit to studying and writing about an ethic of environmental sustainability and the real-world policies and actions that ethic promotes.

In other disciplines, such as forestry, where some courses focus on wood products and profits while others focus on forest sustainability, students may find their personal environmental ethics in conflict with course instruction and assumptions of writing assignments. Disciplines like forestry may be dependent on so-called soft money from both federal grants and industry, raising ethical questions about the extent to which research and curriculum design may be influenced by sources of funding. It is ethical to train students to enter the wood products industry. It is also fair for faculty to help students, through formal and informal inquiry and writing, to think through the possible ethical issues involved in various assumptions, goals, and outcomes of their discipline.

Courses like capstone projects in engineering often address not only their accrediting body (ABET)'s requirement for problem solving but also the standard for collaboration and working in teams. Ethics dwells in both doing the project and in what engineering students call "writing it up." In team endeavors, there is always the question of fair division of labor. The better the student, the greater their concern with getting stuck with the majority of the work, especially the writing. Sometimes out of fear that if they let others do it there will be lower quality of work and a lower grade for the team, one strong student will do the majority of the writing. As research on collaborative writing in the workplace by Andrea Lunsford and Lisa Ede (2012, 128) reveals, this problem continues into the workplace, where a "frequently cited" problem is the equitable division of tasks. Other ethical issues in collaborative writing identified by Lunsford and Ede (2012, 161, 239, 302–3) include differential in power relations among team members, issues of diversity and disenfranchisement, and positive ethical effects of feminist theories of communication.

Training students to take individual responsibility for specific roles and writing tasks and designing assignments that explicitly require a more ethical distribution of work seems crucial to helping them learn ethical ways of doing and writing in group projects. One example is shown in a writing-intensive capstone course in mechanical, industrial, and manufacturing engineering (Robinson, Calvo-Amodio, Parmigiani, and Burton 2015) in which, over a two-term course, students on teams rotate roles and are responsible individually for reporting on and composing initial versions of various parts of the capstone report. Students are assessed individually for their key-role performance and writing. Then the final report is fully collaborative (Robinson, Calvo-Amodio, Parmigiani, and Burton 2015). Other ways to reinforce ethical doing and writing take place in project courses that require students to keep project logs in which they record not only progress with solving the problem but also process information, such as which team members attended each meeting and what they contributed. This informal writing genre encourages students to behave ethically toward and be accountable to their team, and it gives the instructor evidence for final assessment of each student's contribution to the project and the final project report, thus providing a way to base the grade on the amount of ethical practice students have demonstrated.

WRITING ETHICALLY FROM SOURCES

In the humanities, Carter (2007) suggests, the dominant ways of doing involve research from sources rather than from observation, as in empirical research; and the goal of this source-based research is typically not practical problem solving but rather some goal particular to the discipline. Research from sources occurs across the curriculum but particularly in the humanities—history, literature, philosophy, and religion. Where ethics dwells in writing from sources is often thought by students to be in the citation system of a particular discipline, and ethical behavior means avoiding plagiarism. Wayne C. Booth, Gregory G. Columb, and Joseph M. Williams (2003, 202) give an operational definition of plagiarism thus: "In all fields, you plagiarize when you use a source's words or ideas without citing that source. In most fields, you plagiarize even when you *do* credit the source but use its exact words without using quotation marks or block indentation." However, in the field of law, the writer can use a source's exact wording without quotation marks (Booth, Columb, and Williams 2003, 202), showing some variation among disciplines in what counts as ethical practice. A challenge arises with the teaching and practice of ethics in writing from sources because undergraduates typically move among multiple disciplines, even within a single day. They write papers for literature courses requiring MLA style, social science courses using APA, history courses requiring Chicago style, and sciences whose citation style may be tied to a specific journal. The student's motive for ethical use of sources is more often avoiding plagiarism and its penalties rather than respecting the intellectual property of others. Recent research by Rebecca Moore Howard, Sandra Jamieson, and others in the Citation Project has complicated our teaching of research from sources by identifying how much research writing is composed of what Howard and Jamieson (Jamieson 2013, 8) call "patchwriting," defined as "partially restating a phrase, clause, or one or more sentences while staying close to the language or syntax of the source." Helping students see the ethical challenges of paraphrase and giving students tools for articulating ideas in their own words will help reinforce the ethics of doing and writing in these tasks.

When students move from textual sources to living sources, what are the ethics for writers in a field like journalism or creative nonfiction, whose sources are people's lives—their own and the lives of others who may or may not want to be in the story? Lynn Z. Bloom (2003, 278) argues that the writer of creative nonfiction is ethically compelled to tell the truth:

> In contrast to the official story, creative nonfiction presents the unauthorized version, tales of personal and public life that are very likely subversive of the records and thus of the authority of the sanctioned tellers. Although one might ask, "Is it ethical to do so?" the only viable answer is, as it has always been for all writers, "It would be unethical *not* to do so."

Bloom subsequently softens, admitting that an author might take some care with the truth telling that could injure innocent family members who have no desire to have their lives made public, though Bloom (2003, 279) calls Annie Dillard "a Benthamite" for saying in *An American Childhood* that she tried to leave out anything that might trouble her family, "anything at all." Clearly, the matter of ethical writing from sources that are people's lives is, as Bloom says, complicated. A pedagogy of ethics would encourage student writers to understand and consider the costs to others, their responsibilities to family and friends whose stories they know, when creative ambition tempts them to reveal the private lives of people who have not asked to be included. Crafting assignments that specifically encounter and complicate questions of ethics in reporting on people's lives will help students see what are considered virtues in these disciplines, which may contrast with their families' and communities' attitudes toward what can and cannot be shared fairly.

PERFORMANCE AND ETHICAL WRITING

Carter's (2007, 400–403) final metagenre relies on performance as a way of doing, with students educated to produce a certain kind of artifact, whether it be a short story, a dance or music performance, or an architectural design. Interestingly, Carter's research shows that the assessment of student work in performance disciplines typically focuses not on the quality of the artifact (as it might in a capstone engineering project) but on students showing evidence of "enduring knowledge" of the art and the way art is made. Along with the obvious performing arts, Carter includes rhetoric, writing, and even technical writing in this metagenre.

Carter (2007, 400–403) found that the written discourse of performance fields often resides in the genre of critique, whose ethics is vested in fairness. Performance implies an audience, which complicates citation practices in interesting ways. While plagiarism of words and ideas in source-based writing is seen as unethical, visual allusion in one film to an iconic image from another (*ET*-esque bicycles across the moon, for example) enhances the value of the performance and the audience's enjoyment of it. Composers often "sample" snippets of melody from other works. Painters repurpose or reinterpret an image in their own new creation. Booth and colleagues (2003, 285–89) emphasize the writer/performer's ethical responsibility to the community, citing disruptive performance, confusing performance, and troubling display inappropriate for the audience. And yet these negatives are sometimes the actual goals of performance.

Teaching ethical critique might take many forms. At my own land grant university, where many majors require students to complete a course in technical writing, students may encounter an assignment like instructor Sara Jameson's midterm exam on ethical writing. Students are asked to read five source articles (provided by the teacher) on ethics in technical communication. Then, drawing principles from at least two articles, students analyze the ethical or unethical communication of an opaque artifact of workplace technical communication. After the analysis, students must rewrite the artifact in clear, professional prose, following ethical principles they have articulated. The articles provided as sources range from George Orwell (2009 [1946]) ("Politics of the English Language—1946"), Steven B. Katz (1992) ("The Ethics of Expediency: Classical Rhetoric, Technology, and the Holocaust"), and Paul M. Dombrowski's (2000) literature review of ethics in technical communication to Joseph Williams's (2006) instructions on the ethics of style; also Gerald J. Alred and colleagues' (2015, 180) tech writing handbook checklist for ethical writing, which reminds students to:

- Be willing "to take responsibility, publicly and privately" for what they have written
- Be "honest and truthful," with special attention to making sure data support conclusions
- Take care that the document does not violate the rights of others
- Be "ethically consistent" by applying principles of their textbook "and those you have assimilated throughout your life"
- Imagine your reader and whether the message would be received as "acceptable and respectful."

This assignment offers a model that might be adapted across disciplines.

One checklist item offered by Alred and colleagues (2015, 180), not listed above, raises ethical issues in its own right: "Am I acting in my employer's, my client's, the public's, or my own best long-term interest?" What if the employer's interests conflict with those of the public or with the writer's personal ethical principles? Students need practice performing the critical thinking and values clarification needed to answer this question in a particular context. Again, faculty in the disciplines might use informal or formal writing on this topic to scaffold the larger assignment.

WRITING TO UNDERSTAND ETHICAL CODES

We have seen some ways in which ethics dwells in the knowing and doing and within the related genres of disciplinary writing. Some disciplines also have specific ethical knowledge, codes of ethics to which students might be introduced at the undergraduate level. Faculty in the disciplines who are responsible for teaching ethical codes of their field may be introducing a concise statement like the briefly bulleted MBA Oath (n.d.) initiated by members of the Harvard Business School class of 2009, the more elaborate "Academy of Management Code of Ethics" (2006), or the ten-point Code of Ethics of the American Society of Mechanical Engineers (2006); or they may present students with a more complex document like the 16-page "Principles of the Ethical Practice of Public Health" published by the Public Health Leadership Society (2002) or the 114-page International Federation of Accountants (IFAC) "Code of Ethics for Professional Accountants" (2006). WAC pedagogies such as using informal, low-stakes writing-to-learn assignments to unpack and apply these documents (for example, freewriting, looping, cubing, writing for varied audiences, and articulating purpose and context) can be useful for turning abstract ethical principles into concrete situations with ethical implications that a student might confront in the workplace. As with my call for more explicit discussion of the ethics of genres in the disciplines, explicit opportunities to unpack and investigate individual elements of a code of ethics are important for student learning and for the transfer of learning to one's work life.

CONCLUSION

This study of ethics and Writing in the Disciplines reveals a complex activity system in which teachers and student writers encounter, explore, and enact ethical choices informed by such diverse ethical sources as the institution's plagiarism policy (and punishments), the ethical codes of professional organizations, ethical requirements of an accrediting body, and the guidelines of the National Institutes of Health, the United States Patent Office, and other government agencies, among others. To this complexity students may transfer their possible knowledge of Aristotelian ethics from first-year composition (Duffy), a flexible post-modern approach to media and technical communication (Porter), and whatever individual ethics shapes their personal choices and decisions.

As if this were not enough complexity, students arrive in the new and often strange habitat of their major discipline, with its own ethical world and ethical challenges. When we think of ethics in WAC/WID, it may be helpful to remember the story of the ancient Greek travelers who went in search of the famous philosopher Heraclitis, only to find him living in poverty, warming himself by a small stove. In their disappointment, the travelers turned to leave without talking to him. But Heraclitis offered them hospitality and invited them into his humble dwelling place, saying, "here, too, the gods are present" (Hyde 2004, xii). Like Heraclitis, ethical writing may dwell in unexpected places—not only in carefully worded formal codes of ethics but also in humble genres like the lab notebook, the case study, and the performance critique. But students, like the ancient travelers, may not recognize the value of what is before them, thinking mainly of what it takes to get an A. They need to learn what it takes not only to demonstrate academic expertise but also to explore and practice applying ethical principles, coming to recognize ethical challenges that dwell in the genres and the ways of knowing, doing, and writing of their discipline. It falls to faculty teaching Writing in the Disciplines, encouraged and assisted by WAC/WID leaders, to make clear and explicit the ethical principles that abide in disciplinary genres and ways of writing, for "such dwelling places define the grounds, the abodes or habitats, where a person's ethics and moral character take form and develop" (Hyde 2004, xiii).

REFERENCES

Academy of Management. 2006. "Academy of Management Code of Ethics." http://aomonline.org/governanceandethics/aomrevisedcodeofethics.pdf.

Alred, Gerald J., Charles T. Brusaw, and Walter E. Oliu. 2015. *Handbook of Technical Writing*. Boston: Bedford/St. Martin's.

American Society of Mechanical Engineers. 2012. "Code of Ethics." https://www.asme.org/wwwasmeorg/media/ResourceFiles/AboutASME/Get%20Involved/Advocacy/Policy-Publications/P-15-7-Ethics.pdf.

Bazerman, Charles, and James Paradis. 1991. "Introduction." In *Textual Dynamics of the Professions: Historical and Contemporary Studies of Writing in Professional Communities*, ed. Charles Bazerman and James Paradis, 3–10. Madison: University of Wisconsin Press.

Bloom, Lynn Z. 2003. "Living to Tell the Tale: The Complicated Ethics of Creative Nonfiction." *College English* 65 (3): 276–81.

Booth, Wayne C., Gregory G. Colomb, and Joseph M. Williams. 2003. *The Craft of Research.* 2nd ed. Chicago: University of Chicago Press.

Carter, Michael. 2007. "Ways of Knowing, Doing, and Writing in the Disciplines," *College Composition and Communication* 58 (3): 385–418.

Dombrowski, Paul M. 2000. "Ethics and Technical Communication: The Past Quarter Century." *Journal of Technical Writing and Communication* 30 (1): 3–29.

Duffy, John. 2017. "The Good Writer: Virtue Ethics and the Teaching of Writing." *College English* 79 (3): 229–50.

Havelock, Eric. 1957. *The Liberal Temper in Greek Politics.* New Haven, CT: Yale University Press.

Hunter, Ian W., and Barbara J. Hughey. 2007. "Massachusetts Institute of Technology, Department of Mechanical Engineering, Instructions for Using Your Laboratory Notebook." http://web.mit.edu/me-ugoffice/communication/labnotebooks.pdf.

Hyde, Michael. 2004. "Introduction: Rhetorically We Dwell." In *The Ethos of Rhetoric*, ed. Michael Hyde, xiii–xxviii. Columbia: University of South Carolina Press.

International Federation of Accountants. 2006. "Code of Ethics for Professional Accountants." https://www.ifac.org/system/files/publications/files/ifac-code-of-ethics-for.pdf.

Jamieson, Sandra. 2013. "Reading and Engaging Sources: What Students' Use of Sources Reveals about Advanced Reading Skills." *Across the Disciplines* 10. http://wac.colostate.edu/atd/reading/jamieson.cfm.

Jameson, Sara. 2016. "Syllabus for WR 327, Technical Writing."

Jarratt, Susan. 1991. *Rereading the Sophists: Classical Rhetoric Refigured.* Carbondale: Southern Illinois University Press.

Katz, Steven B. 1992. "The Ethics of Expediency: Classical Rhetoric, Technology, and the Holocaust." *College English* 54 (3): 256–75.

Lloyd, Deanna. 2018. "Syllabus for SUS 325: Ag and Environmental Predicaments: A Case Study Approach."

Lunsford, Andrea, and Lisa Ede. 2012. *Writing Together: Collaboration in Theory and Practice, a Critical Sourcebook.* Boston: Bedford/St. Martin's.

"MBA Oath." N.d. http://mbaoath.org/.

Microbiology Writing Guide for Oregon State University. N.d. http://wic.oregonstate.edu/departmental-writing-guide-microbiology.

National Institutes of Health. 2008. "Guidelines for Scientific Record Keeping in the Intramural Research Program at the NIH." https://oir.nih.gov/sites/default/files/uploads/sourcebook/documents/ethical_conduct/guidelines-scientific_recordkeeping.pdf.

Orwell, George. 2009. "Politics and the English Language—1946." http://www.utdallas.edu/~aria/research/resources/orwell.pdf.

Porter, James E. 1998. *Rhetorical Ethics and Internetworked Writing.* Greenwich, CT: Ablex.

Public Health Leadership Society. 2002. "Principles of the Ethical Practice of Public Health" (version 2.2). http://ethics.iit.edu/ecodes/node/4734.

Rice University. N.d. "Guidelines for Keeping a Laboratory Record." http://www.ruf.rice.edu/~bioslabs/tools/notebook/notebook.html.

Robinson, Tracy Ann, Javier Calvo-Amodio, John P. Parmigiani, and Vicki Tolar Burton. 2015. "Capstone Design as an Individual Writing Experience." *International Journal of Engineering Education* 31:6B: 1902–23.

Spellmeyer, Kurt. 1989. "A Common Ground: The Essay in the Academy." *College English* 51 (3): 262–76.

Thaiss, Chris, and Tara Porter. 2010. "The State of WAC/WID in 2010: Methods and Results of the US Survey of the International WAC/WID Mapping Project." *College Composition and Communication* 61 (3): 534–70.

Williams, Joseph. 2006. *Style: The Basics of Clarity and Grace.* New York: Pearson.

11

NOT TO MENTION PLATO
Pedagogical Persuasion

Don J. Kraemer

In a review of the second book I ever read on teaching how to teach writing, William F. Irmscher's 1979 *Teaching Expository Writing*, Walker Gibson (1980) concludes by listing—in a parenthesis—other pedagogical scholarship to which Irmscher refers the reader: "recent books of Kinneavy, D'Angelo, Shaughnessy, and Hirsch." After the parenthesis, Gibson (1980, 93) adds, "And then there's Aristotle, not to mention Plato." Well noted, I think: it is the revisionary zeal in Plato that most relevantly informs this volume and this chapter. Having criticized in the *Gorgias* (1998) rhetoric's separation of effective power from knowledge, Plato uses the *Republic* (1991) to develop a "city" rhetoric that speaks to the threefold being of the soul: (a) *knowledge* of the just, knowledge that is incomplete without also (b) the *zeal* to see justice done and (c) the *desire* for the good things a just order enables. Translated into guidelines for training teachers of writing, Plato's ABCs of the tripartite soul might read like this: we should (a) train prospective teachers in knowledge of writing concepts and practices, the better to distinguish just from unjust concepts and practices; (b) cultivate the zeal, the willingness, these prospective teachers have to teach that knowledge; and (c) encourage the development of their desires—their appetites—that will find satisfaction in such teaching.

The rhetoric to be taught along Platonic lines is a rhetoric for citizens, a rhetoric of "public discourse," discourse that in Gregory Clark's (2002, 111) words remakes acts of "writing and reading [as] acts of citizenship." Writing and reading as acts of citizenship are acts of knowledge and power and desire that are cooperative. The hope is that the transformative effect these cooperative acts have in the classroom will transfer to the "city," and that hope is motivated by what motivates community in general—the fact that "each of us isn't self-sufficient but is in need of much" (Plato 1991, 369b, 46). The *democratic* city, Socrates

DOI: 10.7330/9781607329978.c011

says, is "probably the fairest of the regimes"—a community that gives "license" to everyone to "do whatever one wants," permitting "each man [to] organize his life in it privately just as it pleases him" (quoted in Plato 1991, 557b–c, 235).[1] To help bring about such community is, Plato (1998, 517c, 117) says, the sole duty, "the one work of a good citizen."

As Marina McCoy (2008, 194) understands this duty, it is "based on the understanding of oneself and one's deepest desires. It is not defined by a method or even by a particular intellectual doctrine so much as it is by the practice of living well." To understand ourselves and our "deepest desires" is a (never wholly achievable) precondition for organizing our lives as it pleases us. To organize a pleasing city life, we must understand not only ourselves but also others and their desires. Many different persuasions trying to give each persuasion its due—this is "the practice of living well" in democratic community.

This practice of living well, which frames my teacher training pedagogy and motivates my role in the case study (below), also defines the structure of the MA program I teach in, which is not to say that the program does not offer training in what McCoy calls different methods and intellectual doctrines. Three such doctrinal, methodological differences are offered, in fact: the option of Teaching English to Speakers of Other Languages (TESOL), the option of literature (lit), and the option of rhetoric/composition (rhet/comp). Each option, furthermore, has its distinctive, characteristic "good"—reflected, for instance, in what each option requires for its culminating project. Within the graduate community, each student's option is an intense interest, a passionate identification, a life plan freely chosen, something that gives that life some shape and savor—a big, multidimensional value that most students are deeply attached to, far from eager to detach from. Committed to the practice of living well, however, the program *forces* students outside their option, requiring them to do some other-option coursework. This is the program's way of acting as though no one option is self-sufficient, the program's way of making itself more city-like.

One small subset of the way our program ensures against taking any one art as self-sufficient is the requirement that all students—no matter their option or their interest in teaching—complete one practicum in teaching the kind of literacy perhaps most widely perceived to serve democratic community: first-year composition (FYC) in fulfillment of the general education (GE) written communication requirement.[2] Fostering anything like absolute detachment from what one loves is not the aim. On the contrary, the aim is to put prospective teachers' personal (intellectual, spiritual, recreational/appetitive) attachments into dialogic tension with disciplinary obligations—in particular, that urged by FYC: to teach ways of communing with our interlocutors in reasoned writing and impassioned advocacy, of cooperating with others to try making right the terms on which we and they live freely. These terms affect, if not constitute, the freedom Plato cites above. In democratic community, that is, even as I am free to develop my good, others are free to develop theirs; it is my civic duty to help make that private freedom possible, and doing so will surely affect how my own good develops. In such conditions, Plato (1991, 348b, 26) says, citizens are "both judges and pleaders at once." In a classroom aimed at this civic model, teacher and students might also be "both judges and pleaders at once."

In inviting students as well as teachers to be both judges and pleaders, this curriculum can strain the pedagogical community it is meant to encourage. Although strain is associated with development and growth, it can also be associated with force. A student might feel pressured to judge the case the teacher has made (possibly a case that counters one the student has made). This difference in a student's judgment and a teacher's can take the shape of disagreement, maybe passionate disagreement, and the student is then exposed (as the civic model would seem to require) to the teacher's desire. Insofar as we, like our students, are constituted by passionate identifications, to detach ourselves from the appropriate passion seems too much to ask—not only too much to ask but also, more relevant, the wrong thing to ask.

The right thing to ask, because we also owe something to our students' passions, is whether what we do in *our* passion's name causes harm. The risk of harm is arguably heightened in pedagogical training for GE FYC, where everyone's good—the teacher's, each prospective teacher's—is in play, is pressed into the practice of living well together. Judging others' good while advocating our own—it is this pressure that heightens the risk of harm. Developing the assumption that "what attaches us most deeply to life is also what we are least willing to engage critically," James L. Kastely (1997, 45) writes, "when in noble service of what we love, we are least able to see how we may inadvertently cause suffering." However noble our passionate pursuit, its passion may hurt others—perhaps even if we could see clearly: what we love is hard to give up. Committed to the art she has chosen, a grad student's passion (for linguistics, say) may dominate GE FYC pedagogy, the art it is our assigned duty to teach her to teach.[3] In this chapter, I wish to explore the possibility of causing harm to teachers by training them rhetorically, and to explore that possibility I begin again with Plato.

When it comes to duty, Plato (1998, 517b–c, 117) argues that we must persuade ourselves and others to do what is right and, if persuasion fails, to use force. To rhetorically help citizens better serve the city, one may resort to "persuading and forcing them toward the condition in which the citizens were to be better."[4] If teachers who teach the arts of public discourse imagine that they are also serving democratic community by helping develop better citizens, then it would seem that not only persuasion will be needed; force (of the pedagogical variety) may be needed as well. Readers may recoil on principle from imagining pedagogical force as anything but a last resort. Though recoiling is an appropriate response, let me both give a reminder and make a request. The reminder is that pedagogical force is (as I see it) exercised when we fulfill our duties as teachers of particular subject matter, which the curriculum and our responses dynamically enforce and reinforce. We saw one occasion for such force in the previous paragraph, and I will provide—below, when presenting Clark's "public discourse" syllabus—an example of such force in action.

The request I'd like to make is that we remain open to the possibility that force might exert itself in ways that exceed our persuasive intentions, perhaps all the more so when we refuse to segregate each individual's good from everyone's duty. Our duty, as citizen teachers, includes giving each student's good its due. Goods vary, and what each student is due may differ. Consider a grad student in teacher training who wishes to center her FYC curriculum on the fantasy novels of Terry Prachett (because she really enjoys those novels, thinks the students will connect with them, and claims the novels are so rich they can be used to address every FYC learning outcome). Instead of laying down the verdict that her wish violates the letter of the learning outcomes, I might talk with her about those mandated outcomes, about the customized course theme she has in mind (the civic utility of parody, say) by which to frame those outcomes, about the relations she envisions among reading various kinds of texts and writing in response to those texts, about where literary texts (including Prachett's) might fit in—and how and how much, and so on. Conversation, with persuasive interchange as needed, might settle the conflicts between us. That would be *my* intention, expectation, and hope.

Yet persuasion might fail. My student might insist on teaching the course as Intro to Prachett. That would be, I believe, failure on her part to do right—to do right by the subject matter, by each student, by the relevant community. As her teacher, I then have the duty to see that right is done even when the power of persuasion fails. I might lower her project's grade or grade it highly on its merits but let the student know I cannot recommend her for an FYC teaching fellowship. I see evidence of force in such pedagogical mechanisms as grades and sponsorship; those mechanisms can, however, be understood as more meaningfully toward the persuasive than the forceful end of a continuum. To manage this ambiguity, let me specify that in this chapter, I will not rule out a link between "force" and our acts when we act as *judges*. Where I see our roles as *pleaders*, I will link those with "persuasion."

In the case to be explored below, I present both a way in which I not fully wittingly exerted force and a way—reasonably generalizable, I hope—to mitigate that force, that is, to extend the play of pedagogical persuasion.

THE CASE

In what follows, I will focus on one teacher in training, Bashar Alhoch, who in fall 2016 demonstrated a keen interest in and empirical stance toward discovering "fundamental principles of respectful exchange" (Agnew and Duffy, personal communication, 2016). That empiricism is telegraphed in the first part of his seminar project's title, "Turn, and Become as Little Children: Notes on a Nascent Course in Basic Writing." Addressing the first-year students he might one day teach, Bashar—a grad student in literature but a scientist by undergrad training—writes that in systematically observing and analyzing the good toward which this or that kind of labor is directed, "Aristotle was a scientist." The "child," Bashar adds,

> is also a scientist—one who knows the world by watching it closely and tasting it courageously. One who, observing a practice, knows that, if there are no visible signs of danger, the best way to understand the reason for the practice, and the best way to decide whether the practice should be adopted, is to participate in it and see what happens. The child is an empiricist. (Alhoch 2016, 1)[5]

The course description from which this comes was part of a seminar project in which my students also (1) designed, for a basic writing course, an original curriculum—in the form of a four-assignment sequence—and, in a separate rationale, (2) justified that curriculum's creative accord with and warranted deviation from writing instruction as endorsed by the assigned readings.[6] In his own words, Bashar notes that his materials are influenced by "Douglas Hesse's recently published syllabus 'Occasions, Sources, and Strategies,' David Bartholomae and Anthony R. Petrosky's famous course in Basic Reading and Writing, and Kathleen

Blake Yancey, Liane Robertson, and Kara Taczak's recent study on transfer" (Alhoch 2016, 2). Here are guiding questions from the first draft of Bashar's course description:

- How do written texts work? (How do they function, how do they mean?)
- What is the value of written texts for their creators and readers? (There is this practice in the world: people write and people read. Why do they do it?)
- How can we read and write so as to maximize the value of reading and writing for us? (Just because everyone's doing it doesn't mean that we *should* too. But there is this practice in the world, and all of us are already doing it in some way. Is it possible that we *should* do in a particular way, or that we *should* do it differently from how we previously have?) (Alhoch 2016, 2; emphasis added)

Raising the policy question of whether we *should* accommodate or transform the writing practices that exist ramifies that first part of Bashar's project's title, an allusion (as I later learned) to Matthew 18:3: "Most certainly I tell you, unless you turn, and become as little children, you will in no way enter into the Kingdom of Heaven" (World English Bible).[7] As a teacher of teachers of writing I wonder, if there *is* a way we should turn to enter or create domains of hospitable, just writing practices, whether I know that way, whether I can turn others, and if so, how.

If so, it would help to know what one is turning from. To that end, the design Bashar's course has on his imagined students is to encourage them "to learn about writing by observing, analyzing, and trying it in earnest, all with a view to its affordances for their particular selves" (Alhoch 2016, 2). To support what the course design encourages, Bashar's assignment sequence has other designs on students: first that they inquire into attitudes toward and valuations of reading and writing, next that they study literacy narratives and then draft their own (as well as the criteria by which they themselves will regard their narratives as "successful"), and that they end the sequence with an essay that reflects back and looks forward. A revised version of Bashar's instructions for the reflective essay follows (the arrows denote the main revisions Bashar made in response to others' feedback and mine):

> I'd like us to explore this question a little bit: to what extent or in what ways does your success in meeting your criteria and achieving your purpose depend on your reader's response to your narrative?
>
> First, I'd like each of us to read a narrative and describe, in as much detail and precision as possible, our responses as we read.
>
> Then, I'd like you to read your own narrative and note, in as much detail and precision as you can, how you imagine a reader responding to it.

[Omitted here are the 154 words of guiding questions Bashar provides. They are followed by this:]

> I'll let you know whether I agree with your predictions and why or why not. Where I disagree with you, I'll invite you to consider with me whether it matters that I disagree.
>
> If it doesn't matter, we might proceed by drawing out the implications for the question above: In this practice (of writing and sharing literacy narratives) that we're participating in, what exactly is the point of the sharing? *Is* there such a thing as failure in this practice?
>
> If it does matter that I disagree, we'll consider ways in which writers can improve the likelihood of achieving particular responses. (Alhoch 2016, 15)

In what remains, I'd like to turn toward these revisions, which at the time I held in high regard (and still do)—even as I worried that they were too passive, not sufficiently forthcoming about the teacher's duty (such as in the case of whether the responses a writer claims to want are worthy). But even if that worry were well grounded, it was grounded in how well Bashar's revisions engage (perhaps advance) Kastely's concern about what we love and the suffering it may cause. In an FYC context that foregrounds literacy practices, bringing together personal preferences and public purposes, Bashar asks whether what one loves and knows matters to another. If what I love and know doesn't matter to another—an other, my other—isn't it enough that *I* like it? If what I value does not cause suffering, should I care whether it alleviates suffering at all, let alone enough?

To insist that others engage these questions with us is, I assume, to better the odds that what a citizen desires engages both what a citizen should know to do and the zeal to do it. To "insist" may imply *force*, and it may be the case that Bashar, to be less forceful as well as more prudent, presumes desire rather than makes it an explicit element of rhetorical awareness. That is, the assumption may be in play that the greater the extent to which desire (including the teacher's) is taken for granted, the better a teacher can focus both on students' knowledge of what exists and on their power to enact or change that knowledge. Knowledge and zeal do seem core features of Bashar's curriculum, his rationale for which asserts that "it's important that students make an earnest effort at participating in the practices under investigation. A half-hearted attempt is much less likely to serve" (Alhoch 2016, 9). Knowledge of writing practices through "earnest" participation in them and the will to participate not halfheartedly but wholeheartedly—that's two of the democratic soul's three parts.

But what of that soul's third part, I wonder. In the spirit of rewriting Plato's legacy, I turn now to the question of how that third part might be importantly relevant: that question of how our stance toward and participation in public discourse—academic, civic, disciplinary—is affected by our desire to organize our reading and writing just as it pleases us. After that I end with another look at Bashar's course description and assignment sequence, which as it happens were under-read by my desire to read just as it pleases me.

PLATO'S LEGACY

As part of his inquiry with Callicles into "what way one must live," Socrates argues that "one must use rhetoric thus, always aiming at what is just, and so for every other action" (Plato 1998, 500c, 96; 527c, 128).[8] Aiming teacher training at what is just, we might begin by considering all those affected by this work—a group that includes stakeholders who ask why we can't just teach students to write clearly and effectively. In this last question is the legacy problem Plato poses for rhetoric: while clarity and especially effectiveness are valued qualities, sometimes rhetoric that is clear and clearly effective can ignore questions of justice, can be effective *because* such questions are ignored.

Honoring questions of justice is Plato's positive rhetorical legacy. That legacy, which Socrates calls "noble," concerns "making preparations for the citizens' souls to be as good as possible and fighting to say the best things, whether they will be more pleasant or more unpleasant to the hearers" (Plato 1998, 503a–b, 100). Instead of pandering to the base, rhetoric as "the true political art" can orient us "with a view to the best, not to the most pleasant" (Plato 1998, 521d–e, 122). What is pleasant concerns the body; what is best, the soul (Plato 1998, 513d, 112). Because the properly motivated soul will help the citizen transcend bodily pleasure, Socrates argues that the rhetor must direct "his mind toward how he may get justice to come into being in the citizens' souls and injustice to be removed, moderation to arise within and intemperance to be removed, the rest of virtue to arise within and badness to depart" (Plato 1998, 504de, 102). Soul in *Gorgias* is not body. Soul aims for what's best, the body for what's pleasant. The body involves pleasure, not badness. Badness leaves the soul, not the body. Where justice is concerned, the body is immaterial.

A similar sentiment toward justice, to make choices that lead the soul toward "becoming juster," is expressed in the *Republic* (see, for example, Plato 1991, 618d–e, 301), but with a difference. Soul does not transcend the body but is embodied. Justice as revised in the *Republic* does not require the transcendence of appetite. Appetite, in fact, forms one-third of the soul—knowledge and zeal the other two-thirds. Each dynamism informs the others. After suggesting that in a just city "each one must practice one of the functions in the city, that one for which his nature made him naturally most fit," Socrates adds that "justice is the minding of one's own business and not being a busybody" (Plato 1991, 433a, 111).[9] Minding one's business seems far from the totality of justice—and must have seemed so to Socrates, who qualifies his meaning:

> But in truth justice was, as it seems, something of this sort; however, not with respect to a man's minding his external business, but with respect to what is within, with respect to what truly concerns him and his own. He doesn't let each part in him mind other people's business or the three classes in the soul meddle with each other, but really sets his own house in good order and rules himself; he arranges himself, becomes his own friend, and harmonizes the three parts, exactly like three notes in a harmonic scale, lowest, highest, and middle. (Plato 1991, 443c–d, 123)

This harmonious ordering of the tripartite soul is *justice*, not harmonizing one's desire with the knowledge and zeal one must develop betrays justice. On Plato's terms, Bashar's first-draft curriculum was (as I heard it) not fully harmonious. Because Bashar's desire was not scored, the three-part harmony that is justice was not achieved.

But failing to score or deferring the scoring of desire certainly seems a fair move, and one Socrates raises as a "hard" question: "Do we learn with one [part of the soul], become spirited with another of the parts within us, and desire the pleasures of nourishment and generation and all their kin with a third, or do we act with the soul in each of them once we are started? This will be hard to determine in a way worthy of the argument" (Plato 1991, 436b, 114). Socrates argues, I believe, that once we get going, every cylinder in our soul should be firing—see, for example, the discussion of how it is best that individuals try to become one from many (Plato 1991, 443d–e, 123)—yet even if my reading were absolutely right, that wouldn't mean that a curriculum that defers desire, that in deferring its own desire left student desire alone, would thereby betray the students it serves.

But how *can* one tell whether student desire is betrayed or honored? Here I must return to Plato's words above: "hard to determine in a way worthy of the argument." In teaching and in teaching teachers of writing, we are in argumentation and inquiry with our students. Determining what is just is for Plato a difficult question of persuasion, not of discovery only. This possibility is implicit in Onora O'Neill's reading (1996, 76–77): "In the *Republic* Plato never rescinds the initial account of justice as living by the universal principle of giving each his due, but rather argues that the proper interpretation of that principle shows that what is due to different sorts of human beings differs."[10] I admire O'Neill's "proper interpretation," and one reason I admire it is for the subsequent interpretation it implies: what is due to different sorts of human beings is tied to arguments about which differences *should* matter. If in our rewriting of Plato's community everyone and their differences could matter, then every person's desire might matter—their dispositions might also be material, then, as well as which domain of justice their spirits rise to, the kinds of knowledge they construe as *good* reasons. Student desire must thus matter to a teacher of teachers. A teacher trainer should have the appetite—the stomach—to help teachers in training persuade others that their desire can count as a good reason.

The power imbalance is reason to be careful, however. Engaging in didactic persuasive exchange with teachers in training, we do not decide for them—not even if it is, as we may believe, for their own good. We do not outlaw nonconformity or paternalistically name their desire but, rather, help them assume responsibility for theirs—and so they with ours, inasmuch as, in trying to compose just communal ends, we win and lose together. This is pedagogy in a Platonic spirit, as Marina McCoy (2008, 194) says, an approach "based on the understanding of oneself and one's deepest desires. It is not defined by a method or even by a particular intellectual doctrine so much as it is by the practice of living well." In this practice is something individually indelible, one's understanding of oneself and one's deepest, most critically important desires.

But living well is also public practice, requiring at that level an equal concern for others. No matter the private desires motivating a teacher, a teacher must also be motivated by public obligation, by the questions that (as we'll see) motivated Bashar: *what* to be didactic about—that which a teacher must know, must teach, must do and must not do. These help constitute our duty. When it comes to duty, Plato (1998) says, we must be willing—in case persuasion fails—to use force. To help citizens—including first-year writers and teachers in training—better serve the community, one may resort to "persuading and forcing them toward the condition in which the citizens were to be better" (Plato 1998, 517b–c, 117).[11] Persuasion and muscle are paired, testing a liberal-humanist rhetoric's commitment to the unforced force of the better reason. Sometimes even the most rhetorically congenial pedagogy suggests the use of force to secure the better reason—as in the syllabus Clark designed for Brigham Young University's composition program. Devoted to "public discourse," the syllabus represents public discourse as "acts of citizenship" (Clark 2002, 111). As rendered in the syllabus, the desire-driven conception that students tend to bring with them—"writing and reading as skills that individuals develop and master in order to produce their own texts that appropriate knowledge and credentials for themselves" (Clark 2002, 106)—must be transformed into "genuinely communicative and thus collaborative action" (Clark 2002, 107). Discourse as such is so important that "careful theoretical discussion will be required throughout the course to keep students from slipping back into prior conceptions of writing and reading" (Clark 2002, 107). This requirement—a strenuous preventive measure "to keep students from slipping back"—seems to entail force, force exerted by a teacher lest students regress. That force might take the form of (to elaborate the pedagogical force reminder above) refusing to accept a response to an assignment, requiring revision of that response, or failing that response outright.

It can be objected that "theoretical discussion" does not necessarily rule out *persuasion*. Neither, the response might go, does such discussion promise a place for persuasion, a forum for teachers and students to exchange, advocate, revise commitments to their good.[12] To move on, if only to the next section, let us say that even if one's curriculum forces certain issues, force is not all there is and what force there is can be reduced. That's what we want. And because we want that, we continue our inquiry into "fundamental principles of respectful" *persuasive* exchange.

TOWARD THE INVITATIONAL MODE IN PEDAGOGICAL PERSUASION

Early in the fall quarter 2016, my grad students wrote two "passage-based papers" (PBPs) in response to Kathleen Blake Yancey, Liane Robertson, and Kara Taczak's *Writing across Contexts: Transfer, Composition, and Sites of Writing* (2014).[13] Bashar wrote PBPs that posited a strong distinction between the humanities and the sciences. My written feedback on his PBPs pressed him on that distinction, and although no response to my response was required, Bashar chose to write back:

> I do see your point about invention in both the sciences and the humanities and will have to ponder it. It just seems that in the humanities, or at least in literary studies, much more so than in the sciences, we're asked to start inventing before we've even surveyed the "residue" of other people's work. My sense is that as undergraduates, we don't exactly "throw ourselves into projects in hopes of mastering established knowledge by a process (writing)." Instead, we're thrown into the process (the writing)

without a clear sense of what exactly we're trying to master or why we're trying to master it, and without much hope of actually discovering anything new. (Alhoch, personal communication, 2016)

An excerpt from my response follows (a response Bashar used in his final project):

You raise the question of what we think with. Let's say we think with knowledge in situations with other people for some reason. You refer [above] to "without a clear sense of what exactly we're trying to master or why we're trying to master it, and without much hope of actually discovering anything new." WHAT to master, WHY master it—may we call these knowledge—knowledge of what to master, knowledge of why we're trying to master it? How do we get such knowledge? Why would reading and especially writing about that reading not be part of getting such knowledge—internalizing it, appropriating it? If appropriating it, for what? Might that "what" lead to the new discovery you also refer to?[14]

Reviewing the exchange to this point, whatever else I now see, I still see mutual ends-driven inquiry, not push and shove. So far so good.

But not so fast. My words—perhaps especially "if appropriating it, for what," where "what" fails to exclude an individual's or group's interest-laden ends—appeared to Bashar to restate, not resolve, the problem. In his final draft, Bashar describes his course as more investigative than parliamentary or sermonic—a course of inquiry into an appropriate body of knowledge, an opportunity for each student to empower herself with that knowledge—promising (as I then saw it) protection from persuasion:

Neither do I intend to turn you into lovers or even enjoyers of any particular kind of reading or any particular kind of writing, not even the kinds that I'll require in this course or the kinds that you'll continue to encounter throughout college. There's certainly a case to be made for enjoying one's work and doing one's duties in good cheer, and I'll cheerfully share why I enjoy the reading and writing that I practice, and I'll give you the best advice I have for being a successful student in college. But the main goal of this course is for us to broaden our understanding of reading and writing and to engage, partly for the sake of understanding but also in order to adopt as everyone sees fit, certain reading and writing practices. (Alhoch 2016, 10)

The problem such a stance raises for me is whether leaving student desire alone, in this case attraction to this or that kind of discursive practice, implies a kind of vagueness about ends: "to broaden our understanding of reading and writing and to engage, partly for the sake of understanding but also in order to adopt as everyone sees fit, certain reading and writing practices." If these practices are the duty—the sole duty, "the one work of a good citizen" (Plato 1998, 517c, 117)—then why not be more explicit, more directive? Why not follow Plato farther, bringing into more intense focus what the "common good" entails? The common good does, after all, make a cameo in Bashar's revised course description, separated from individual interests by an "or":

> How can we read and write so as to maximize the value of reading and writing for us? (Just because everyone's doing it doesn't mean that we should too. But there is this practice in the world, and all of us are already doing it in some way. Is it possible that we should do it in a particular way that best serves our interests *or* the common good?) (Alhoch 2016, 10, emphasis added)

I made an issue of this separation, asking Bashar whether if what we ought to do is imperative as well as attractive (note the two *should*s his revision retains), that direction could be more directly pointed to as *the* direction, that is, as the direction toward justice, that direction toward which we should orient our development, becoming the kind of people who desire greater knowledge of that direction, who participate in that project with zeal.

To engage Bashar in this issue, I selected the following moment from his Assignment #4: "Where I disagree with you, I'll invite you to consider with me ways in which you can improve the likelihood of achieving the responses that you wish to achieve." To connect readers' responses to the writer's wish fulfillment seems a kind of persuasion to me. And so it seemed to me then that it must to Bashar as well, for in the same assignment he also asks his students: "To what extent or in what ways does your success in meeting your criteria and achieving your purpose depend on your reader's response to your narrative?" Thinking that this question might be an overly circumspect approach toward the Platonic "one work of a good citizen," I asked Bashar in my written response whether he was endorsing rhetoric that is clear and effective while deliberately setting aside rhetoric that fights "to say the best things" (Plato 1998, 503a–b, 100).

A return to the revisions Bashar made to Assignment #4 will help me explain my concern, as well as bring to light something I'd missed, so intent had I been on maneuvering Bashar into revealing what he'd been withholding from students: that, like Plato, he cared about students' caring about everyone else's good:

> I'll let you know whether I agree with your predictions and why or why not. Where I disagree with you, I'll *invite* you to consider with me whether it matters that I disagree.
>   If it doesn't matter, we might proceed by drawing out the implications for the question above: In this practice (of writing and sharing literacy

narratives) that we're participating in, what exactly is the point of the sharing? *Is* there such a thing as failure in this practice?

   If it does matter that I disagree, we'll consider ways in which writers can
improve the likelihood of achieving particular responses. (Alhoch 2016,
16, first emphasis added)

The invitational mode—part of which I've emphasized above, though
now I see that mode everywhere in Bashar's project, from his rationale
to his course description and throughout his assignment sequence—is
something I'd not picked up on until early November 2017. I then had
the pleasure of reading Bashar's rhet/comp portfolio (part of his culminating project for his master's degree, which also included comprehensive exams in literature). Until then, I had been pretty confident in my
belief that Bashar had given priority to knowledge and zeal, so much so
that his own desire was subordinated. Desire was acknowledged, to be
sure, but not otherwise freed—not given that license without which a
just harmony is impossible. What Bashar had done, as I saw it, was suggest that his students consider with him whether it could matter that
he agrees or disagrees with their predictions, but although his students
were directly addressed, their judgment was not *forcefully* invoked. Bashar
might pose, I thought, other questions, questions like "Does it matter to
you that I disagree" and "Shouldn't it matter to you that I *cannot* join the
audience you appear to be addressing?" These are questions of desire,
questions I thought would help Bashar in situations like the following:
What if a student says that some insult to equality does not matter and
the teacher strongly disagrees, so passionately believing it should matter
as to destabilize Bashar's "we might proceed by drawing out the implications for" whether rhetorical exchange has a point, for whether it's possible to fail at such exchange?[15]

   But reading Bashar's portfolio exposed my pedagogy's way (or one
of its ways) of mistaking force for persuasion—a mistake that matters
because it violates what I now better see as a fundamental principle
of persuasive exchange that is respectful. When enrolled in the pedagogical practicum with me, Bashar was concurrently enrolled in other
classes, among them a survey of rhetorical theory. That survey included
invitational rhetoric, which had appealed to Bashar as an alternative not
merely to persuasion but to academic bullying. This insight illuminated
something in Bashar's project that my own project had displaced: his concern that too often academics label students' views "the stuff of sloppy,
senseless, half-dead minds that take up the drivel of the streets, of their
parents, of their churches, like simple animals"; in doing so, academics
mask "disagreement as moral difference" and figure "non-academics,

non-readers, and non-writers as cognitively underdeveloped and unreal-
ized, as though ninety-year-old grandparents who happen not to read,
or ancient bards who happen not to write, need not neighborhood nor
family nor church but Professor Jones to teach them right from wrong,
truth from untruth, wisdom from folly" (Alhoch 2016, 5–6).

What I'd under-read, in other words, was Bashar's desire, his desire
to circumvent persuasive exchanges that edge into bullying. He desired
more comprehensively respectful exchange—exchange more patiently
invitational than I had imagined it. Taking that desire into consideration
has helped me acknowledge ways I had imposed *my* image of respectful exchange (imposing it pretty much as if I had already seen the
justice—the one and only kind of justice—that would have to follow).
Presuming that our seminar already represented democratic community, I had been far less than fully open to how such community is an
undertaking—an undertaking that has begun before any seminar (that
has been begun by bards and grandparents), that takes place outside it
as well as in it (that takes place in neighborhoods and churches), and
that has to continue well beyond it (well into city life and beyond that).
In being less open than was appropriate, I probably required my students to suffer me more than was necessary, and I surely mitigated the
force of my privileged position less than I could have. (For one, I could
have shown more interest in and made more connections to their past
and concurrent coursework—perhaps especially to that coursework with
which they passionately identify, that coursework which informs how
they organize their lives as it pleases them.)

Rewriting Plato with others, not least with teachers in training like
Bashar and with all the students and colleagues whose work I wish I had
the space to include, does *not* imply a dismissive stance toward "training." Quite the opposite is implied by Plato's aspirational draft of democratic community. We train in many things because we need to: none of
us is "self-sufficient"; each of us "is in need of much" (Plato 1991, 369b,
46).[16] I am in need of much as a teacher of teachers—in need of many
more of the city's tales, of more understanding (as I have tried to show
here) of what my students know, of what they want, of what will move
them and what should move me. If I am to do my part in extending the
community I compose with them, then I had better mind *my* business
better. It is my business to better know what they are asking of me—to
know why, in FYC as they imagine teaching it, it pleases them to focus on
ethnography or grammar or lit or writing about writing. If I am going to
help them give each student her distinctive due, then I ought to always
mind giving them theirs.[17]

Easier said than done—Bashar, after all, chose to extend reflective exchange with me, overtly expressing that aspect of his desire; had that aspect not been more explicitly restated a year later, I would have missed it altogether. That would have been regrettable—regrettable less because pedagogical persuasion violated pedagogical hospitality than because an opportunity was unwittingly deferred. That opportunity is to let our students' desire speak, to see whether it is something our community building can help (re)form. If Plato's legacy is rewritten as it should be—not only with our students but also with knowledge of, zeal for, and desire for the invitational—then there is good reason to hope that such persuasive hospitality will engage, and little fear that it will deny, the chaotic moments of making just policy and living it well.

NOTES

1. Using Plato's (and his translators') default to the male referent seems a decent way to acknowledge this limitation. Here I'm assuming that "organize his life in it privately" encompasses, among other things, both privately organizing one's public life and organizing that fit between public and private in a way one finds pleasing.
2. As of 2017–18, this graduate-level requirement could also be fulfilled by taking the basic writing practicum, which focuses on the "stretch" portion of the FYC GE curriculum.
3. In spring 2018, in an informal survey conducted by my colleague Kristin Prins, nearly every one of her fifteen graduate students had had, as first-year students themselves, first-year composition classes that were literature-*based*—that is, GE writing classes in which literary study was the objective rather than GE writing classes in which the readings included literary as well as other kinds of texts.
4. In discussing the place in rhetoric of "recourse to force," Chaïm Perelman (1982, 11) makes it clear that persuasion "tries to gain a meeting of minds instead of imposing its will through constraint or conditioning."
5. I use the present tense for Bashar's final draft, past tense for his rough drafts and our online exchanges. (In my reading, Bashar's reference to "tasting" alludes to our seminar's commitment to each person's good, including exploration of tastes.)
6. This is an assignment I've been working with and on since 1990, when it was introduced to me by Bill Hendricks.
7. In a reading of a draft of this chapter, Bashar brought to my attention a passage from *The Republic* that has affinity with Matthew 18:3: Socrates's words on education as "an art of this turning around," not "an art of producing sight" but an "art [that] takes as given that sight is there, but not rightly turned nor looking at what it ought to look at" (quoted in Plato 1991, 519d, 197). Persuasion may overlap with conversion—the implications of which ought to turn a teacher's head.
8. On justice as constitutive of rhetoric, see Crosswhite (1996, 36); Kastely (1997, 4, 34).
9. Rewriting Plato's legacy also means rewriting Plato's revisions. Plato's account of the division of labor is not merely deficient but unjust. An example of a revisionary response is Adam Smith's, in which Smith sees the division of labor as "the *origin* of differences in talent, not the consequence of such differences" (quoted in Fleischacker 1999, 134).

10.   For another side of this coin—being the kind of person who gives such due—see Kastely (2015, 183).

11.   Plato (1998, 536e, 216), however, would have *children* enjoy their education, learning by play: "No forced study abides in a soul." Although Socrates advocates using the means of "play" rather than force in educating children, in educating children about force as an end, force can be a means: "The children must be led to war on horseback as spectators; and, if it's safe anywhere, they must be led up near and taste blood, like puppies" (Plato 1998, 537a, 216). There, alas, is the importance of "taste" again.

12.   To be clear, I think that in such exchanges, views like Clark's—of FYC as symbolic civic action—*must* have a voice.

13.   For an explanation of such papers, see Carillo (2015, 132–35). Students are asked to choose a short passage (three to five sentences) from an assigned text and write a short paper (one to two pages). The papers provide students with the opportunity "to engage in close textual analysis and to grapple with difficult ideas that come up"; such grappling means it is acceptable for papers to "represent an attempt at developing an argument through close reading as opposed to a fully-developed argument" (Carillo 2015, 133).

14.   In Bashar's own words: "My motivation for explaining the exercise to students in this way is the doubts that I sometimes had throughout college about the value of the work that I was doing—doubts that experience suggests to me are shared by others. My work seemed to float free of ends and values, and the result was a sense that the work was oppressively arbitrary. The solution that I'm attempting here was inspired by a comment that Professor Kraemer made when I shared such concerns:

>   WHAT to master, WHY master it—may we call these knowledge—knowledge of what to master, knowledge of why we're trying to master it? How do we get such knowledge? Why would reading and especially writing about that reading not be part of getting such knowledge—internalizing it, appropriating it?

What I've added here is the natural metaphor of the child—that greatest of knowers and appropriators—and the explicit grounding of the work in actual practices that exist outside the classroom." (Alhoch 2016, 8–9)

15.   And so for the flip side, discussed above via Clark's (2002, 107) pedagogy: that is, when a student resists a teacher's attempts "to keep students from slipping back into prior conceptions of writing and reading."

16.   The pedagogical topics in which we train (inquire into, question, practice) include, but are not limited to, academic discourse, assessment, assignment sequences, basic skills, classroom management, conventions/correctness, difference, directed self-placement, formative and summative feedback, genre, justice, L1 and L2/m-l students, politics, process (invention, arrangement, revision), prominent pedagogical approaches, reading; research, style, teacher persona.

17.   For several rounds of generous, helpfully directive feedback, I thank Lois Agnew and John Duffy. I must also acknowledge Bashar's careful, incisive reading of an earlier draft of this chapter, as well as one of the many questions his reading posed that I could not get to: "whether persuasion does or should take particular, distinctively pedagogical forms in pedagogical encounters—forms different from those appropriate to the courtroom, say, or the laboratory or the home."

REFERENCES

Alhoch, Bashar. 2016. "Turn, and Become as Little Children: Notes on a Nascent Course in Basic Writing." Seminar Project for ENG 587, Teaching Basic Writing. California Polytechnic State University, Pomona.

Carillo, Ellen C. 2015. *Securing a Place for Reading in Composition: The Importance of Teaching for Transfer.* Logan: Utah State University Press.

Clark, Gregory. 2002. "Departmental Syllabus: Experience in Writing." In *Strategies for Teaching First-Year Composition,* ed. Duane Roen, Veronica Pantoja, Lauren Yena, Susan K. Miller, and Eric Waggoner, 102–13. Urbana, IL: National Council of Teachers of English.

Crosswhite, James. 1996. *The Rhetoric of Reason: Writing and the Attractions of Argument.* Madison: University of Wisconsin Press.

Fleischacker, Samuel. 1999. *A Third Concept of Liberty: Judgment and Freedom in Kant and Adam Smith.* Princeton, NJ: Princeton University Press.

Gibson, Walker. 1980. "Review of *Teaching Expository Writing.*" *College Composition and Communication* 31 (1): 91–93.

Kastely, James L. 1997. *Rethinking the Rhetorical Tradition: From Plato to Postmodernism.* New Haven, CT: Yale University Press.

Kastely, James L. 2015. *The Rhetoric of Plato's* Republic: *Democracy and the Philosophical Problem of Persuasion.* Chicago: University of Chicago Press.

McCoy, Marina. 2008. *Plato on the Rhetoric of Philosophers and Sophists.* New York: Cambridge University Press.

O'Neill, Onora. 1996. *Towards Justice and Virtue: A Constructive Account of Practical Reasoning.* New York: Cambridge University Press.

Perelman, Chaïm. 1982. *The Realm of Rhetoric.* Trans. William Kluback. Notre Dame, IN: University of Notre Dame Press.

Plato. 1991. *The Republic of Plato.* 2nd ed. Trans. and with new introduction, notes, and interpretive essay by Allan Bloom. New York: Basic Books.

Plato. 1998. *Gorgias.* Trans. and with introduction, notes, and interpretive essay by James H. Nichols Jr. Ithaca, NY: Cornell University Press.

Yancey, Kathleen Blake, Liane Robertson, and Kara Taczak. 2014. *Writing across Contexts: Transfer, Composition, and Sites of Writing.* Logan: Utah State University Press.

12

MINDFUL ETHICS AND MINDFUL WRITING

Paula Mathieu

The 2015 Pixar film *Inside Out* takes viewers inside the brain of Riley, a twelve-year-old girl whose family has just moved from Minnesota to San Francisco. Running the console inside Riley's brain (and everyone's brain) is a team of emotions, each personified as a separate character: Joy, Anger, Sadness, Fear, and Disgust. As Riley struggles to adjust to her new surroundings, Joy and Sadness get lost, leaving Fear, Anger, and Disgust to run her console, directing her actions and responses—which signifies a big change from her childhood when Joy had been the dominant emotion. Fear causes Riley to be too cautious during hockey tryouts, failing to earn a spot on the local team of her beloved sport. Disgust causes her to spurn her father's goofy attempts to comfort her. Anger causes her to speak harshly to her parents, steal money from them, and run away from home. With each of these actions, Riley's thoughts about her own core values crumble: she doubts friendships back home, decides hockey is stupid, doubts her family's love, and believes that leaving San Francisco will solve her problems. Eventually, Riley is so lost and overwhelmed that her console gets jammed. No emotions are in control. She acts utterly without awareness as she boards a bus heading out of town.

What saves Riley by bringing her awareness back to the current moment is not Joy, the emotion who felt she should be in charge, but Sadness. Sadness gently takes control of the console and allows Riley for the first time to be present with what she had been experiencing all along: sorrow over leaving family and friends and moving to a city that seems new and scary. Present with her emotions, Riley cries and returns home where her parents comfort her.

What's revolutionary about this film is the way it explains and responds to Riley's actions, especially the harmful and dangerous ones. They are shown as arising out of Riley's lack of awareness of her own

DOI: 10.7330/9781607329978.c012

emotions and the unconscious thoughts and actions connected to that lack of awareness. In other words, Riley doesn't choose unethical actions; she acts unconsciously, without mindfulness: an awareness of her own "thoughts, the intentions underlying conduct, and the emotions, body sensations, and behaviors they precipitate" (Riskin 2009, 8).

The film resolves *not* by having Riley punished for her actions or experiencing shame. Instead, Riley becomes present, allowing herself to be aware of the sadness she is feeling and to sit with that sadness. Once she does this, her choice of actions becomes conscious and purposeful. She races home to her parents and shares the sadness she had been trying to hide from them after years of being praised for being a cheerful kid. In return, her parents remain present and accepting of Riley's sadness and offer her love and comfort. Even after behaving recklessly, Riley remains the deeply beloved character her parents—and the audience—support and cheer on.

Simply put, *Inside Out* is a movie about mindful ethics. Mindfulness, borrowing Beth Berila's (2016, 4) definition, is "the process by which we become more self-aware through particular practices." Mindful ethics, as I'm defining the concept, maintains that people act most ethically when we are conscious and fully present with our thoughts and emotions, when we slow down the time between stimulus and reaction, and when we act out of a place of self-awareness and equanimity. A mindful approach to ethics would contend that a person's least ethical actions arise from reactions to pain, driven by often painful thoughts and tacit storylines, undertaken without reflection or awareness. People's unethical actions arise when they act unconsciously, cut off from their own capacity to love and be loved, even when they choose to do something hurtful or reckless,

In this chapter I overview the rationale behind a mindful or contemplative[1] approach to ethics; I connect that approach to writing by exploring writing as one way to practice mindfulness and to view mindful practices as useful tools for developing ethical writers. I argue that writing is an important tool for living that can help us have healthier relationships with ourselves, those with whom we are in relationships, and the wider world.

MISGUIDED, NOT UNETHICAL

Pema Chödrön (2009, 5–6), a well-known writer and American Buddhist nun, writes that humans possess three natural qualities: intelligence, warmth, and openness. Natural intelligence, an intuitive sense of what is right to do, arises when we are no longer caught up in self- and society-created storylines fueled by anger, fear, or self-pity. Natural warmth is "our shared capacity to love, to have empathy, to have a sense of humor" as well as gratitude and appreciation (Chödrön 2009, 5). Natural openness means that fundamentally, human minds are open, curious, and flexible before they become narrowed into "a fear-based view where everyone is either an enemy or a friend" (Chödrön 2009, 6). Contemplative practices, which draw from a range of secular and spiritual traditions, share underlying beliefs that all beings are worthy and capable of love and that we hurt each other out of mis-guided attempts to ease pain and fear or because of storylines fueled by such emotions.

According to the spiritual writer Eckhart Tolle, even the concept of Christian sin can be interpreted to accord with a contemplative approach: "Literally translated from the ancient Greek in which the New Testament was written, to sin means to miss the mark, as an archer who misses the target, so to sin means to *miss the point* of human existence. It means to live unskillfully, blindly, and thus to suffer and cause suffering" (Tolle 2005, 9, original emphasis).

Understanding sin as missing the target aligns with Chödrön's conten-tion that all humans have the capacity for natural intelligence, warmth, and openness. The ethical challenge then becomes as follows: How do we call on the best and truest versions of ourselves to create less rather than more suffering in the world? Do we live in a way that "adds further aggression and self-centeredness to the mix, or are we adding some much-needed sanity" (Chödrön 2009, 2)? And what practices help us bring our most aware, intelligent, warm, and open versions of ourselves to our daily encounters?

There are myriad ways to respond to these questions, and these answers and practices form a large body of contemplative thought and practices that includes meditation, yoga, listening, writing, movement, and speaking (see figure 12.1).

What unites contemplative work is its desire to help us slow down our reactions, become aware of our thoughts and emotions, and engage in a process with those thoughts and feelings in compassionate ways. The practice is not about trying to banish feelings or thoughts; quite the opposite. The contemplative call is to show up fully present with whatever arises inside us, to be with our pain and emotions—and the ridiculous stories of revenge or self-hatred fueled by them—with aware-ness, compassion, and a realization that thoughts and feelings do not define who we are.

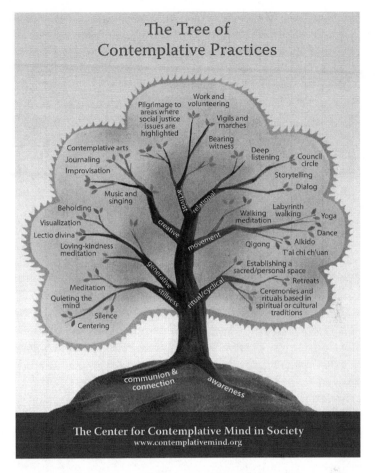

Figure 12.1. A list of contemplative practices, described by the Center for Contemplative Mind in Society

A central focus of contemplative practice is to realize that humans are creatures of habits, and often our habits involve running away from what is unpleasant, thus avoiding what is present. We seek pleasure by becoming numb, acting aggressively, obsessing, procrastinating, and becoming self-absorbed. Chödrön describes humans as like young children afflicted with poison ivy. Wanting to eliminate the discomfort of life, we try to make it go away; we scratch what itches, which seems to make perfect sense: "Scratching is our habitual way of trying to get away, trying to escape our fundamental discomfort, the fundamental itch of restlessness and insecurity, or that very uneasy feeling: that feeling that something bad is about to happen" (Chödrön 2009, 15).

While scratching seems helpful and temporarily eases the itch of poison ivy, it also causes the poison ivy to spread. The more we itch, the more we suffer. But if we can allow the itch to be present, apply some balm (perhaps with the help of doctors), and resist scratching, eventually the itch subsides and we heal. But we must be aware enough to recognize that habitual itching brings us continued suffering and love ourselves enough to resist scratching. This act of itching, of running away from all that is unpleasant, can also be called "ego" (Chödrön 2009, 17).

For Chödrön, itching is a metaphor for the unease and pain of everyday life. Instead of being present with whatever we are feeling, we seek to scratch away our unease through distraction or reaction. Sometimes these responses can be relatively benign: a bit of procrastination here, a slight critical complaint there. But if we cling to our fear of the present moment, the cycle of distraction and reaction can escalate dangerously and result in violence.

An example of reaction turned to violence can be seen in the acts of Alexandre Bissonnette, who in 2017 walked into a mosque in Quebec City with a gun, opening fire on a group of worshippers who had just completed evening prayers. He killed six men and injured two, including paralyzing Aymen Derbali, who distracted Bissonnette long enough to allow others to get free. Friends of Bissonnette said he "had become fascinated by extreme right-wing politics and frequently expressed hateful anti-immigrant views" prior to the shooting (Perraux 2018). Bissonnette's actions show the violent ends of feeling pain, fueling it with stories that blame others for that pain, and reinforcing it with views that encourage extremism and violence. But Bissonnette's story is also notable for how it points to a possible way out of this unhealthy cycle.

Rather than responding to this horror with hatred, the Quebec Muslim community responded with messages of love, welcoming, and neighborliness, even as vandalism and threats to the mosque continued and a local town refused to allow the murdered victims to be buried in its cemetery. The grieving community refused to mirror the violence aimed at them. In court, the victims and families of victims "filled the room with dignified calm and sadness, some taking a moment to comfort Mr. Bissonnette's own stricken parents" (Perraux 2018).

Perhaps even more remarkable than this behavior or perhaps because of it, as some journalists speculate, Bissonnette eventually changed his plea to guilty after vehemently denying his guilt for months. In a three-minute statement delivered in court, Bissonnette took full responsibility for the shooting, saying that pleading guilty was "the only decent thing he could do" and expressing remorse for the crime: "I'm ashamed of what I've done . . . [I] was a person carried away by fear, negative thoughts and a horrible form of hopelessness" (Perraux 2018). While many survivors are understandably skeptical of Bissonnette's statement, especially when he claimed he was not Islamophobic but instead fearful and hopeless, I think his words explain very clearly what leads people to extremism and committing hate crimes—a compulsive, self-reinforcing cycle of pain and scape-goating thoughts toward a person or people who are believed to be responsible for that pain.

What led Bissonnette to claim responsibility for his actions and spare the victims a long, painful trial? The prosecutors confirmed that there was no plea deal. His lawyers repeatedly tested his mental state. Many seemed incredulous that such a transformation had taken place. One reporter speculated that "maybe even a murderer can witness enough decency to set aside hate" (Perraux 2018).

Seen through a lens of contemplative ethics, this situation is a desired yet not surprising outcome. Stripped of his story that Muslims were the cause of his pain, Bissonnette likely still experienced pain. And perhaps by seeing that those he had harmed did not respond with violence or hatred, he had trouble fueling his toxic story. When one no longer clings to a hateful story (because one must cling, one must repeat, renew that story constantly to keep it alive), the present moment can reveal itself. Like Riley in *Inside Out*, perhaps Bissonnette became aware, realizing that the sources of his pain were his own fears and sense of hopelessness and not others trying to live peaceful lives.

Neither this realization nor a guilty plea excuses Bissonnette's actions; nor do they undo the pain he caused. But what I find hopeful in this story is that the cycle of pain-hate-retribution was broken. The perpetrator no longer sees himself as the victim. The victims grieve but don't seek vengeance. Two family members of victims found enough compassion to whisper to Bissonnette's parents, "You have my sympathies" (Perraux 2018). Those are mindful ethics in action.

Mercifully, many of us writing for and reading this volume haven't had to face the kind of devastating, violent loss as the victims of Bissonnette's shooting. If a grieving widow can offer sympathy to the parents of her husband's killer, how much easier should it be for any of us to wish well the person who cuts us off in traffic or who holds political view we abhor? Or how much easier should it be to feel compassion for a spouse, child, student, or friend who responds to us with an unkind or careless remark? Easier perhaps, but it's not easy. Too often we get hooked.[2] We take the bait. We react quickly and fuel that reaction with a story: "This always happens to me." "Why can't he or she ever treat me better?" That story, if not examined and questioned, can grow and feed reactivity. But if it is examined, if we slow down, realize what we are feeling, notice that we are going down a familiar road, and perhaps even smile at ourselves and feel compassion for our own habitual responses, perhaps we can break that cycle and find equanimity in the current moment.

MINDFULNESS AND ITS CONNECTION TO WRITING

While I have discussed a mindful approach to ethics, I have not yet discussed explicitly how mindfulness can, and I would argue should, constitute a central practice for teachers of writing and rhetoric. I will try to make that case now.

I begin by drawing on Aristotle's (1991, 36, emphasis added) definition of rhetoric: "an ability in each [particular] case to *see* the available means of persuasion." What strikes me about this well-cited definition is its relationship to action: the goal is to see, to observe, to become aware before acting. Rhetorical action should follow a considered and deliberate act of looking and seeing. Rhetorical training, then, should include learning tools and strategies for engaging others in persuasive acts *and* having the wisdom to know when and how to act and, conversely, when *not* to act, when to remain silent, when to listen.

Acts of restraint, slowing down, waiting, listening, and being aware of one's situation *before* acting rhetorically are essential to a mindful approach to writing. But I would also argue that teachers and writers spend more time focusing on teaching rhetorical action than we do on teaching the moments of restraint and listening.

Shortly, I will discuss the ways our field has and continues to offer scholarship related to mindfulness, but I first want to walk through a few concrete writing practices that can help cultivate mindful, curious writers.

VALERIE KAUR AND REVOLUTIONARY
LOVE AS WRITING PRACTICE

The best example I can find of mindful, ethical writing practices can be found not in a textbook or a journal article but in a TED talk by Valerie Kaur, an American attorney and civil rights advocate. She describes a process she calls "revolutionary love," which entails curiosity, listening, and self-care. I see these as valuable habits for any writing classroom.

Kaur, a California native, grew up brown-skinned in the Sikh faith, which led her childhood classmates to call her a "black dog." When the twin towers fell in New York in 2001, Kaur's family friend whom she called uncle, Balbir Singh Sodhi, also a Sikh, was the first casualty of post-911 hatred, murdered at the gas station he owned in Arizona by a white man who mistook Sodhi as a Muslim and called himself a patriot. Rather than allow this incident to turn her toward bitterness, Kaur strived to keep an open, curious mind. She decided to listen to and tell stories, to seek for herself and others the ability to "see no stranger" as her Sikh faith called her to do. She went to Sodhi's widow with a camera to record her story. When Kaur asked what Sodhi's wife wanted to tell the American people, she replied, "Tell them, 'Thank you.' 3,000 Americans came to my husband's memorial. They did not know me, but they wept with me." Kaur (2017) learned that after local media had shared Sodhi's story, thousands of people joined together to mourn his loss. For Kaur, this became her first lesson in what she calls *revolutionary love.* "Stories can create the wonder that turns strangers into sisters and brothers."

As writing teachers, we can seek to teach the kind of curiosity and storytelling that helps students "see no stranger" through question-driven writing, interview assignments, and acts of mindful listening. Curiosity and listening can help us and our students turn moments of pain into opportunities for learning and growth.

Kaur (2017) sees curiosity as the first step of revolutionary love, which she defines as "the choice to enter into labor for others who do not look like us, for our opponents who hurt us, and for ourselves." A lawyer, Kaur soundly rebuffs the idea that her call is a misty-eyed notion that "love is the answer." Instead, it's a call to do the hard work of being present, even with people we might prefer to avoid.

Fifteen years after her uncle's death, Kaur stood with his brother on the spot of the killing and felt a sense that little had changed. Kaur asked, "Who have we not loved yet?" This question caused her brother and her to phone Balbir's killer in prison and forgive him. Yet Kaur (2017) has a clear and specific definition of forgiveness:

> Forgiveness is not forgetting. Forgiveness is freedom from hate. Because when we are free from hate, we see the ones who hurt us not as monsters, but as people who themselves are wounded, who themselves feel threatened, who don't know what else to do with their insecurity but to hurt us, to pull the trigger, or cast the vote, or pass the policy aimed at us. But if some of us begin to wonder about them, listen even to their stories, we learn that participation in oppression comes at a cost. It cuts them off from their own capacity to love.

While there is deep compassion and possibly selflessness in Kaur's action, she argues that listening deeply to others' stories must not come at the cost of loving oneself:

> Loving our opponents requires us to love ourselves. Gandhi, King, Mandela taught a lot about how to love others and opponents. They didn't talk a lot about loving ourselves. This is a feminist intervention. Because for too long have women and women of color been told to suppress their rage, suppress their grief in the name of love and forgiveness. But when we suppress our rage, that's when it hardens into hate directed outward, but usually directed inward. But mothering has taught me that all of our emotions are necessary. Joy is the gift of love. Grief is the price of love. Anger is the force that protects it. (Kaur 2017)

In this passage, Kaur emphasizes the self-care and self-love necessary to be mindful and to be a deep listener to others. A writing classroom can encourage acts of self-care, especially by having students write a letter to themselves exploring thoughts or fears they hold about themselves as writers or as college students, stories filled with anxiety and self-recrimination. Very early last semester, after having students hand in such a letter, I took two sentences (one filled with fear, the other a hopeful statement) from each student's letter and pieced it together to form a group essay that I shared with the class called "Which Wolf Are We Feeding?" As a group, we were surprised by two things: one, that all students shared a similar belief that they were uniquely unqualified or challenged at writing, and two, that as a class the group had deep collective wisdom about what makes a good writer. So, we discussed: Do we want to feed the wolf of fear or the wolf of kindness and wisdom? And how, as a community, can we support each other in feeding the right wolf?

In short, Kaur's idea of revolutionary love enacts practices that are mindfully ethical, which are also solid intellectual habits for writing: curiosity instead of certainty, listening deeply to stories of others, and tending to the pain in ourselves are all habits and practices that can be cultivated in a writing classroom. We can strive to be curious rather than fixed in our thinking, to practice listening with openness to others, to record and circulate complex and rich stories of others, and to attend to the wounds in ourselves with care and compassion. Such writing practices would be mindful ethics in action.

MINDFUL PRACTICES IN WRITING STUDIES

Contemplative or mindful practices can be used in myriad ways in writing classrooms, and a handful of teacher/scholars in our field have been writing about these connections for many years. Mary Rose O'Reilley's *Peaceable Classroom* (1993) directly connects ethics and pedagogy when she poses a central question for all times: "Is it possible to teach English so that people stop killing each other?" She followed up with *Radical Presence: Teaching as Contemplative Practice* (1998), which argues that the keys to good teaching are contemplative in nature, and the secrets of good living are hidden in plain sight: "seeing one's self without blinking, offering hospitality to the alien other, having compassion for suffering, speaking truth to power, being present and being real" (O'Reilley 1998, ix). Another critically important book from the 1990s related to mindfulness is Alice Glarden Brand and Richard L. Graves's edited volume *Presence of Mind: Writing and the Domain beyond the Cognitive* (1994). This collection has sections on Silence, Wisdom of the Unconscious, Wisdom of the Body, Images, and the Open Door and features essays by Peter Elbow, Donald Murray, Sondra Perl, Kristie Fleckenstein, and others. While an interest in contemplative practices and their connection to writing pedagogy is not new in the field, the need this collection argued for in 1994, I would argue, still holds true today: "The greatest need for growth in composition studies lies now in the ways we create meaning beyond what is currently considered acceptable knowledge . . . call them unconscious, automatic, ineffable, inexplicable" (Brand and Graves 1994, 5). Brand and Graves (1994, 5) argue that writing evolves from a "discursive mind" that should be regarded as a mystery and that "our full psychological life" lies beyond verbal reasoning. In other words, a focus on emotions, bodily responses, and unconscious motivations can and should be at the heart of writing studies and is especially critical at this moment in history.

A growing body of contemporary scholarship in the field explores explicit connections between contemplative practice and writing. Several notable books include Barry Kroll (2013), Christy Wenger (2015), Robert Yagelski (2015), and Krista Ratcliffe (2006). Kroll uses ideas and exercises from the martial art of Aikido to teach forms of argument that focus on cooperation and empathy. Wenger draws on feminist thought and yoga practice to advocate pedagogy that includes body-generated knowledge and embraces a range of contemplative practices. Yagelski critiques writing studies' implicit embrace of Cartesian dualism ("I think, therefore I am"), which posits the self as an autonomous being separate from the world. The reliance on this dualism, according to Yagelski (2011, 45), occludes connections we have with each other, with other living beings, and with the planet itself. He argues that despite advances in our theorizing, most writing classes still value textual production over the experience of writing itself. When writing becomes a gerund and not a verb, we teach writing as a thing to be learned, texts to be produced and evaluated. When writing is taught as an activity that can help us attune more mindfully to the world, it can become a useful tool for living.

Ratcliffe's (2006) work on rhetorical listening also dovetails with mindful approaches to teaching writing. Ratcliffe shows that listening is a skill that can be cultivated and taught and that helping students become curious and active listeners is a key rhetorical skill.

Geared to writers of many disciplines, Daniel Barbezat and Mirabai Bush (2014) outline a variety of contemplative teaching practices including deep listening and beholding, mindfulness practice, movement, and contemplative approaches to reading, which are rooted in the Benedictine practice of Lectio Divina.

Beyond published scholarship, several professional organizations support instructors across the disciplines who seek to bring mindful, contemplative practices to their teaching and scholarship. The Association for the Contemplative Mind in Higher Education (ACMHE 2015) and the Advancement of Expanded Perspectives on Learning (AEPL) are two organizations that help highlight contemplative or mindful approaches to teaching through publications, conferences, and online events for instructors. The ACMHE explicitly states as its goal "the transformation of higher education through the recovery and development of the contemplative dimensions of teaching, learning and knowing." It holds an intensive summer institute for faculty, an annual conference, and many online webinars for members, who span a wide range of academic disciplines. The AEPL is an assembly of the National Council of Teachers of English that invites English teachers from all grade levels to explore the boundaries of teaching and learning beyond traditional disciplines and methodologies. The AEPL invites participation in its many events, including its annual summer conference, the *Journal for the Advancement of Expanded Perspectives on Learning*, the AEPL Newsletter, national conference workshops, panels, and special interest groups at the Conference on College Composition and Communication and in the National Council of Teachers of English.

WRITING AS MINDFUL PRACTICE

I increasingly seek to incorporate mindful practices into all my classes, scholarship, and program administration.[3] To offer a concrete example, I focus on one elective writing class I have taught. Mindful Storytelling is a senior capstone course that asks students to examine their relationship with self, family, society, spirituality, and career through these guiding questions: What are the stories we tell ourselves and others that bring us to greater well-being, and what are the stories we tell that encourage distraction, fear, and pain? What *is* a mindful story? How do we tell ourselves and the world more mindful stories?

Mindful Storytelling begins by inquiring into the nature of our mind and its tendency to tell incessant stories to explain the world. By drawing on cognitive research, we learn that the voices in our heads produce a nonstop stream of stories that are not always true: "The storytelling mind is a factory that churns out true stories when it can but will manufacture lies when it can't" (Gottschall 2012, 103). Like me, most students have long believed that the thoughts our minds create, especially the self-critical ones, are true. Realizing that our thoughts aren't reality can be comforting: "What a liberation to realize that the 'voice in my head' is not who I am," writes Tolle (2005, 22). Once we see our mind's stories as unreliable and understand that storytelling is what minds do, we can become curious about our thoughts and stories, observe them, ask questions of them, and try to process them without attachment or shame.

One way we process our often tacit stories is to write about them, borrowing from practices highlighted by Byron Katie (2002). What she calls the Work is a process of writing out and processing the incessant stream of stories our mind tells. Katie (2002, 16) writes:

> You can't stop the story inside your head, however hard you try. It's not possible. But when you put the story on paper and write it just the way the mind is telling it, with all your suffering and frustration and rage and sadness, then you can take a look at what is swirling around inside you. You can see it brought into the material world, in physical form. And finally through The Work, you can begin to understand it.

The Work includes four questions about any story our minds tell: Is it true? Can you absolutely know it to be true? How do you react when you think this thought? Who would you be without this thought? During the course, I ask students to pick a story about themselves, someone else, or the world that they feel causes them pain and to write about that story and engage in the Work as defined by Katie. The purpose of the assignment is to see our beliefs and thoughts as tentative and revisable and that as writers, we can take control of the stories of our lives and change them in ways that are more compassionate to ourselves and others. As an example, one student wrote the following to begin her essay about what story she would like to revise:

> I would like to change the idea that I am not enough. The "what" I am
> not enough of changes from time to time. It can be not pretty enough,
> or smart, or interesting . . . I am often angered and disappointed when I
> buy into this narrative. It frustrates me that I am an intelligent person but
> still cannot shake those stupid thoughts of being less than others and can't
> improve my self-esteem rationally . . . I know these thoughts aren't true. I
> also know that "enough" isn't a real concept. In turning it around I would
> say, "I need to be enough for myself." I need to love who I am and stop
> finding details I could change and thinking that would make me happier.
> Changing this narrative would allow me to be better fulfilled with my life
> and myself.

As this example shows, this assignment might invite students to
make themselves vulnerable and write about feelings of shame, inad-
equacy, or fear. To try to help create a space to allow this work to
occur without too much stress or self-censoring, I did several things:
I incorporated mindful practice into the beginning of each class,
whether it be ten minutes of silence, breath-awareness meditation,
loving-kindness meditation, or the mindful eating of an orange, based
on practice by Thich Nhat Hanh.[4] After a few weeks, I asked the students to lead class for the first hour, and each week students chose to
begin the class with their own mindful practice, including walking our
campus labyrinth, coloring a mandala, or lying on the floor listening
to a guided full-body meditation. Second, I collected all student writings in hard copy, wrote my comments on them in ink, and returned
the papers to the students for them to keep. Instead of workshopping
these papers directly, every few classes the students met in groups and
chose something out of their weekly writing to share. Each week had
a new writing prompt focused on exploring a different kind of story
we tell, such as a story about our bodies, a family story, a story about
our relationship with technology, our spiritual story, and so on. I told
students that I chose to collect and share their writing in this way for
this course because I wanted them to feel comfortable exploring topics
meaningful to them without deciding (yet) how publicly they wanted
their stories to be circulated. For the end of the semester, I asked each
student to create a public-facing final project and send me a paragraph
from their writing that they were willing to share anonymously. I compiled these paragraphs into a four-page publication called "Wise Words
from Mindful Students."

Another aspect of this course was mindful listening: learning to listen
deeply to others, and practicing listening without interrupting. Each
student had the assignment of interviewing "an elder," someone who
was at least a generation older than they were. Their main goal was to

be present and learn something valuable from their deep listening during a face-to-face interview seventy-five minutes or longer. Some students interviewed faculty members, and others interviewed family members. One student chose to share the following paragraph about his interview with his grandfather:

> Every year as the ground begins to thaw, he puts his mind, energy and love into caring for his garden. I never really knew what a mindful activity it is for him. It is a way to keep busy, but also a way to reflect, bringing him closer to my Nonna who passed away 15 years ago . . . I was able to see the suffering he has had, from losing a wife and a son, and the way he can still find joy and continue loving all the people around him . . . I have also learned about the importance of the memories we have and the stories we tell. They are powerful; helpful for those who hear them and healing for those who tell them.

The final projects included a children's book about mindfulness, handwritten letters to friends and family who helped the writer navigate college, a 100-days-of-gratitude compilation and reflection, and a creative nonfiction essay about a writer's grandmother and the family's immigration from Korea. Other projects included forgiveness letters to family members who had hurt the writer (sending them was not required) and a mindfulness book filled with photos, favorite passages from our readings, drawings, and messages to the writer to be consulted during challenging times. I was impressed at how creative and deeply meaningful the final projects seemed to be.

This class was taught to seniors in their last semester of college. After the course, I wondered how useful the lessons were after graduation and whether any of the ideas from the class stuck with the participants. I sought IRB approval for an anonymous, online survey of those students, conducted ten months after the course ended. The results indicated that the practices of mindful storytelling had remained useful navigation tools for many of the students.

One third of the students responded to the survey, and of that group, 80 percent said they still practiced awareness or mindfulness activities (27% of the class) either daily or regularly. The top practices they used were simply Awareness of the Present Moment (80%), Silent Meditation, and Walking Meditation (60% each).

I asked an open-ended question: If you engage in these practices, what do they offer you? These are some of the answers I received:

- They offer me the realization that my thoughts aren't truth. When I engage in these practices, I instantly feel energized. Like actually *less* tired. It's pretty awesome/strange.

- In college, I was also so busy that I felt that I couldn't truly meditate or take walks without letting my mind race or use my phone to further plan my day. However, I find that I can't even get through my work day without having a block of time to myself, where I either eat mindfully, sit in my car in silence and try to appreciate the present moment, or take walks/hikes with my dogs. These practices offer me an escape from my worries and fears and let me focus on the present moment, without worry or anxiety.

- These exercises give me a sense of calm. After graduating, I often feel panicked and lost and meditation offers a feeling of calm and an understanding of myself.

- They offer an instant of calm in the chaotic world I have created for myself. If I didn't want a chaotic world, I would change something about it. Mindfulness practices help me cope with the demanding environments in which I prefer to place myself.

- In college, I felt I had to really make the effort to engage in these practices, whereas now I can't get through a day without them.

Of those who said they didn't practice, one said that mindful practices sometimes increased stress. The other expressed a desire to practice more but cited time as a limiting factor.

Finally, I asked about a connection between mindfulness and ethics: Do mindful practices help you in any way to live a more ethical life? Why or why not? These are the answers I received:

- These practices absolutely help me live a more ethical life. Before . . . I was very self focused and did not consider the views of those around me . . . I feel as though I am more mindful and considerate in my actions. It is extremely humbling to go from being on top of the world as a senior in college to the bottom of the totem pole in the real world.

- It hasn't affected my moral compass, but it has certainly forced me to become more reflective on my morals and self.

- Sound decisions should also be ethical and just. Thanks Ignatius.

- I'm not sure if it makes me make more ethical decisions, but it helps me be more true to myself and not feel sorry or guilty about my decisions.

I realize that this study included a small group of students, so no conclusions can be made. Even so, these responses hint at the value of mindful awareness, listening, and self-care, not just for students but in everyday life after graduation. Also, as my teaching has turned more toward contemplative work, it has increased my awareness that dysfunction is built into any process involving human interaction. Being mindful of our own stories and emotions, slowing ourselves down, listening better, and embracing silence can sometimes be our most ethical form of action.

WRITING AS A TOOL FOR LIVING

In recent years, I have engaged in many conversations with my colleague and friend Robert Yagelski, whose remarkable book *Writing as a Way of Being* I refer to above. We have discussed that we know, deep in our bones, that writing is about more than writing, more than academic success, and more than transferable knowledge or concepts learned. We have discussed how writing can be a vital tool for living in and navigating as minds and bodies in the world. I increasingly try to focus all my writing classes around ideas of curiosity, awareness, listening, and compassion for self and others. And I deeply value my talks with Bob and the support of many ACMHE and AEPL colleagues who see the ethical value of intangible ideas like mindfulness, presence, awareness, full-body listening, compassion, and love. I help my students and myself seek balance and a sense of equanimity in the world and teach them how to act skillfully, rhetorically, and compassionately in the world.

I agree with Valerie Kaur that in our divided world, revolutionary love is our best hope for acting toward a better future. I believe that mindful practices help cultivate more ethical writers, and mindful writers are "better" writers, in the sense of being more curious, aware, and observant of the world around them. Like my students, I am working on and practicing telling more compassionate stories about myself and others in today's world.

NOTES

1. In this chapter I use "mindful" and "contemplative" as synonyms, even though their meanings are somewhat different. In figure 12.1, contemplative refers to a broader range of practices including mindfulness, but here I use the words interchangeably to underscore that the goal of contemplative practice is to bring more awareness or mindfulness. It's important, when introducing any contemplative approaches in teaching, to use the terms or ideas that work best in your local context. For example, working at a Jesuit university, I find that terms like *contemplation* and *reflection* are comfortable for students and faculty. A colleague who works at a secular campus chooses to talk about "breathing exercises" to enhance learning. Mindfulness is a term (and practice) with its own baggage, as it has been co-opted by corporations to eke out more efficiency from workers. (See the critique by Ron Perser and Edwin Ng [2016].)

2. "Hooked" is how Pema Chödrön describes the term *shenpa*, a feeling in which the words or actions of others irritate and engage us, often leading to mindless reaction.

3. See Mathieu 2014, 2016.

4. Many versions of this practice are available online. One is at https://www.lionsroar .com/the-moment-is-perfect/.

REFERENCES

Aristotle. 1991. *On Rhetoric: A Theory of Civic Discourse*. Trans. George Kennedy. New York: Oxford University Press.

Association for the Contemplative Mind in Higher Education (ACMHE). 2015. "Mission." http://www.contemplativemind.org/programs/acmhe.

Barbezat, Daniel, and Mirabai Bush. 2014. *Contemplative Practices in Higher Education*. San Francisco: Jossey-Bass.

Berila, Beth. 2016. *Integrating Mindfulness into Anti-Oppression Pedagogy*. New York: Routledge.

Brand, Alice Glarden, and Richard L. Graves, eds. 1994. *Presence of Mind: Writing and the Domain beyond the Cognitive*. Portsmouth, NH: Boynton/Cook Heinemann.

Chödrön, Pima. 2009. *Taking the Leap: Freeing Ourselves from Old Habits and Fears*. Boulder: Shambhala.

Gottschall, Jonathan. 2012. *The Storytelling Animal: How Stories Make Us Human*. New York: Houghton Mifflin.

Inside Out. 2015. Directed by Peter Docter. Pixar Animation Studios, Emeryville, CA.

Katie, Byron. 2002. *Loving What Is: Four Questions That Can Change Your Life*. New York: Three Rivers.

Kaur, Valerie. 2017. "3 Lessons of Revolutionary Love in a Time of Rage." November. TED Video, 22.13. https://www.ted.com/talks/valarie_kaur_3_lessons_of_revolutionary _love_in_a_time_of_rage.

Kroll, Barry. 2013. *The Open Hand: Arguing as an Act of Peace*. Logan: Utah State University Press.

Mathieu, Paula. 2014. "Excavating Indoor Voices: Inner Rhetoric and the Mindful Writing Teacher." *Journal of Advanced Composition* 34 (1–2): 173–90.

Mathieu, Paula. 2016. "Being There: Mindfulness as Ethical Classroom Practice." *Journal for the Assembly of Expanded Perspectives on Learning* 21, article 5.

O'Reilley, Mary Rose. 1993. *The Peaceable Classroom*. Portsmouth, NH: Boynton/Cook Heinemann.

O'Reilley, Mary Rose. 1998. *Radical Presence: Teaching as Contemplative Practice*. Portsmouth, NH: Boynton/Cook Heinemann.

Perraux, Les. 2018. "Quebec Mosque Shooting Suspect Alexandre Bissonnette Pleads Guilty." *Globe and Mail*, March 28. https://www.theglobeandmail.com/canada/article -bissonnette-pleads-guilty-to-first-degree-murder-in-quebec-shootings/.

Perser, Ron, and Edwin Ng. 2016. "Cutting through the Mindfulness Hype." *Huffington Post*. https://www.huffingtonpost.com/ron-purser/cutting-through-the-corporate -mindfulness-hype_b_9512998.html.

Ratcliffe, Krista. 2006. *Rhetorical Listening: Identification, Gender, and Whiteness*. Carbondale: Southern Illinois University Press.

Riskin, Leonard L. 2009. "Awareness and Ethics in Dispute Resolution and Law: Why Mindfulness Tends to Foster Ethical Behavior." *South Texas Law Review* 50: 493–99.

Tolle, Eckhart. 2005. *A New Earth: Awakening to Your Life's Purpose*. New York: Plume.

Wenger, Christy I. 2015. *Yoga Minds and Writing Bodies: Contemplative Writing Pedagogy*. Anderson, SC: Parlor.

Yagelski, Robert. 2011. *Writing as a Way of Being: Writing Instruction, Nonduality, and the Crisis of Sustainability*. New York: Hampton.

13

RHETORICAL PIVOTS
Contending with the Purpose and Value of Higher Education in Prison

Patrick W. Berry

A few years had passed since Project Justice, a college-in-prison program offering upper-level courses to incarcerated men, had begun at the Midwest Correctional Center. To recognize students' creative works and, by extension, the value of higher education in prison, the program held an annual symposium in which incarcerated students, community members, and teachers gathered at the prison for a few hours of readings, performance, and conversation. When the program first began, I had organized a similar symposium, and it had been overwhelmingly celebratory of the program's work, but something had changed. While this year's symposium featured moments of appreciation and recognition for Project Justice and the notable work it was doing, there were also moments in which incarcerated students questioned how this program might help them in the future.

Sarah, a teacher and tutor, recalled sitting at the symposium at the prison watching a rap performance in which students depicted themselves "back on the streets of Chicago" facing countless hurdles and struggling to survive.[1] "You've got the parole officer, and you still can't get a job," she recalled one student saying, "and you can't feed your family." Then another group of students was introduced whose performance indicated that they had "gone back into drug trading and were making a fine living." Students were vocalizing their fears about life after prison as well as concerns about how their work in the program might benefit them. Sarah was unsettled by these performances and observed that others in attendance were, too. For some, education in prison was not the lifesaver it had once been imagined to be. Describing this moment as a major pivot point for her, Sarah interpreted the students' performance as saying:

DOI: 10.7330/9781607329978.c013

"You know what? Higher education is great. We love it. But it's really our problem now. You guys don't know what we have to deal with . . . We need to pick it up now and really decide how the heck are we going to use this when we get back out, or what does it do?" And it really—it had the effect for me and the audience of [making us think], *This really is their problem. I can't help with this.* I mean, what we bring only goes so far.

Sarah was jolted by the symposium, seeing it as a shift from what she called the "naive early days of the program" (just two years before), when many students and teachers had seen endless potential for achievement through higher education in prison. Early on, she ex- plained, she had had the mistaken notion that all the men would leave prison and be on campus taking classes at the leading public research university that sponsored the program. While such enthusiasm was hardly absent from this symposium, some students highlighted their concerns about life after prison and the problems they would likely face post-release.

What was reasonable to expect from this college-in-prison program? Should the program offer rehabilitation, transformation, employment, or something else? The students' writings and performances suggested various answers to these questions as well as shifting attitudes toward higher education in prison and its purpose. I argue that we need to listen rhetorically to how discussions about higher education in prison are framed, interrogate the cultural logics that inform them, and create spaces for alternative understandings. "If rhetorical listening is to facilitate cross-cultural communication," writes Krista Ratcliffe (2005, 47), we need to extend discussions of identification "to include troubled identifications, that is, those identifications troubled by his- tory, uneven power dynamics, and ignorance." Focusing on rhetorical pivots—those moments when discourses shift or are challenged—this chapter urges a more expansive understanding of the value and pur- pose of higher education in prison, one that emphasizes the ethical dimensions of listening, learning, and writing in carceral spaces. The chapter (1) highlights competing discourses about education in prison, (2) explores rhetorical listening as an ethical imperative for understanding both higher education in prison and the students it serves, and (3) focuses on Sarah, a teacher and tutor whose early com- mitments to higher education in prison were challenged by her expe- riences with the incarcerated men she taught. Her story illuminates how totalizing rhetorics of prison education are enacted, engaged, and challenged in a local context.

WHAT IS THE PURPOSE OF HIGHER EDUCATION IN PRISON?

Whether we understand prison as a place of punishment or as one of rehabilitation influences what pedagogical possibilities are available and can affect how incarcerated students see and express themselves. In prison education research, ethics is often evoked to argue for a range of practices that include how we represent and talk about the lives of the incarcerated (see, for example, Hinshaw and Jacobi 2015), how we create positive learning environments (see, for example, Lockard and Rankins-Robertson 2018), and how we conceive of the purpose and value of higher education in prison (see, for example, Berry 2018). Ethics becomes synonymous with a commitment to recognizing power differentials, listening to the voices and desires of the incarcerated, and doing (or at least striving to do) "the right thing." Rather than relying on a set of moral codes, ethics involves an ongoing interrogation of our own dispositions and those of others with the hope of, as John Duffy (2014, 224) writes, achieving honesty and fair-mindedness. Thus is ethics grounded in humility and generosity.

In the opening vignette, Sarah found herself coming to terms with how her understanding of higher education in prison had been challenged. She, like many other teachers who worked with the program, was focused less on issues of reduced recidivism and jobs than on the transformative potential of such work. Reflecting on the early years of the program and the first symposium, Sarah noted that she and other teachers had been gratified by and felt proud of their work: "Wow, you know, we're rock stars. They just can't get enough of what we offer, of what we bring . . . higher education is their salvation." While she laughed at this overstatement, she recognized that such claims were not shared by all. She would come to see how such discourses needed to be tempered and how she, following Ratcliffe (2005), would need to listen to the lives and experiences of the men with whom she worked.

"Why are rhetorical listening and its places of identification, dis-identification, and non-identification necessarily linked to ethics?" asks Ratcliffe (2005, 76). Drawing on the work of Nietzsche and Derrida, she discusses the function of the ear. For ethics to exist, Ratcliffe (2005, 76; original emphasis) suggests, "a listener must be imagined with an agency that enables him or her to *choose* to act ethically, either by listening and/or by acting upon that listening." A listener must also cultivate "a lexicon and tactics for listening and for acting upon their listening." In the context of Sarah's account, this involved coming to terms with competing rhetorics that circulated about higher education in prison and attending to those moments when the dominant narrative about this college-in-prison program had been called into question.

Project Justice began in 2008, offering advanced courses at the Midwest Correctional Center to incarcerated men who had completed the equivalent of an associate's degree. It served a large number of African American and Latino students, in line with the general composition of the population at the Midwest Correctional Center.[2] Students took a wide range of courses, including ones focused on literature, writing, history, and religion. Learning was positioned as a rigorous and intellectual pursuit with transformative potential, as the program offered students a chance to earn college credit from a top public research university while experiencing a curriculum attentive to the whole person.

Students were provided with a resource room, including access to books and laptops. They worked one on one with tutors and peers as well as on their own. Sarah managed the resource room, served as a lead tutor, and often found herself working with students on their writing. In addition, the program offered workshops and reading groups on a range of topics. Unsurprisingly, Project Justice was met with a great deal of enthusiasm by students and teachers, most of whom worked as volunteers. I have written elsewhere (Berry 2018) about my experiences as a teacher, tutor, and researcher with the program, which I saw as one that valued written and oral communication and was committed to providing a broad-based liberal education. Many of the students and teachers saw the program as an oasis, a space where students were seen apart from their crimes and where learning was, for many, invested with the potential to transform lives. Like many other teachers, Sarah and I admired the work of Project Justice, which made the students' questioning of it all the more challenging.

An ethics of listening involves interrogating deeply held beliefs and being open to alternative perspectives. In this case, it involved questioning discourses about a program that many of us were invested in and knew on a personal level. Through listening, Sarah was able to cultivate a more nuanced understanding of the program and, by extension, to practice what Duffy (2014) calls *ethical dispositions*, revisiting her own beliefs and generously considering the expressions of others.

This contrasts with the way higher education in prison is often conceived in professional discourse. As Erin L. Castro and Mary R. Gould (2018, 2) assert, it is often cast as a corrective—hence the tendency to position such education under the umbrella of *correctional* education. While some may say a broad-based liberal education is about change, too, there are significant differences. "When all programming efforts inside prisons are understood as 'correctional' in nature," Castro and Gould (2018, 2) write, "the meaning, purposes, and possibilities of education broadly, and higher education in particular, are narrowed." Listening rhetorically to such discourse can help us see the limiting and problematic ways incarcerated students are often evoked.

The work of Michael D. Maltz (1984) as well as that of Castro and Gould (2018) suggests that a rehabilitative orientation is linked to a medical model of intervention that limits the possibilities of understanding the full potential of higher education in prison. Whereas some of our best colleges and universities are conceived of as places of discovery and personal growth, incarcerated students are given education as a way to repair their lives. Such a medical-model focus is familiar to literacy researchers who must also contend with the tendency to see literacy as a remedy for the criminal mind (Graff 1979, 240; 1987).[3] I see the questioning of such discourses as central to ethical practice because it asks us as readers to come to terms with how we are evoking the incarcerated and their needs in our arguments.

Even when medical-model rhetoric does not come into play, researchers have tended to rely on a few common justifications for higher education in prison, including reduced recidivism and job readiness for the incarcerated after their release (see, for example, Davis et al. 2013). Making such claims is a rhetorical tactic used by many, including those who work in higher education in prison, because it tends to generate, as Castro and Gould (2018, 5) explain, "'buy-in' from a diverse range of stakeholders." While recognizing the usefulness of such rhetoric, Castro and Gould (2018, 5) note its limitations:

> It isn't that using such studies and citing their findings (some of the most common being: investing $1 in education saves $5 in corrections or education in prison reduces the likelihood of returning to prison by 43%) to bolster support for broadening access to higher education during incarceration is necessarily bad; however, when the purposes of higher education in prison are framed as and often bound to reduced recidivism or cost savings, higher education is subject to commodification and vulnerable to predatory market forces.

Here we see a rhetoric that can limit our understanding of higher education in prison. By analyzing such discourses, as Castro and Gould do, we can see how incarcerated students are imagined and begin to explore alternative understandings. This process of listening, questioning, and challenging is central to understanding how rhetoric and ethics can work in discourses about college in prison. By seeking to understand the cultural logics at work (Ratcliffe 2005), we are engaging in an ethical practice of interrogating dominant discourses and comprehending the thinking behind them.[4]

The distinction between education as a cure and education as a transformative force is sometimes missed when discussing higher education in prison. Some of our best colleges and universities present the educational experience as one of (at least potential) personal growth and transformation. Such rhetoric is different from a medical-model approach, yet the difference is not always easy to see given that both involve the changing of people. As I see it, the use of the word *transformation* in prison education is not problematic in and of itself. Incarcerated students often see their lives transformed by writing and learning, and such perspectives need to be acknowledged even if transformation cannot be guaranteed for all. What Sarah began to understand was that in advocating for the program, she needed to temper her claims and be attentive to the experiences of the students therein.

RHETORICAL LISTENING AS AN ETHICAL IMPERATIVE

Defined by Ratcliffe (2005, 1) as a "trope of interpretive invention and a code of cross cultural conduct," rhetorical listening is a pragmatic and ethical practice.[5] It involves, as Ratcliffe (2005, 26; original emphasis) explains, a series of moves that include "promoting an *understanding* of self and other . . . proceeding within an *accountability* logic . . . locating identification across *commonalities* and *differences*," and "analyzing claims as well as the *cultural logics* within which these claims function." In this section, I focus on two examples from my meeting with Sarah to illustrate the troubled identifications that can circulate around incarcerated people, with the intent of further elucidating how rhetorical listening can function as an ethical practice.

Given that most of us who worked with Project Justice were doing so at a medium-high security prison, we knew on some level that the men we were working with had committed serious crimes. Still, most of us did not know the specific crimes they had committed,[6] and we refrained from looking up the students on the Department of Corrections website. The men did not usually talk about their criminal pasts, but one exception was Alex, a gifted writer who found himself in the resource room on a regular basis, working with Sarah to reflect through composition on his arrest fifteen years earlier when he was eighteen years old.

"I was sitting in a very small holding cell, chained to a steel chair, and facing what was sure to be an extended prison term," he wrote. "How could things have possibly gotten this bad?" When he was just thirteen, he had begun a battle with substance abuse, and he had since spent a great deal of time reflecting on and writing about his life. He felt he had learned something about factors that contribute to substance abuse and its prevention that was different from, and certainly more complicated than, the "Just Say No" campaign that had been prevalent during his youth in the 1980s. Alex would return to this piece of writing again and again, ultimately publishing it in the National Council of Teachers of English's (NCTE) National Gallery of Writing.[7]

As Sarah read the final piece at her home, she wept, moved by its beauty, but she was also jolted by it. "In the spring of 1995," Alex wrote, "I [pleaded] guilty to the murder of a drug dealer, a man who would never get the chance to change his life around because of what I had done." Despite his remorse, Sarah described herself as having been shocked by the revelation: "It was the first time I had to . . . quit denying that these guys were in for serious crimes." She noted how this understanding raised multiple issues for her. She thought, "Well, if this is a murderer, then I don't think all the categories I've been working with—they all need to be rethought."

In Sarah's discussion of Alex, we see her attempting to understand him—or more precisely, as Ratcliffe (2005, 28) suggests, to stand under her own discourses and the discourses of others, considering how they might affect her understanding of the person she had come to admire. As she read Alex's powerful words, she had to come to terms with categories (or cultural logics) that shaped her image of incarcerated people. In reflecting on her understandings, she was being accountable to herself and those around her, recognizing that all people are connected.

Sarah remembered telling Alex how moved she was by his writing and performances and, more broadly, how his writing appeared to be helping him and no doubt would help others who read his work. Despite her progressive stance, however, the label "murderer" conjured for her an image that was at odds with her perception of Alex as she knew him. Such reductive labeling is all too common when we imagine incarcerated people. As Bryan Stevenson (2014, 15) powerfully writes:

> We've institutionalized policies that reduce people to their worst acts and permanently label them "criminal," "murderer," "rapist," "thief," "drug dealer," "sex offender," "felon"—identities that cannot change regardless of the circumstances of their crimes or any improvements they might make in their lives.

Sarah was a dedicated teacher and activist committed to supporting students, but labels such as "murderer" still found a way to color her understanding, and this gave her pause.

As Ratcliffe (2005) helps us see, listening is not just something we do but also something we need to *learn* to do. "When practicing rhetorical listening," Ratcliffe (2005, 32; original emphasis) notes, "we are invited to consciously locate our identifications in places of commonalities *and* difference."[8] Ratcliffe (2005, 51) stresses that identification and identity should not be understood as one and the same, for to fail to separate them creates the risk of stereotyping in much the same way Stevenson (2014) describes. I appreciate Sarah's reflections because they show the complexity of the identifications and disidentifications that were present for her, even if they did not result in her taking any particular action. Her realization of this is where I see the intersection of rhetorical listening and ethics. Sarah was carrying a viewpoint that she took with her into prison and also, as I would learn, into her work with restorative justice.

A commitment to restorative justice had led Sarah to Project Justice. Through her church, she had invited Howard Zehr (2002), practitioner and theorist of restorative justice, to her town; she met the director of Project Justice at one of the events and would ultimately learn more about the program and its value. "I was very interested in peace and alternative ways of resolving conflicts than violence and punishment," she said. What appealed to her about restorative justice was that it was grounded in a new way of understanding how people respond to crime. She explained how the US justice system "really takes the focus away from the people who are involved in the crime," separating the offender and the victims and leaving them little to no possibility of talking with one another. "They're in fact counseled *not* to talk to each other," she explained. Rather than talking about crime as the act of causing harm to another person, she continued, we tend to talk about it as "breaking the law," erasing the opportunity for connection and listening.[9] She continued:

> So [Zehr] began to wonder, what would justice look like if we said that crime was about breaking a relationship between people, and what if the resolution to that was trying to find a way to restore that relationship? So it came out of listening to victims—what do victims really need? And it turned out [that] victims don't really need their offenders to suffer and be punished a lot. They need them to listen.

Here, too, Sarah attempts to practice a form of rhetorical listening by considering the cultural logics that inform our current justice system and by imagining the healing that might come from restoring relationships. By tracing different beliefs, exploring the cultural logics behind them, she was illustrating the reasoning behind different perspectives, including those with which she disagreed. She saw restorative justice as very much about conflict resolution and transformation.[10] Whether

confronting her understanding of the term *murderer* or the cultural logics that inform how we think about justice, she was opening up space for
new ways of learning about herself and the world.

These two examples illustrate rhetorical listening and, by extension,
the ethical imperative to question and interrogate dominant discourses
as well as our own perspectives. In the first account, Sarah illustrated the
tension between Alex, the student in front of her, and the label *murderer*.
We see her coming to understand her own beliefs and her experiences
working with a man she had come to admire. In the second account,
Sarah bravely tries to understand alternative responses to crime. An ethical disposition is enacted by way of Sarah's coming to understand and
rearticulate a relationship with a person about whom and a topic about
which she had previously had limited knowledge.

WRITING ACROSS BOUNDARIES

In exploring the ethical decisions writers make and the relationships
they form through composing, John Duffy (2019, 10) identifies three
questions raised by moral philosophers: "What does it mean to be a
good person? What kind of person do I want to be? How should I live
my life?"[11] The importance of such questions is intensified in the prison
classroom, where students often attempt to rewrite their lives and form
relationships with others both inside and outside prison. Such work is
about ethics, and it is also about listening.

As Ratcliffe (2015, 76) suggests, by focusing on identifications, disidentifications, and non-identifications, we are revisiting our assumptions about others. In listening to Alex, Sarah attempted to understand
him in ways that challenged beliefs she had carried with her since childhood. Her reflections illustrate how rhetorical listening is an ongoing
process of attempting to listen beyond our comfort zone. In this section,
I focus on Sarah's early experience with and knowledge of issues of mass
incarceration and higher education because I believe that one's location in the world informs one's ability to cross boundaries and engage
in the ethical practice of deep listening. I also return to Alex's writing,
which provided Sarah and others with an alternative way of understanding incarcerated people and higher education in prison. Such reflective practice has the potential to function as what Paula Mathieu (this
volume) calls mindful ethics—that is, "when we are conscious and fully
present with our thoughts and emotions, when we slow down the time
between stimulus and reaction, and when we act out of a place of self-
awareness and equanimity."

Prior to meeting Alex, Sarah had little exposure to incarcerated people. She grew up in a Midwest town, in a home in which her family never felt the need to lock the doors. As a child, when she had trouble sleeping, she remembered her mother telling her there were "no robbers in Smithtown" to calm her fears. When she was a child, prison was "another world" to her. Only later, when she got involved with the Mennonite church, did she begin to think about restorative justice.

As an undergraduate she said, "I went to a liberal arts church college, and my dad taught religion at a church college." Though her father did not have a doctorate, he was invited to teach because of his strength in working with undergraduates and families of different faiths, and he also served as an ordained minister for a Lutheran church. She continued, laughing, "Growing up, it was sometimes hard to tell whether the Gospel was liberal arts education or salvation through Christ." This experience influenced Sarah's understanding of education and its role in transforming lives. From the church's perspective, she said:

> Education serves the whole purpose of nurturing and supporting whole human beings living together . . . So, education is itself something that's a blessing, a gift. It's something that you would expect to play an important role in changing people's lives, teaching them to get along better, and so on.

This was the type of work she saw both Project Justice and herself doing—a stance that was in some ways aligned with the goals of a liberal education.

After completing her undergraduate degree, Sarah attended a theological school on the East Coast and earned a master of divinity degree. Rather than pursuing ordination, she saw her calling "in doing religion in a classroom." But this aspiration was put on hold as her husband began his academic career and they started a family. When her kids were old enough, she returned to the idea of teaching. She remembered a professor of religion asking her, "Would you ever consider teaching in a prison?" Her initial response was "okay, so I'm a total loser at this point. There's no possible teaching career if I have to go to a prison." She went on to say, "And then—you know . . . the joke's on me." She would come to recognize that her earlier ideas about the prospect of teaching in prison had been wrong, for in prison she would find an extremely gratifying teaching experience.

During Project Justice's second semester, Sarah taught a course in religion. "I think for a lot of the students," she said, "it was the first time that they had really wrestled with religion as an academic exploration and not a religious [one]." She had the sense that talking and writing about religion without preaching or "fighting with somebody or being defensive was something they didn't have much occasion to do." Like her father, she had learned to effectively carry out such dialogues and help students listen to diverse perspectives. Though she had initially hoped the class would cover far more material than was the case, Sarah reported that many of the students commended her on the course and urged her to teach it again.

What stood out for her about her teaching and the program more broadly was that she felt many of the students had gained a greater sense of confidence through it. They recognized, she thought, that "I have something to say," and she was excited to observe this because she saw how students were able "to change their self-conception, the role that they thought they had to play in society." Often, as in the case of Alex, this change came through writing.

In one of Alex's essays, he reflected on his crime and on the role of writing in helping him find his way out of prison, both figuratively and literally. Composing had played a critical role in helping him make sense of the past and connect with others, including Sarah. During the years in which he had been incarcerated, he had come to see that those he had imagined would be there for him, those he had thought might write him letters, were no longer around. He imagined the world moving on as he was in prison with "an almost palpable atmosphere of indifference." What kept him going were "shimmers of light" in the "books, teachers, and loved ones . . . who have encouraged me to think critically about who I am, and who I want to become." The value he placed on education and its importance in his life could not be overestimated.[12]

A central narrative in Alex's essay concerned his effort to make amends in some way, "to help other kids avoid making some of the mistakes" he had made. He wrote:

> As the pieces of paper in front of me soaked in years of mistakes, I began to realize how distracted I had become in my life, and what little attention I had paid to how significantly the world was changing around me. I caught glimpses of my childhood friends, my brother and sister, aunts, uncles, and even my mom, all fading away, and replaced by kids who were just as lost as me.

When the prosecutor read what Alex had written, Alex was asked if he would be willing to read his words in front of a camera, and he agreed. This was a way to reach out to kids he did not know who might be facing some of the same challenges he had faced. His sixth-grade teacher was among those who asked to share the video with students.

Alex's participation in college-in-prison programs was central to his growth, as he found education "the best chance for people in here to learn how to truly change their lives." "In the end," he wrote, "maybe writing can't erase what happened in the past . . . but it has helped me transform my life." He said:

> I still may be a little unsure when I think about what the future holds, but one thing I am certain of is that I feel strongly about helping others avoid suffering the way my family, my victim's loved ones, and I have suffered . . . Yes, I believe a wonderful future awaits me, and that somehow a fresh sheet of paper will always have a connection to it all.

This was a belief shared by Sarah, one connected with her early experiences with education and spirituality and consistent with her observations at the prison, and it made her comfortable arguing for the value of Project Justice and higher education in prison more generally. I appreciate her attention to learning in the present moment, a view I describe in other work (Berry 2018, 38) as the *contextual now*, which involves attending to the present moment without losing sight of issues like the numerous obstacles incarcerated people face once they are released from prison. In this section, we see how our histories can shape our beliefs and the words we construct, our ability to write across boundaries, and our identification with others or lack thereof. Such considerations are, at the core, ethical ones that resist the drawing of easy conclusions. Yet through reflective practices, through efforts to see beyond ourselves, writers can work toward constructing ethical dispositions toward others. They can also interrogate rhetorical pivots in public discourse about incarcerated people and their education.

CONCLUDING THOUGHTS

The ways we identify, disidentify, or non-identify with the incarcerated play a significant role in our understanding of higher education in prison. The rhetorics of mass incarceration name the crimes, and those crimes replace the individuals, making it easy to disregard them and their circumstances. When we imagine higher education in prison, those whom we are trying to serve are not always discussed. While I agree with those who argue that we should not provide one type of education for the incarcerated and another for those on the outside (Karpowitz 2017), education is not homogeneous. When we refer to everything as "corrections," we narrow our potential for understanding nuance and possibility.

Following the symposium mentioned at the opening of this chapter, Sarah recalled meeting with students in the resource room to reflect on what had taken place. They anxiously asked what she had thought about the symposium. "I said . . . I felt like there was this huge pivot where you guys . . . said, 'Look, we have to wrestle this one to the ground. We have to figure this out.'" They agreed, Sarah thought, that they were all still figuring out what higher education was and how it might help them both in the present and in the future. I appreciate the humility expressed by the students, particularly their recognition that they were dealing with complex issues, some without easy resolutions. Such a disposition strikes me as a central component in understanding rhetoric and ethics.

Many incarcerated students have, like Alex, found higher education and writing to be transformative. Despite the naïveté sometimes associated with such rhetorics, we need to acknowledge that such possibilities do arise from time to time, especially among students like Alex who attend programs like Project Justice that embrace a liberal education as central to their missions. When Alex writes about how "an ordinary pen became [his] lifeline back to the world" and how through writing he "found a place free of the restrictions that threatened to close [him] off from the world, a place where the only rules that existed were [his] own, no one else's," it should get educators' attention. We know that this is not everyone's story, but it is Alex's and no doubt that of others like him.

Higher education, whether for those incarcerated or for those on the outside, would do well to be concerned with, as Jacqueline Jones Royster and Gesa Kirsch write (this volume), "teaching students about discovering beauty and joy in citizenship, about engaging in meaningful work, about fostering curiosity and wonder in life, and about the genuine friendship and love that emerges from a commitment to community and to a good that is greater than ourselves." The sharing of such stories is important for rhetorical listening and the fostering of ethical practices. Sarah would come to recognize her disidentification with the category "murderer"; as she learned about Alex's substance abuse and the struggles he had experienced, she began to reconsider her internal categories. Through working with Project Justice, she came to better understand incarcerated students and thereby to understand more about the possibilities (and challenges) of higher education in prison. Such rhetorical listening remains critical for supporting incarcerated people and their families and is part of cultivating an ethical disposition grounded in humility and fairness.

NOTES

1.   Interview with Sarah, a pseudonym, May 28, 2011.
2.   As Barack Obama noted at the 2015 NAACP conference, "African Americans and Latinos make up 30 percent of our population; they make up 60 percent of our inmates. About one in every 35 African American men, one in every 88 Latino men is serving time right now. Among white men, that number is one in 214." In the class I taught, African Americans and Latinos made up the majority of the students.
3.   See also Graff (1987, 337), in which he writes: "The reduction of crime and disorder via controlled schooling and transmission of literacy ranked high among education's presumed socializing functions. Ignorance was considered the first cause of criminality, and schooling was to eradicate ignorance. The extent of literacy marked success, in theory."
4.   The concern about "predatory market forces" is, of course, not confined to prison education. In fact, I found that Project Justice tended to avoid such framings (at least in general communication), which allowed it to talk about higher education in broader and more transformative ways.
5.   Ratcliffe (2005, 26; original emphasis) writes: "Dismissing rhetorical listening as too idealistic presumes a focus only on its obvious limitations. That is, rhetorical listening cannot solve all the world's problems, nor can it guarantee perfect communication or even productive communication in *all* instances. Then again, neither can Aristotle's enthymeme."
6.   I worked as a teacher, tutor, and researcher for approximately two years.
7.   Unfortunately, these contributions are no longer available.
8.   See Ratcliffe (2005), chapter 2, for a valuable discussion of theories of identification, disidentification, and non-identification as related to rhetorical listening.
9.   See also Winn (2018, 20), in which she powerfully discusses the need for restorative justice approaches in our schools: "If teachers are prepared to think about access to language, literacies, the sciences, history, art, music, and mathematical reasoning as both civil and human rights, it might be possible for them to think about the moral and ethical obligations of addressing harms and needs that stem from education debt."
10.   See also Angela Davis (2003, 114–15), in which she describes how Linda and Peter Biehl responded to their daughter's murder in 1993. Davis (2003, 115) quotes Peter Biehl as saying: "We tried to explain that sometimes it pays to shut up and listen to what other people have to say, to ask 'Why do these terrible things happen?' instead of simply reacting."
11.   See also Duffy (2017).
12.   In other work (Berry 2018, 86), I talk about what one teacher called the "dark side of prison teaching"—that is, the irony that many teachers found in having prison students who were much more interested in them and their scholarship than were their students on traditional campuses.

REFERENCES

Berry, Patrick W. 2018. *Doing Time, Writing Lives: Refiguring Literacy and Higher Education in Prison.* Carbondale: Southern Illinois University Press.

Castro, Erin L., and Mary R. Gould. 2018. "What Is Higher Education in Prison? Introduction to Radical Departures: Ruminations on the Purposes of Higher Education in Prison." *Critical Education* 9 (10): 2–15.

Davis, Angela Y. 2003. *Are Prisons Obsolete?* New York: Seven Stories.

Davis, Lois M., Robert Bozick, Jennifer L. Steele, Jessica Saunders, and Jeremy N.V. Miles. 2013. *Evaluating the Effectiveness of Correctional Education: A Meta-Analysis of Programs That Provide Education to Incarcerated Adults.* Santa Monica, CA: Rand Corporation. http://www.rand.org/pubs/research_reports/RR266.html.

Duffy, John. 2014. "Ethical Dispositions: A Discourse for Rhetoric and Composition." *JAC: A Journal of Rhetoric, Culture, and Politics* 34 (1): 209–37.

Duffy, John. 2017. "The Good Writer: Virtue Ethics and the Teaching of Writing." *College English* 79 (3): 229–50.

Duffy, John. 2019. *Provocations of Virtue: Rhetoric, Ethics, and the Teaching of Writing.* Logan: Utah State University Press.

Graff, Harvey J. 1979. *The Literacy Myth: Literacy and Social Structure in the Nineteenth Century City.* New York: Academic.

Graff, Harvey J. 1987. *The Legacies of Literacy: Continuities and Contradictions in Western Culture and Society.* Bloomington: Indiana University Press.

Hinshaw, Wendy Wolters, and Tobi Jacobi. 2015. "What Words Might Do: The Challenge of Representing Women in Prison and Their Writing." *Feminist Formations* 27 (1): 67–90.

Karpowitz, Daniel. 2017. *College in Prison: Reading in an Age of Mass Incarceration.* New Brunswick, NJ: Rutgers University Press.

Lockard, Joe, and Sherry Rankins-Robertson, eds. 2018. *Prison Pedagogies: Learning and Teaching with Imprisoned Writers.* Syracuse, NY: Syracuse University Press.

Maltz, Michael D. 1984. *Recidivism: Quantitative Studies in Social Relations.* Orlando, FL: Academic.

Obama, Barack. 2015. "Remarks by the President at the NAACP Conference." White House, July 14. https://www.whitehouse.gov/the-press-office/2015/07/14/remarks-president-naacp-conference.

Ratcliffe, Krista. 2005. *Rhetorical Listening: Identification, Gender, Whiteness.* Carbondale: Southern Illinois University Press.

Stevenson, Bryan. 2014. *Just Mercy: A Story of Justice and Redemption.* New York: Spiegel and Grau.

Winn, Maisha T. 2018. *Justice on Both Sides: Transforming Education through Restorative Justice.* Cambridge, MA: Harvard Education Press.

Zehr, Howard. 2002. *The Little Book of Restorative Justice.* Intercourse, PA: Good Books.

14

TOWARD A COMMON TONGUE
Rhetorical Virtues in the Writing Classroom

John Duffy

Let us imagine a conversation. We are at the Conference on College Composition and Communication (CCCC) conference in, say, Pittsburgh or Kansas City or maybe Portland. It's the end of another satisfying conference day. We've been to a breakfast committee meeting, browsed the exhibit hall, and attended several stimulating sessions. Now we find ourselves at the hotel bar. A group of us is sitting around a long table: friends, some friends of friends, and a few people whose work we've read but never previously met. In the clamor of the room, it's hard to catch every word, but we soon establish that the conversation concerns different approaches to teaching writing.

A man at one end of the table—did you meet him at a conference two years ago?—is explaining that in his program, teachers focus on teaching first-year students how to write academic arguments: formulating claims, presenting evidence, assessing audience, and the rest. A woman seated nearby counters that argument, professing that writing should be taught in a broader critical context that addresses questions of power and ideology. The writing classroom, she says, is a venue for promoting social change. A friend puts in a word for teaching students how to write collaboratively. In her classes, she tells the group, students create their own projects, negotiate writing tasks, and grade themselves. Someone else argues for teaching genre awareness, helping students learn to identify and write in diverse genres. A young man at the opposite end of the table—a graduate student?—asks how these different approaches address the new media environments in which students live and write. And on it goes. Someone catches the bartender's attention, and the company orders another round.

Depending on one's perspective, the diversity of pedagogical approaches to the teaching of writing may be understood as:

DOI: 10.7330/9781607329978.c014

- An expression of the deep, possibly irreparable fissures in disciplinary conceptions of how and why to teach writing
- An affirmation of the seemingly boundless creative energies of writing teachers and scholars
- A rational response to the different needs, goals, and resources of students, teachers, institutions, and communities.

Perhaps the best answer is, all of the above. Nor is there any discernible reason to choose among the various approaches to teaching writing—at least not in the sense of deciding which, in the abstract, is better than the others. As Amy Rupiper Taggart, H. Brooke Hessler, and Kurt Schick (2014, 1) observe in the introduction to *A Guide to Composition Pedagogies* (Tate, Taggart, Schick, and Hessler 2014), teachers and scholars of writing can take comfort in the fact that "there is no single way to teach writing, nor even one unified set of goals all writing teachers need to help students achieve." Instead, the authors suggest, teachers of writing choose among the various pedagogical approaches based on what they hope to accomplish in their classes and what they understand the needs of their students to be (Taggart, Schick, and Hessler 2014, 10).

Yet the sharp differences in our many approaches to teaching writing—the critical and the collaborative, the expressive and the community-engaged, the process and the genre-based approaches—challenge those of us in writing studies to articulate what is common in the ongoing work of teaching students to write. Each of the pedagogies we might choose to adopt comes with its own distinctive language of arguments, methods, and bodies of knowledge. These we know and can elaborate on, defend if need be. Yet what are the connections, if any, among these diverse languages?

What is common, for example, in the work of teaching basic writing to immigrant students at a community college in New York City and teaching community-based writing to first-year students at a religious college in Texas? What is shared in teaching personal narrative to writing majors at a private liberal arts university in Tennessee and teaching argument to engineering students at a large Midwestern state university? Is there a language that speaks across diverse contexts and pedagogical boundaries to widely accepted disciplinary values? Is there a common tongue, so to speak, in which we can explain—to students, to colleagues in other disciplines, to deans and provosts, to the general public—what we teach, why we teach it, and why, in the present cultural moment, our work is so critically important?

In this chapter I argue that there is such a language. Regardless of the pedagogical approach we adopt in our respective writing classrooms, I propose, whether we see ourselves as teaching critical literacy or cultural studies, second-language writing, or Writing Across the Curriculum, we are necessarily teaching a language grounded in ethics and ethical discourse practices. The teaching of writing, to say it another way, is inseparable from the teaching of ethical rhetoric. In making this claim, I do not mean we should be teaching ethical discourse, that the world would be a better, happier place if we did so, and so forth. Rather, I mean that in teaching writing we are always and inevitably teaching practices of ethical communication, and this is true regardless of the pedagogical approach we adopt.

First, some definitions. When I say "writing," I am referring to the various kinds of writing commonly taught in postsecondary writing programs. So, for example, "writing" as I mean it in this chapter can refer to academic argument, to personal narrative, or to what is termed "basic writing," whether these are taught at universities, colleges, community colleges, or elsewhere. "Writing" as I use it here refers as well to writing taught in writing-intensive courses, in writing majors programs, and in Writing Across the Curriculum classes. In short, when I say "writing," I am talking about the sorts of writing many readers of this chapter teach on a regular basis.

Next, when I refer to "ethics" and the "ethical," I am locating myself in a particular ethical tradition, one in which "the good" is expressed in such qualities, dispositions, and habits as truthfulness, accountability, fair-mindedness, intellectual generosity, intellectual courage, righteous indignation, and other such qualities that moral philosophers have called "virtues" and that today are the subject of the branch of philosophical inquiry known as "virtue ethics." When writing teachers provide students with opportunities to express such qualities in their speech and writing, I propose, we are teaching what I have elsewhere called "rhetorical virtues," or the discursive enactment of the virtues (*Provocations*). And it is in the discourse of rhetorical virtues that we find our common language, one that speaks across pedagogical boundaries to the shared values of our discipline and to the urgency of our work.

By way of illustrating these claims, I shall consider two contrasting approaches to the teaching of writing outlined by Gary Tate and colleagues (2014): community-engaged pedagogy (Julier, Livingston, and Goldblatt 2014), and new media pedagogy (Brooke 2014). I argue that while each approach has its own set of assumptions and objectives, there is common to both an inherent and implicit virtue-based ethical discourse. In making this case, I do not mean to obscure the meaningful, often enlightening differences in the many distinctive approaches to teaching writing. Our pedagogical choices can tell us much about the particulars of our students, our institutions, our material and political contexts. I do not mean to discount these. Rather, my aim is to demonstrate that regardless of the pedagogical approach we adopt, regardless of the differences in our institutional and material contexts, we are nevertheless teaching the language and practices of rhetorical virtue.[1] Before turning to the pedagogies, however, let me briefly review, since they are central to my discussion, what I mean by the terms *virtue* and *virtue ethics*.

WHAT IS VIRTUE AND VIRTUE ETHICS?

One way to begin conversations about the concept of virtue is to think of its exemplars. Rosa Parks, Muhammad Ali, Dorothy Day, Nelson Mandela, the Dalai Lama, Malala Yousafazi—these individuals are widely admired for their courage, compassion, resolve, humility, and generosity of spirit. They exhibit the qualities, dispositions, or traits, as virtue theorist Linda Zagzebski describes exemplars, of "a paradigmatically good person," a person whose actions or life fills us with feelings of admiration. "Exemplars are those persons," Zagzebski (2010, 49) writes, "who are most imitable, and they are most imitable because they are most admirable." We may revere such historical and religious figures as Buddha, Jesus, and Socrates; or admire someone we know, such as a parent, teacher, or friend; or find exemplary such fictional characters as Scout Finch, Hermione Granger, and Lisbeth Salander. What is common to exemplars is that they demonstrate those "*qualities that make one an excellent person*" (Battaly 2015, 5, original emphasis).

Let us define virtue, then, as an excellence of character, a quality, disposition, or trait that is characteristic of a good person, one who can be counted on to act in the right way at the right moment for the right reasons. Virtues are not hard and fast rules of conduct—do this but not that—but rather should be understood as patterns or tendencies that, much like rhetoric, call for adjustment to particular and changing circumstances.

While virtue is commonly associated with individual character—Julia Annas (2011, 9) argues that a virtue is "a deep feature" of a person, "a disposition which is central to the person, to whom he or she is, a way we standardly think of character"—virtues are equally contextual and communal. Annas (2011, 21) notes that we learn to be virtuous "in a multitude of embedded contexts, which can stand in various relations, from overlapping to conflicting: family, school, church, employment, siblings, friends, neighbourhoods, the internet." What we count as a virtue, then, reflects the values, traditions, memories, and narratives of the communities and cultures in which we live.

Alasdair MacIntyre, one of the most influential figures in the modern revival of virtue-based ethical theories, makes the point that the heroic virtues of Homeric society differ from the catalog of virtues that might be found in the novels of Jane Austen or the writings of Benjamin Franklin or our own conception of a good life. "For we would now seem to be saying," MacIntyre (2007, 182) writes, "that Homer's concept of an *arête*, an excellence, is one thing and that our concept of virtue is quite another since a particular quality can be an excellence in Homer's eyes, but not a virtue in ours and *vice versa*." Or as Deirdre N. McCloskey (2006, 364) writes of the virtue of courage, "'Courage' does not mean the same thing to a Roman knight as to a Christian knight, or to a samurai as to a cowboy, or to a free man in Athens of 431 BC as to an adult woman in the Paris of AD 1968."

In multi-cultural, trans-global societies such as our own, questions of what is considered a virtue and who gets to define virtue are not easily resolved. At worst, such discussions may result in exclusion and oppression. At best, however, such questions may be generative, offering opportunities to explore how conceptions of such virtues as tolerance, wisdom, and justice may be interpreted in culturally specific ways. Regardless of whether we make space for these discussions in our classrooms, "it is hard to envision a human community," David Carr has written, "in which these qualities are not needed, or recognized, held to be of any value at all" (quoted in Lapsley and Narvaez 2006, 256).

If virtues are, as Richard White (2008, 1) writes, "the ways in which we typically grasp the nature of goodness," virtue ethics is "the ethical system that takes 'virtue' or 'the virtues' as its primary ethical category" (Cafaro 2015, 442n1). Virtue ethics offers an alternative to ethical traditions of deontology, the ethics of absolutes, and consequentialism, the ethics of outcomes. Where the former asks "What categorical rules should I follow," and the latter demands "What outcomes will result from my actions," the primary questions of virtue ethics concern how best to live: "What kind of person do I want to be? How should I live my life? What does it mean to be a good person?"

In comparison to rival theories, writes Rosalind Hursthouse (1999, 3), virtue ethics offers a broader landscape of moral inquiry, one that makes a place for addressing "motives and moral character, moral wisdom and discernment, friendship and family relationships, a deep concept of happiness, the role of emotions in our moral life, and the questions of what sort of person I should be, and of how we should live." Daniel C. Russell (2013, 2) argues that what distinguishes virtue ethics from other moral theories is its concern with the whole of one's life, in which the focus "is not so much on what to do in morally difficult cases as on how to approach all of one's choices with such personal qualities as kindness, courage, wisdom, and integrity." The theologian William Mattison has argued that what most distinguishes virtue ethics from rival moral theories is its attention to a final end, the overall purpose of one's life. The virtues, according to Mattison, are "qualities of persons" that "dispose toward action that is *constitutive of happiness*" and make possible "a life well lived" (personal communication, November 7, 2016, original emphasis).

There is, of course, a good deal more I might say about virtue and virtue ethics, space permitting. A fuller treatment of the subject would review, among other things, the foundational theories of Confucius, Plato, and Aristotle, the latter of whom Dorothea Frede (2015) has described as "*the* protagonist of virtue ethics." We would examine how virtue ethics has been applied to contemporary moral problems in diverse fields, including psychiatry (Radden 2007), animal rights (Walker 2007), and environmental studies (Treanor 2014), among others. Certainly, we would acknowledge the historical baggage of the term, its associations with the subjugation of women, regressive politics, and an exclusively Christian tradition. Responsive to these, we would consider the development of new narratives of virtue, such as feminist virtue ethics (McLaren 2001), critical virtue ethics (Tessman 2005), and non-Western virtue ethics (Angle and Slote 2013). A complete account of virtue and virtue ethics would make time for these discussions and more.[2]

This chapter is not meant to serve as that account. I am interested here in examining how different pedagogical approaches to the teaching of writing, despite their distinctive practices, methods, and bodies of knowledge, share a common language of rhetorical virtues—a language that speaks both to the ethical dimensions of teaching writing and the significance of the work in our current cultural moment. So I turn to those pedagogies now, beginning with community-engaged pedagogy.

COMMUNITY-ENGAGED PEDAGOGIES

Laura Julier, Kathleen Livingston, and Eli Goldblatt (2014) organize their informative discussion of community-engaged pedagogies around five questions: What is community-engaged pedagogy and how does it benefit students? How does one find community partners? What sorts of writing assignments work best in the community-engaged classroom? How can faculty assess student learning? Finally, how does community-engaged pedagogy benefit the communities in which it is taught? The answers Julier and colleagues (2014) offer to these questions speak to the virtue-based ethics of community-engaged pedagogies.

Julier and colleagues (2014, 56) define community-engaged pedagogy as "a kind of experiential learning grounded in the understanding of writing as a situated social act." The roots of this understanding, the authors contend, are to be found in the hands-on learning philosophy of John Dewey, the liberatory pedagogies of Paulo Freire and bell hooks, and the truth-telling qualities of expressivists such as Ken Macrorie and Peter Elbow. Collectively, such approaches to education were defined by "the desire to connect personal commitments to social and political realities" in the hope that "writing could address problems the writer recognizes in the world" (Julier, Livingston, and Goldblatt 2014, 56). Community-engaged pedagogy is a contemporary legacy of these theories.

While there are many forms of community-engaged learning courses, what is common to all, the authors write, "is that students work in a relationship" with a community-based organization and write for purposes "shaped or defined by the public sphere" (Julier, Livingston, and Goldblatt 2014, 57). Establishing such relationships, caution Julier and colleagues, requires that educators listen carefully to community needs to negotiate sustainable, ethical, mutually beneficial partnerships.

While relationships are the common currency of community-engaged pedagogies, such courses are nonetheless diverse in their purposes and audiences, their forms and goals, their conceptions of community, and their means of assessment (Julier, Livingston, and Goldblatt 2014, 57). In some community-engaged courses, for example, students write as a form of service, authoring documents that serve the needs of the organization. In other courses, students write about their service, perhaps in the form of weekly responses or research papers. As students interact with others outside the classroom, they are called upon to "explore and negotiate the complexities of rhetorical exigencies: the way in which audiences differ, words work, and meanings multiply in various social settings" (Julier, Livingston, and Goldblatt 2014, 59).

While teaching practices are not the focus of their essay, Julier and colleagues (2014) provide examples of assignments for the community-engaged course. In some versions of the course, for example, students might "interview residents of a nursing home to record personal histories, tutor underserved school kids in after-school reading and writing programs, help elementary students write and illustrate school newspapers or zines, or produce media that does work on behalf of non-profit organizations. In [other versions of the course], students partner with an organization or community group to learn about and advocate on behalf of particular civic and social issues in that community" (Julier, Livingston, and Goldblatt 2014, 57).

Underscoring the diversity of approaches to community-engaged education, Julier and colleagues (2014) describe several of the distinctive contexts, assignments, and purposes of the community-engaged classroom. Students in Linda Flower's course at Carnegie Mellon, for example, served as mentors to urban teens and adults at a community literacy center, using writing and public dialogue to address issues confronting the urban neighborhood (Julier, Livingston, and Goldblatt 2014, 58). In the course developed by Jonathan Alexander, Janell Haynes, and Jacqueline Rhodes (2010), students researched issues related to HIV/AIDS and published texts on sexuality and sexual health for college-age audiences (Julier, Livingston, and Goldblatt 2014, 65). In Gwendolyn Pough's course, in which students were introduced to Black Panther Party autobiographies and documents as a way of providing them with a framework for analyzing their own experiences and for using literacy as a vehicle for social change, students were called upon to read, write weekly responses, complete a research paper, and author a proposal for change—resulting in several students establishing a student group dedicated to discussing diversity issues at their university (Julier, Livingston, and Goldblatt 2014, 65).

In sum, community-engaged pedagogies as described by Julier and colleagues (2014) are varied, imaginative, and socially responsive. They are equally pedagogies that enact practices of rhetorical virtue. Consider that fundamental to each of the venues, courses, and assignments reviewed in Julier and colleagues (2014) is *service*, the act of doing something for another, perhaps for a community. Service becomes a virtue, Gregorio Guitián (2017, 177) writes, "if it means a habitual disposition of doing good" for others. Students in the community-engaged classroom are given opportunities to develop the "habitual disposition of doing good" for others through the relationships they form and the literacy practices they perform. The community-engaged classroom, in other words, invites students to engage in discursive enactments of the virtue of service.

Yet service is not a single, stand-alone virtue in the community-engaged classroom. Rather, service functions as a sort of banner under which other virtues may be gathered and developed. So, for example, when Julier and colleagues (2014) recommend syllabuses that call upon students to interview residents of a nursing home, tutor children in after-school programs, or produce media for nonprofit organizations, they are inviting students to reflect on the virtues of selflessness, or putting others before ourselves; of empathy, or identifying with the concerns of others; and of compassion, or caring for the plight of other sentient beings.

The writing assignments in the community-engaged classroom further promote the teaching and practice of rhetorical virtues. For example, the research students conduct for Alexander, Haynes, and Rhodes's course on sexuality and for Pough's course on empowering rhetoric encourages students to cultivate the virtues of knowledge in learning about a topic, integrity in providing evidence for their claims, open-mindedness when engaging arguments that contradict their own, and discernment in revising their papers. Similarly, the reflective writing assignments required of students in many community-engaged courses, generally in the form of journals or perhaps a blog (Julier, Livingstone, and Goldblatt 2014, 66), invite students to enact discursive practices of truthfulness in recounting one's experiences, understanding when reflecting on the actions of others, and practical wisdom, or *phronesis*, when making sense of one's experiences in the community setting.

Faculty, too, are called upon in community-engaged courses to speak and write in ways that may express the discursive enactment of virtues. So, for example, when Julier and colleagues (2014, 61) stress the importance of faculty listening to community partners and negotiating with them when initiating relationships, they are encouraging the virtues of respectfulness and cooperation. When the authors acknowledge that assessing the benefits of the community partnership to both students and the community partner is a complex task requiring instructors to "understand their limitations and knowledge about the textual practices and rhetoric of the sites with which they partner" (Julier, Livingston, and Goldblatt 2014, 67), they are implicitly suggesting that faculty practice the virtue of humility. And when they recommend that faculty make regular visits to the community site "to make sure the learners and their sponsor organizations are getting what they want from the partnership" (Julier, Livingston, and Goldblatt 2014, 68), they are advocating communications grounded in the virtues of attentiveness and responsibility.

In the community-engaged classroom, in sum, students learn to understand writing as a social act, to connect personal commitments to social and political realities, and to use writing as a means of addressing issues of social justice outside the classroom. Toward those ends, students may be asked to participate in such activities as volunteering in a soup kitchen, tutoring in a prison, or assisting immigrants with their paperwork. Such assignments, I have suggested, do more than promote reading and writing skills. Beyond these, such assignments encourage students to speak and write in language that expresses, implicitly or explicitly, such virtues as selflessness, empathy, compassion, and others. More broadly still, the assignments of the community-engaged classroom invite students to reflect on the central questions of virtue ethics: What kind of person do I want to be? How should I live my life? What does it mean to be a good person?

Such questions are foundational to community-engaged pedagogies. Yet they are equally intrinsic, as we shall see, to the theories, purposes, and practices of a different sort of pedagogy—what Collin Gifford Brooke (2014) calls new media pedagogy.

NEW MEDIA PEDAGOGY

Brooke begins by acknowledging the dramatic changes over the last few decades in the shifting, tumultuous landscape of new media. "In the late 1990s," Brooke (2014, 177) writes, "applications like 'electronic mail,' online discussion platforms, the Web, and hypertext/media were (with some exceptions) the province of a small subset of the field, a community mostly of graduate students and assistant professors." Since then, however, there has been a proliferation of information and communication technologies, including such things as corporate course management systems, plagiarism detection software, and mobile devices. Such technologies have changed the way we interact with one another and with knowledge, argues Brooke (2014, 178), and while those of us who teach writing may resist such changes, "we can no longer ignore them."

By way of engaging the changes, Brooke (2014, 179) lays out a set of principles and challenges relating to the uses of new media, which he defines as "a site where the long history of multiple modalities intersects with recent developments in technology, but it also includes important shifts in audience, institutions, and context." Under the heading "New Media Principles and Attitudes," Brooke (2014, 180–83) offers the following:

- New media pedagogy is more than teaching to the text.
- New media function as a writer's laboratory, a site of experimentation.

- New media operate in "Internet Time" (and so must we).
- New media replace expertise with exploration and engagement.

Brooke's discussion of these principles and attitudes is more compelling than this brief review admits, but it seems fair to say that he frames much of his analysis in terms of exploration and change. So, for example, in describing the new media classroom "as a writer's laboratory, a site of experimentation," Brooke (2014, 180) writes, "'add technology and stir' is perhaps a poor way to improve education in general, but on the smaller scale of the writing classroom, it can be a positive source for experimentation and innovation." Calling for teachers to encourage "invention and experimentation" (2014, 181), Brooke (2014, 181n) offers the example of a student who composed a long-form essay using Storify, the online application that enables users "to curate stories by allowing them to embed a range of online sources from social media like Facebook, Twitter, Instagram, YouTube, etc." The student's essay, which drew upon activity theory to understand the use of Kickstarter in video game development, addressed issues of "credibility, agency, audience, and community" (Brooke 2014, 181) while at the same time raising questions, Brooke writes, of how students negotiate the relationships of citation and source use, argumentation and curation. The responsibility of the new media writing teacher in responding to such innovation, contends Brooke (2014, 181), is to create "classroom spaces that can encourage our students to experiment."

Toward that end, Brooke exhorts teachers of writing to "replace expertise with exploration and engagement" or to collaborate with students in navigating the multi-layered landscapes of new media technologies. By promoting reflection on the uses of technology in our classrooms and writing assignments, Brooke (2014, 183) proposes, we make it "easier to invite our students to investigate and experiment with new media."

If the qualities, dispositions, and habits associated with community-engaged pedagogies, such as service, selflessness, compassion, humility, and the like, are largely familiar to us as virtues, as conventional conceptions of "the good," the qualities Brooke ascribes to new media pedagogy—such as experimentation, exploration, and innovation—may not appear to stand in the same light, sharing the same virtuous stage. While we might admire the inventor who experiments, the voyager who explores, the designer who innovates, we may not conceive of such activities as "ethical" or associate them with the qualities and practices of the good.

Yet I would argue that just as new technologies have changed the ways we "interact with one another and with knowledge," new media technologies are changing and expanding our catalog of virtues. Recalling our definition of virtue as "an excellence of character, a disposition, quality, or trait that is characteristic of a good person," we may see experimentation, exploration, and innovation as "excellences" characteristic of the person who is willing to question traditional assumptions, take risks for the sake of new knowledge, and disrupt unproductive practices, attitudes, and values.

So, for example, we may say that the teacher who challenges assumptions about what her "disabled" students can learn, who takes risks by introducing new technologies to the classroom, and who disrupts unproductive practices by abandoning lessons and methods that fail to motivate is the kind of teacher we admire and would imitate. And we would admire and imitate that teacher precisely because she exhibits the virtues of experimentation, exploration, and innovation characteristic of the new media classroom. Just as Brooke describes an approach to teaching writing that differs significantly from that of the community-engaged classroom, so, too, does his essay invoke a strikingly different set of rhetorical virtues.

We can, of course, think of situations in which the qualities of experimentation, exploration, and innovation are not construed as virtues but as their opposites. Experimentation, for example, is not a virtue but an evil when it causes suffering, as in the morally abhorrent examples of the Nazi medical experiments or the Tuskegee Syphilis Experiment. Similarly, for countless numbers of people across the planet, the exploration of indigenous cultures by Western powers in the eighteenth and nineteenth centuries resulted not in moral excellence and lives well lived but in exploitation, environmental destruction, and enslavement. And do we celebrate or condemn the innovation of weapons manufacturers who develop ever more lethal means to kill human beings? What counts as a virtue, in other words, is never absolute; it is shaped by the particulars of history, culture, economics, and ideology. This is true whether we are talking about qualities conventionally thought of as virtues, such as honesty, compassion, and humility, or about the qualities of experimentation, exploration, and innovation associated with new media pedagogy.

Brooke (2014) concludes his essay with a discussion of the challenges and obstacles to integrating new media pedagogies into the writing classroom, specifically the issues of access, infrastructure, accessibility, and assessment. The issue of access, Brooke tells us, refers to the social, cultural, and economic divide between those who have access to new technologies and those who do not. While the field has long been attentive to problems of access, Brooke (2014, 183) writes, "there remain a number of important dimensions that separate certain groups of users from others, and these differences can enter our classrooms in unpredictable ways." Similarly, the challenge of infrastructure refers to differences on college campuses relating to "equipment, maintenance, resources, and support" that can affect how new media might be used in a given class (Brooke 2014, 184). Accessibility, in turn, refers to the design of new media products and environments and whether they will be inclusive or "leave intact," as Sean Zdenek (2012) writes, "a set of normative assumptions about students' bodies, minds, and abilities" (quoted in Brooke 2014, 185). Finally, there is the challenge of assessing new media products in the writing classroom. "How does a three- to five-page paper," Brooke (2014, 186) asks, "translate to blog entries or Twitter updates?"

These are material, technological, and educational questions. They are equally ethical questions. Should we endeavor to address the challenges Brooke identifies, we are again drawn into deliberations and discussions grounded in the ethics and language of virtue. In advocating that students should have equal access to new technologies, that infrastructure should not exacerbate existing inequalities, that new media should be accessible and inclusive, and that assessment practices ought not disadvantage students in new media classrooms, Brooke is essentially arguing for fairness—the exercise of which requires that one group of people not be treated more favorably than another group—and for equality, which refers to the equal distribution of resources. Fairness and equality, in turn, are elements of justice, which White (2008, 75) notes is often described as the "highest of all the virtues, the master virtue that animates the others and makes them virtues to begin with." Underlying and fundamental to conversations about the challenges of access, infrastructure, accessibility, and assessment, in other words, is the discourse of rhetorical virtues.

OUR STORY, THIS MOMENT

Both new media and community-engaged pedagogies offer distinctive visions of the writing classroom, its activities and assignments, its goals and guiding principles. Yet as I have tried to demonstrate in this chapter, common to both pedagogies—and, I would argue, to all the approaches considered in Tate and colleagues' *A Guide to Composition Pedagogies*

(2014)—is the teaching of discursive ethics, or what I have called rhetorical virtues. More, I have proposed that in the discourse of rhetorical virtues, teachers of writing find a common language, one that tells the story of our discipline and speaks to the urgency of our work in the current cultural moment.

As best I understand that story, the teaching of writing inevitably and invariably engages us in questions of honesty, compassion, judgment, justice, and other such virtues. In the narrative I am proposing, we are teaching students how to express themselves in ways that will help them succeed in college, find jobs after college, and participate in the democratic process. Beyond these, however, we are offering them opportunities to speak and write in ways that are consistent with those qualities, dispositions, and habits we commonly associate with "a paradigmatically good person," a person whose actions or life we admire and would emulate. The writing classroom, in this perspective, becomes a setting for composing such lives, a venue in which the everyday work of formulating arguments, keeping journals, or developing multimodal texts helps us, teachers and students, discern the kind of people we wish to become, how we should live, and what sorts of communities we would create and sustain.

To be clear, I do not mean to suggest that we are introducing students to those dispositions and habits of honesty, compassion, judgment, and the rest. Students arrive in our classrooms with complex moral lives that have already been formed, as Annas (2011, 21) noted, in the embedded contexts of "family, school, church, employment, siblings, friends, neighbourhoods, the internet." Rather, what I understand us to be doing as teachers of writing, if we so choose, is sharing with students the idea that writing always and inevitably involves ethical deliberations and decision-making that speak to the kind of people we are or wish to become and the character of the communities in which we wish to live.

The urgency of our work in the current moment seems plain enough. We are living through a period in the United States, but in other countries as well, in which truth is under assault, reason is discredited, racism is intensifying, conspiracies are rampant, and authoritarianism is on the rise. There has never been a more important time, I submit, to teach what we teach. Our work has never mattered more. When we explain to students why truthfulness is essential to a claim, why claims must be accompanied by evidence, why open-mindedness is an intellectual responsibility, or how righteous indignation functions as a virtue, we are, in effect, engaging in acts of resistance. We are rejecting the illiberalism and irrationality of the current climate, and we are teaching practices of rhetorical ethics through which we might work—students and teachers—toward a more decent, compassionate, and just society. We are engaged in this effort, I have tried to suggest in this chapter, regardless of the pedagogy we adopt.

To speak this way in our classrooms, however, to speak, write, and teach in the language of rhetorical virtues, calls for a conscious commitment on our part. It requires that we make *explicit* and *intentional* that which is *inherent* and *implicit* in the teaching of writing. It challenges us to redefine the good writer as one whose work is characterized by ethical as well as rhetorical awareness. It necessitates that we speak and write candidly, fearlessly, and without irony in defense of those qualities, dispositions, and habits—those virtues, in other words—that are at the heart of our common enterprise.

We will not always agree on what those virtues are or how they might be enacted in our classrooms and communities or whether we should be talking about virtues at all. We will not always speak the same language of ethics. If nothing else, this book makes that abundantly clear, offering, as it does, multiple ethical perspectives and languages: feminist, transnational, non-Western, and others. Perhaps the next great project for writing studies is to define our ethical commonalities and irreconcilable differences and to articulate how they influence the work we do each day in the classroom. Our common tongue, to recall the guiding metaphor of this chapter, has many varieties.

I have argued in this chapter that the ethical language that most closely corresponds to the work we perform each day in our classrooms is the language of rhetorical virtues, the discursive enactments of those qualities said to be emblematic of paradigmatically good people. Regardless of the ethical perspective we embrace, however, and regardless of the pedagogical approach we adopt, we are ultimately and necessarily speaking, writing, and teaching in a language grounded in ethics and ethical discourse practices. And that is the language, I propose, in which we can best explain who we are, what we do, and why the writing classroom remains so important in the twenty-first century.

NOTES

1.   For an earlier version of this argument, see Duffy (2014).
2.   The literature on virtue and virtue ethics is vast. For a wide-ranging tour of the landscape, see Besser-Jones and Slote (2015).

REFERENCES

Alexander, Jonathan, Janell Haynes, and Jacqueline Rhodes. 2010. "Public/Sex: Connecting Sexuality and Service Learning." *Reflections: A Journal of Public Rhetoric, Civic Writing, and Service Learning* 9 (2): 1–19.

Angle, Stephen C., and Michael Slote. 2013. *Virtue Ethics and Confucianism.* New York: Routledge.

Annas, Julia. 2011. *Intelligent Virtue.* Oxford, UK: Oxford University Press.

Battaly, Heather. 2015. *Virtue.* Cambridge, UK: Polity.

Besser-Jones, Lorraine, and Michael Slote, eds. 2015. *The Routledge Companion to Virtue Ethics.* New York: Routledge.

Brooke, Collin Gifford. 2014. "New Media Pedagogy." In *A Guide to Composition Pedagogies,* ed. Gary Tate, Amy Rupiper Taggart, Kurt Schick, and H. Brooke Hessler, 177–93. New York: Oxford University Press.

Cafaro, Philip. 2015. "Environmental Virtue Ethics." In *The Routledge Companion to Virtue Ethics,* ed. Lorraine Besser-Jones and Michael Slote, 427–44. New York: Routledge.

Frede, Dorothea. 2015. "Aristotle's Virtue Ethics." In *The Routledge Companion to Virtue Ethics,* ed. Lorraine Besser-Jones and Michael Slote, 17–29. New York: Routledge.

Guitián, Gregorio. 2017. "Service in the Catholic Social Tradition: A Crucial Virtue for Business." In *Handbook of Virtue Ethics in Business and Management,* ed. Alejo José G. Sison, Gregory R. Beabout, and Ignacio Ferrero, 177–87. Dordrecht: Springer Science-Business Media.

Hursthouse, Rosalind. 1999. *On Virtue Ethics.* Oxford, UK: Oxford University Press.

Julier, Laura, Kathleen Livingston, and Eli Goldblatt. 2014. "Community-Engaged Pedagogies." In *A Guide to Composition Pedagogies,* ed. Gary Tate, Amy Rupiper Taggart, Kurt Schick, and H. Brooke Hessler, 55–76. New York: Oxford University Press.

Lapsley, Daniel K., and Darcia Narvaez. 2006. "Character Education." In *Handbook of Child Psychology,* vol. 4: *Psychology in Practice,* ed. William Damon, Richard M. Lerner, and Irving I. Sigel, 248–96. Hoboken, NJ: John Wiley and Sons.

MacIntyre, Alasdair. 2007. *After Virtue.* 3rd ed. Notre Dame, IN: University of Notre Dame Press.

McClaren, Margaret A. 2001. "Feminist Ethics: Care as a Virtue." In *Feminists Doing Ethics,* ed. Peggy DesAutels and Joanne Waugh, 101–17. Lanham, MD: Rowman and Littlefield.

McCloskey, Deirdre N. 2006. *The Bourgeois Virtues: Ethics for an Age of Commerce.* Chicago: Chicago University Press.

Pough, Gwendolyn D. 2002. "Empowering Rhetoric: Black Students Writing Black Panthers." *College Composition and Communication* 53 (3): 466–86.

Radden, Jennifer. 2007. "Virtue Ethics as Professional Ethics: The Case of Psychiatry." In *Working Virtue: Virtue Ethics and Contemporary Moral Problems,* ed. Rebecca L. Walker and Philip J. Ivanhoe, 113–34. Oxford, UK: Oxford University Press.

Russell, Daniel C. 2013. "Introduction: Virtue Ethics in Modern Moral Philosophy." In *The Cambridge Companion to Virtue Ethics,* ed. Daniel C. Russell, 1-6 7–28. Cambridge, UK: Cambridge University Press.

Taggart, Amy Rupiper, H. Brooke Hessler, and Kurt Schick. 2014. "What Is Composition Pedagogy? An Introduction." In *A Guide to Composition Pedagogies,* ed. Gary Tate, Amy Rupiper Taggart, Kurt Schick, and H. Brooke Hessler, 1–19. New York: Oxford University Press.

Tate, Gary, Amy Rupiper Taggart, Kurt Schick, and H. Brooke Hessler. 2014. *A Guide to Composition Pedagogies.* New York: Oxford University Press.

Tessman, Lisa. 2005. *Burdened Virtues: Virtue Ethics for Liberatory Struggles.* Oxford, UK: Oxford University Press.

Treanor, Brian. 2014. *Emplotting Virtue: A Narrative Approach to Environmental Ethics.* Albany: State University of New York Press.

Walker, Rebecca L. 2007. "The Good Life for Non-Human Animals: What Virtue Requires of Humans." In *Working Virtue: Virtue Ethics and Contemporary Moral Problems*, ed. Rebecca L. Walker and Philip J. Ivanhoe, 173–89. Oxford, UK: Oxford University Press.

White, Richard. 2008. *Radical Virtues: Moral Wisdom and the Ethics of Contemporary Life*. Lanham, MD: Rowman and Littlefield.

Zagzebski, Linda Trinkaus. 2010. "Exemplarist Virtue Theory." *Metaphilosophy* 41 (1–2): 41–57.

Zdenek, Sean. 2012. "College Astusenrs on the Margins in the New Media Classroom." *Accessible Podcasting*, May 26.

POSTSCRIPT
(Epilogue)

Frederick Antczak

Why do you go away? So that you can come back. So that you can see the place you came from with new eyes and extra colors. And the people there see you differently, too. Coming back to where you started is not the same as never leaving.

—Terry Pratchett

In the short period of one scholar's lifetime, the place of ethics in writing studies has hugely shifted, expanded, deepened. In some cases it has been pulled by the thread of theory, but in many others it has been pricked and driven by events in the worlds of politics, business, medicine, education. From the rhetorical efficacy of Hitler's propaganda to Nixon's invocations of the law to Clinton's slips and slides with "what 'is' is" to Trump's challenges to fact-based discourse, ethics has always been drawn into topics that have a kind of pre-heated and occasionally partisan inspiration. From the rhetorical process of corporate life to the relationships among advertising, desire, and reality to boycotts to the ethical status of plastics and industrial by-products in an increasingly stressed physical environment, ethics became a more sophisticated consideration for business writing and communication. From the responsibilities of translating medical talk about conditions and treatments to reviving more agency in (and even collaboration with) the patient, medicine became more richly, and urgently, a scene for ethical inquiry. And today, from the twinned issues of free speech and hate speech on campus to their disproportionate impacts on different student audiences across various forms of symbolic action, contention is becoming more richly contentious. It turns out that exactly now is a particularly exciting moment for the scholarship this volume represents, a time when its inquiries are likely to welcome new minds and perspectives; the scholarly originality, variety, elegance of these authors and many others working in the field bring new sensibilities and greater depth to a place that is now both invigorating and oddly familiar.

DOI: 10.7330/9781607329978.c015

One of the irresistible perquisites of living a scholar's lifetime is the satisfaction brought by the sense that everything old is new again—albeit in different and more flexible forms for different audiences and more complicated situations. Or is it that everything new is old? For students (and the remaining survivors) of the 1960s, it may seem so. Once again, there are urgent purposes for "truth"—some intersubjectively verifiable, if not in older senses *objective*, "truth"—to measure mendacious political discourse or advertising claims or medical prognoses. "Fact" is now no simpler or easier a term to invoke or apply, but again it has a siren song attraction in at least some of these discussions. "Agency" is a concept that has gone through decades of transformative critique and revision, but its updates are no less germane in contemporary thinking about communicating and interacting with patients or customers, citizens or students. Means and ends are still both elusive and essential to sort out. Costs and consequences, the perspectives from which they are recognized, and the languages in which they are assessed all remain stubbornly and sometimes more enlighteningly pivotal to the critical conversation.

To admit the durability of such issues and concepts and their resistance to being solved or settled once and for all by one theory or perspective or ethical code is not to deny that understandings can grow and deepen; nor is it to be skeptical about whether debates can progress. Indeed, sometimes they progress so much that they begin to connect to, even anticipate, other contemporary discussions. Scholarly inquiries into the ethics of rhetoric in writing studies and in communication ramify so often and powerfully that they practically career toward interdisciplinarity. These sorts of connections seem like signs of making real headway, as well as a rough map of future directions—although, of course, it was ever thus.

Perhaps the lesson of this scholarly lifetime is that timelessness and timeliness can coexist and can even progress together—tugging, staggering, and rebalancing all the way. Over time, quite remarkably over the last four decades, ethics has waxed and waned in the number of participants and the seeming liveliness of the topics. Undeniably, there have been long periods when it seemed an unpromising place for finding genuinely new and engaging scholarly discussion; yet the kinds of scholars we see engaged in it in this volume are expert at bringing change just as a vein of inquiry threatens to grow sclerotic. The reader, moving through the different inquiries in this volume, can't miss the invigorating sense that the horizon of inquiry grows broader and the applications of new insights bring new color to the grayest of arguments. Just as some of us were thinking of decamping, things get interesting again.

Judging from this volume, the vitality of scholarly debates in which each chapter participates will inexhaustibly open themselves to scholarship of discovery and scholarship of application in equally significant measure. Whether it's been a conversation for your scholarly lifetime or you're new to the territory, please let us welcome you in.

ABOUT THE AUTHORS

Lois Agnew is professor of writing and rhetoric and associate dean of curriculum innovation and pedagogy in the College of Arts and Sciences at Syracuse University. She regularly teaches graduate and undergraduate courses in writing and rhetorical history and is the author of two books, "*Outward, Visible Propriety*": *Stoic Philosophy and Eighteenth-Century British Rhetorics* (2008) and *Thomas De Quincey: British Rhetoric's Romantic Turn* (2012), as well as a number of journal articles.

After taking his AB from the University of Notre Dame, **Frederick Antczak** matriculated into the ideas and methods doctoral program at the university, where he worked with Wayne Booth and Robert Streeter and became a scholar of American political rhetoric. He taught in the Rhetoric Department at the University of California–Berkeley, the Rhetoric and Communication Studies Department at the University of Virginia, and the University of Iowa's Rhetoric Department. It was at Iowa where he began to explore leadership roles as department chair, associate dean, editor of the *Iowa Journal of Communication*, and president of the Rhetoric Society of America. He was given the extraordinary opportunity to help shape a new college of liberal arts and sciences and has spent more than fifteen years as its founding dean at Grand Valley State University, during which he has grown to appreciate the applicability of Niebuhrian ethical concepts like pride, community, and irony to academic administration. When possible, he still teaches a section of first-year writing.

Patrick W. Berry is associate professor of writing and rhetoric at Syracuse University, where he serves as chair of the Department of Writing Studies, Rhetoric, and Composition. He has published on literacy narratives, digital media and production, and higher education in prison. His publications include *Doing Time, Writing Lives: Refiguring Literacy and Higher Education in Prison* (2018) and *Transnational Literate Lives in Digital Times* (coauthored with Gail E. Hawisher and Cynthia L. Selfe, 2012), which received the College Composition and Communication (CCCC) Research Impact Award and the CCCC Advancement of Knowledge Award. He teaches courses in writing and rhetoric on campus and in prison.

Vicki Tolar Burton is professor of English and director of the Writing Intensive Curriculum Program at Oregon State University. She is the author of *Spiritual Literacy in John Wesley's Methodism: Reading, Writing, and Speaking to Believe* from Baylor University Press and is the co-producer of the Telly Award–winning documentary film *Writing across Borders*. Her articles have appeared in *College English, College Composition and Communication, Rhetoric Review*, and others.

Rasha Diab is associate professor in the Department of Rhetoric and Writing and a faculty affiliate of the departments of English and Middle Eastern studies at the University of Texas at Austin. Her work centers on the rhetorics of peacemaking, Arab-Islamic rhetorics, and revisionist historiography. Her book *Shades of Ṣulḥ: The Rhetorics of Arab-Islamic Reconciliation* (University of Pittsburgh Press, 2016) won the 2018 Conference on College Composition and Communication (CCCC) Outstanding Book Award. She has articles and chapters published and forthcoming on peacemaking rhetoric and Arab-Islamic reconciliation rhetoric, as well as violence/microaggressions and social justice in rhetoric and writing studies. She is writing a book tentatively titled *On Word Weaving and Peacemaking* that focuses on the interconnectedness of Arab-Islamic traditions of conciliation, legal-political rhetoric, and rhetorical historiography.

John Duffy is professor of English and the O'Malley director of the University Writing Program at the University of Notre Dame. His published works include *Provocations of Virtue: Rhetoric, Ethics, and the Teaching of Writing, Literacy, Economy, and Power* (co-editor) and *Writing from These Roots: The Historical Development of Literacy in a Hmong-American Community,* for which he was awarded the 2009 Outstanding Book Award by the Conference on College Composition and Communication. He has published essays in *College Composition and Communication, College English, Rhetoric Review, JAC: A Journal of Rhetoric, Culture, and Politics, McSweeny's,* and elsewhere.

William Duffy is associate professor and coordinator of the Writing, Rhetoric, and Technical Communication Program in the English Department at the University of Memphis. His scholarship focuses on the intersections of rhetoric and writing with philosophies of language. His work has most recently been published in *Present Tense, Literacy in Composition Studies,* and *College English.* His book *Beyond Conversation: Collaboration and the Production of Writing* is forthcoming from Utah State University Press.

Norbert Elliot is professor emeritus of English at New Jersey Institute of Technology and research professor at the University of South Florida. With Mya Poe and Asao B. Inoue, he is co-editor of *Writing Assessment, Social Justice, and the Advancement of Opportunity.* Most recently, with Richard Haswell, he is coauthor of *Early Holistic Scoring of Writing: A Theory, a History, a Reflection* and, with Alice S. Horning, he is co-editor of *Talking Back: Senior Scholars and Their Colleagues Deliberate the Past, Present, and Future of Writing Studies.* With Robert J. Mislevy, between 2017 and 2020 he worked on a program of research exploring connections between psychometrics and writing assessment. Their chapter is a result of that collaboration.

Gesa E. Kirsch is professor of English at Bentley University. Her research focuses on feminist rhetorical studies; qualitative and archival research methods; ethics, gender, and diversity; and theories of creativity and innovation. Her publications include *Feminist Rhetorical Practices: New Horizons for Rhetoric, Composition, and Literacy Studies* (coauthored with Jacqueline Jones Royster), *Beyond the Archives: Research as a Lived Process* (co-edited with Liz Rohan), and *More Than Gold in California: The Life and Work of Dr. Mary Bennett Ritter,* a critical edition of a memoir written by Dr. Ritter, a nineteenth-century California physician, civic leader, and women's rights activist. She has won a National Endowment for the Humanities summer fellowship, the Winifred Bryan Horner Award from the Coalition of Feminist Scholars in the History of Rhetoric and Composition, and the Richard Braddock award from CCCC.

A professor in the English and Modern Languages Department at California State Polytechnic University, Pomona, **Don J. Kraemer** is at work on a book-length project tentatively titled "Paradoxes of Substance, Terms of Addiction." This project, like this collection's "Not to Mention Plato," extends related work of his on the rhetoric of value judgments, recent examples of which can be found in *College Composition and Communication, Journal of Basic Writing, Philosophy and Rhetoric, Rhetoric Society Quarterly,* and *WPA: Writing Program Administration.* He can be reached at djkraemer@cpp.edu.

Paula Mathieu is associate professor of English at Boston College and director of first-year writing. She teaches courses in writing as social action, first-year writing, composition pedagogy, mindful storytelling, creative nonfiction, and rhetoric as cultural study. She is author of *Tactics of Hope: The Public Turn in English Composition* and coeditor of three essay collections, including *Circulating Communities: The Tactics and Strategies of Community Publishing,* coedited with Tiffany Rousculp and Steve Parks. With Diana George, she has written about the rhetorical power of the dissident press. She has also published several articles on the intersections between writing and contemplative practice.

Robert J. Mislevy is Frederic M. Lord chair in measurement and statistics at the Educational Testing Service and professor emeritus at the University of Maryland at College Park. His research applies advances in statistics, technology, and psychology to practical problems in educational assessment. His most recent book is *Sociocognitive Foundations of Educational Measurement* (Routledge, 2018). With Norbert Elliot, between 2017 and 2020 he worked on a program of research exploring connections between psychometrics and writing assessment. Their chapter is a result of that collaboration.

Michael A. Pemberton is professor of writing and linguistics at Georgia Southern University and director of the University Writing Center. A past president of the International Writing Centers Association, he has published six books and more than fifty articles on writing center theory, tutoring ethics, and the ethics of text recycling in journals such as *College Composition and Communication, Computers and Composition,* and the *Writing Center Journal,* as well as numerous book chapters. He serves on the editorial and review boards of the WAC Clearinghouse, *Praxis, Prompt,* and the *Journal of Writing and Pedagogy*; is associate publisher for scholarly journals at the WAC Clearinghouse; and is series editor of *Across the Disciplines Books.* Since 2015, he has also served as associate director of the CWPA Consultant Evaluator Service.

James E. Porter is professor of rhetoric and professional communication at Miami University, with a joint appointment in the Departments of English and Emerging Technology in Business and Design. His research focuses on rhetoric, ethics, and interaction, particularly human/machine communication. His most recent book—*Professional Communication and Network Interaction: A Rhetorical and Ethical Approach,* coauthored with Heidi McKee—was published by Routledge in 2017.

Jacqueline Jones Royster (former dean of the Ivan Allen College of Liberal Arts at the Georgia Institute of Technology and Ivan Allen Jr. Dean's Chair in Liberal Arts and Technology) is professor of English in the School of Literature, Media, and Communication. Her research focuses at the intersections of the history of rhetoric, feminist studies, and cultural studies with a primary interest in the connections between human and civil rights. She has authored, coauthored, edited, or co-edited six book publications and two textbook series. She has authored numerous articles in rhetorical studies, literacy studies, and women's studies and has received several prestigious awards, including most recently the Winifred Bryan Horner Award from the Coalition of Women Scholars in the History of Rhetoric and Composition and being named a fellow of the Rhetoric Society of America.

Bo Wang is Lüka chair professor at Ocean University of China and professor of English at California State University, Fresno. A historian, she works in the intersections of comparative/cultural rhetoric, feminist/gender studies, postcolonial studies, and transnationalism. Her writing has appeared in the journals *Advances in the History of Rhetoric, College Composition and Communication, College English, Rhetoric Review,* and *Rhetoric Society Quarterly* and in the books *Rhetoric and Writing Studies in the New Century: Historiography, Pedagogy, and Politics; Comparative Rhetoric: The Art of Traversing Rhetorical Times, Places, and Spaces;* and *Representations: Doing Asian American Rhetoric.* Her co-edited Symposium on Comparative Rhetoric received the 2015 Theresa J. Enos Anniversary Award (Special Recognition).

Xiaoye You is Liberal Arts Professor of English and Asian studies at Penn State and Yunshan chair professor at Guangdong University of Foreign Studies. Specializing in multilingual writing, comparative rhetoric, and World Englishes, he has published three monographs on teaching writing in transnational contexts: *Writing in the Devil's Tongue: A History of English Composition in China*; *Cosmopolitan English and Transliteracy*; and *Inventing the World Grant University: Chinese International Students' Mobilities, Literacies, and Identities*.

INDEX